INDIGENEITY:
A POLITICS OF POTENTIAL
Australia, Fiji and New Zealand

Dominic O'Sullivan

First published in Great Britain in 2017 by

Policy Press
University of Bristol
1-9 Old Park Hill
Bristol
BS2 8BB
UK
t: +44 (0)117 954 5940
pp-info@bristol.ac.uk
www.policypress.co.uk

North America office:
Policy Press
c/o The University of Chicago Press
1427 East 60th Street
Chicago, IL 60637, USA
t: +1 773 702 7700
f: +1 773-702-9756
sales@press.uchicago.edu
www.press.uchicago.edu

British Library Cataloguing in Publication Data
A catalogue record for this book is available from the British Library

Library of Congress Cataloging-in-Publication Data
A catalog record for this book has been requested

ISBN 978-1-4473-3942-7 hardcover
ISBN 978-1-4473-3944-1 ePub
ISBN 978-1-4473-3945-8 Mobi
ISBN 978-1-4473-3943-4 ePdf

Cover design by Policy Press
Front cover image: Billy Alexander
Printed and bound in Great Britain by CPI Group (UK) Ltd, Croydon, CR0 4YY
Policy Press uses environmentally responsible print partners

For my mother Tui and my father Vincent
Kia nui te aroha

Contents

Acknowledgements

This book was financially supported by Charles Sturt University.

My father Vincent and mother Tui helped with editing the text. I am always grateful for their support and interest in my work and privileged to dedicate the book to them. *Ka nui te aroha ki a korua.*

My wife Cara's street level indigenous policy work has provided a practical reference point for thinking about the complex relationships that develop indigeneity as a politics of potential. Always ready with a bottle of beer and acceptance of my aversion to cooking, Cara has made an important contribution to the book.

Like King Tawhio, my 12-year-old daughter, Lucy, born in Waikato, will 'build her own house'. I am very grateful for her love and support of me and my work. My 7-year-old son, Joey, born in Wiradjuri country will make a special contribution to *yindyamarra winhanga-nha* [the wisdom of knowing how to live well in a world worth living in].

The book honours my daughter, Sarah Therese, whose memory inspires us all.

Introduction[1]

Indigeneity is a politics of potential that transcends neocolonial victimhood. The book's principal purpose is to explain how and why. It does so by showing that indigeneity's relationships with discourses of reconciliation, self-determination and sovereignty allow people to find ways of asserting their culturally framed political rights of prior occupancy. These rights are potentially realised through differentiated liberal citizenship, or 'belonging together differently', in a single non-colonial state (Maaka and Fleras, 2005). Thus the book's unifying concern is with the intersection of ideas about the terms of indigenous peoples' belonging to the state, and the nature of their citizenship and participation in public life. It is also concerned with the preservation of independent indigenous political authority. The Introduction explains these theoretical perspectives, their context and the reasons for the book's comparative approach.

The politics of indigeneity seeks space for indigenous political structures to emerge and enjoy meaningful policy influence. Indigeneity itself is grounded in neither class nor ethnic minority politics. It challenges and transforms postcolonial understandings of power, politics and justice to take an expansive view of what counts as fair and reasonable. In particular, it makes citizenship a 'political practice…not just…a legal or administrative status' (Stokes, 2000, p. 232). It challenges the Left's traditional preoccupation with class and gender politics, and its 'excessive faith in the ability of democratic participation [alone] to solve the problems of citizenship' (Kymlicka and Norman, 1994, p. 359), while also calling into question the Right's emphasis on the individual, often without reference to the collective claims that are, for indigenous peoples, preliminary to personal liberty. The book contests the argument that liberalism's concern for the individual prevents institutional attention to difference. Instead, it affirms Kymlicka's position that 'membership in a cultural community may be a relevant criterion for distributing the benefits and burdens which are the concern of a liberal theory of justice' (Kymlicka, 1989, p. 162).

The Australasian states are compared with Fiji to demonstrate that historical constraints on political authority are not removed with the withdrawal of the colonial power alone. Nor does the restoration of collective indigenous majority population status, on its own, serve meaningful self-determination. Conversely, this cross-jurisdictional comparison shows that negative power relationships in Australasia are not simply a function of minority status in majoritarian democracies. The comparison demonstrates the complexity and diversity of the environments in which indigenous peoples pursue their political aspirations and highlights the argument that the claims of indigeneity, which are concerned with permanent rights rather than short-term measures to address material inequality, must hold equally well whatever the postcolonial indigenous population status. This is because, as the comparison shows, political vulnerability is the outcome of indigeneity itself, and it is colonial experience that sets indigenous claims apart from those of migrant minority groups. Indeed, migrant groups have no moral claim on the state to protect and uphold their cultures or especially guarantee their political participation in different forms from other citizens, as is the case in New Zealand, where Maori parliamentary representation is guaranteed and where public policy routinely requires Maori input into decision making (O'Sullivan, 2007).

Indigeneity gives theoretical context to *particular* political relationships, agendas and ideas beyond the social and cultural priorities of the multicultural claims of ethnic minorities. States may offer special recognition to minority groups in the interests of social cohesion, but only with reference to theories of justice distinct from those in which indigenous peoples find arguments for recognition of inherent rights of prior occupancy. The minority/majority indigenous population comparison helps to illuminate this distinction.

Indigenous political status is a function of how postcolonial societies conceptualise and articulate prevailing liberal concepts of justice and political organisation. Relationships among indigeneity, citizenship and liberal democracy suggest, along with Fijian political experience, that indigeneity's transformative capacity for majority indigenous populations is conditional upon a fuller conception of power than simple collective dominance of public institutions. The restoration of power and influence is not an inevitable outcome of parliamentary dominance, nor the institutionalisation of indigenous entities into the national political system. Fijian indigeneity's fervent religiously inspired nationalist expression does, however, highlight the moral limits of indigeneity as well as the pragmatic imperative to admit self-determination's relative and relational character, within the context of ordered, shared and stable national sovereignty.

For minority indigenous populations, political aspirations are distinguished by a sense of nationhood that defines a claim to independent sovereignty within and over their own communities. On the one hand, maximum possible independence is claimed, and on the other, guaranteed and substantive influence in the national polity is sought. In other words, the politics of indigeneity is a politics of 'shared sovereignties' (Maaka and Fleras, 2005, p. 187) intended to restore some degree of indigenous power and authority. Liberal political arrangements need not, then, presume sameness as the basis for equality. Their inclusive capacity is formed by deeper underlying values and conceptions of what it means to belong; what it means to be a citizen.

Indigeneity's intellectual significance is that it broadens the lens through which political claims can be made and examined. It engages notions of independent political status with western liberal theory to set a framework for thinking about how power and authority ought to be conceptualised for an inclusive acceptance of Locke's (1887) 'people' whose consent is required for legitimate government. Like Tully, indigeneity 'waves no flag for liberalism' (Scott, 2003, p. 96), but simply recognises its importance as the prevailing and politically secure paradigm under which national politics occurs in Australia and New Zealand and which the international community seeks to impose on Fiji.

The distinctive relationship between indigenous peoples and the state is distinguished by the dispossession of resources, usurpation of political authority and affronts to human dignity. Substantive self-determination requires that these transgressions of justice are acknowledged and, as far as possible, corrected. In short, reconciliation, which has, in different ways, in each jurisdiction, transcended religious metaphor to become an important contemporary goal in secular politics.

Reconciliation provides a rationale for public expressions of sorrow for affronts to human dignity. It is a theological response to colonisation's impact that was brought into secular discourse to help public policy admit indigenous perspectives on matters such as land rights, health and wellbeing and apology and restitution for state sanctioned violence. It provides a founding rationale for secular reconciliation beyond the legal and political arguments raised in the Canadian Supreme Court's *Mitchell v. Minister of National Revenue*'s reference to reconciling indigenous and state political authority through 'merged sovereignties', for example (Supreme Court of Canada, 2001).

Reconciliation's foundational significance to this book is explained further by the strength of religious interconnectedness with Fijian ethnic politics and by the role of the Australian Christian churches in establishing reconciliation as a theological/political nexus in that country's indigenous public policy during the 1990s. In New Zealand, reconciliation is less prominent in public debate, but remains an always acknowledged principle in iwi [tribal] settlements with the Crown for breaches of the Treaty of Waitangi.

Reconciliation means that political theory must see the state and indigenous peoples as equal participants in the creation of a just political order. From this perspective, politics ought not concern itself only with how the state might act justly, but with how indigenous peoples might find the political capacity to work out for themselves what constitutes justice in the relationships and aspirations that they wish to define and pursue. In this way, when it is juxtaposed with the politics of indigeneity, reconciliation's foundation in human equality challenges state accounts of absolute and indivisible sovereignty; discourses that are 'neither natural nor neutral [but which]…reproduce a space for politics that is enabled by and rests upon the production, naturalization and marginalization of certain forms of "difference"' (Shaw, 2008, p. 9). In this way sovereignty becomes an absolute, incontestable and indivisible vesting of political power in the state. Alternatively, the legal scholar and former New Zealand Prime Minister, Geoffrey Palmer (1995), argues that:

> Notions of sovereignty are collapsing all over the world… Far from being the indivisible omnipresent concept that Hobbes made it in *Leviathan*, sovereignty is more like a piece of chewing gum. It can be stretched and pulled in many directions to do almost anything. Sovereignty is not a word that is useful and it should be banished from political debate. (pp. 153–4)

For many indigenous peoples, however, sovereignty is neither absolute nor meaningless and, perhaps, rather than notions of sovereignty collapsing, indigenous political aspirations might be positioned among those that are re-configuring the meaning and practice of political authority, with particular reference to relationships between the state and indigenous citizens.

Indigenous experiences of sovereignty are contests over political power. Sovereignty's emancipatory potential, its capacity as 'an instrument of escape from rule by outsiders' (Jackson, 1999, p. 10) occurs only in so far as it is located with the people as an all-encompassing construct, rather than vested in some individual or institution from which indigenous peoples are excluded. If sovereignty belongs to the people it must, in the interests of cohesion, order and justice, belong to all the people.

Exclusion from full and equal membership of the polity, either by virtue of race or alienation from the centre of military power, undermines capacity for independent indigenous political authority.

If sovereignty is 'popular' then the populace must be defined either as an homogenous whole where minority voices are rightly subsumed, or as a body comprising many parts requiring some political solution to the question of how these disparate parts ought to share power and authority. The theoretical engagement of democracy with indigeneity offers one way of thinking about this question. It suggests that some rearrangement of sovereignty is implicit in the creation of more inclusive democratic orders while balancing the rights and expectations of indigenous peoples vis-à-vis all others.

Liberal democracy requires checks on unbridled majoritarian rule meaning that there must be constraints on popular sovereignty so that one group's liberty is never at the expense of another's. State sovereignty is always constrained by international acceptability; 'it depends on conditions that operate above the level of the individual states themselves' (Hindess, 2000, p. 31), which is why this book especially analyses the possibilities for indigenous authority and self-determination beyond the state; within indigenous institutions, and through the security that comes from independent economic development. Indigeneity's local geopolitical focus is also underpinned by global theoretical developments in law and politics that make it a movement of resistance but also one of transformation concerned with pragmatic yet meaningful opportunities for self-determination through differentiated citizenship, where indigenous peoples share substantive equality as citizens *within* the state and *beyond* it as members of their own political communities with authority over their own affairs.

New Zealand and Fiji are former British colonies, while Australia is a political federation, established in 1901, comprising six former colonies. The origins of contemporary Australian government lie in the self-proclamation of British sovereignty, based on the contention that the continent was in Locke's theory of labour, *terra nullius*, or unoccupied land. *Terra nullius* was in Reynold's phrase a 'self-serving Eurocentric jurisprudence' of convenience (Reynolds, 1996, p. xii) on which government proceeded until 1992 when the High Court found that when settlement occurred in 1778: 'The lands of this continent were not…practically unoccupied' (*Mabo and Others v. Queensland*, 1992). The *Mabo* decision enjoyed landmark significance and together with Royal Commission reports into *Aboriginal Deaths in Custody* (Johnston, 1991) and the *Separation of Aboriginal and Torres Strait Islander Children from their Families* (Dodson and Wilson, 1997), the case made the decade a turning point in indigenous/state relationships. The 1997 report's explicit promotion of reconciliation as a political aspiration brought the concept into public policy discourse and helped to frame the ways in which the political claims of an indigenous population comprising less than 3 per cent of the national total might be addressed. For indigenous people, statements of apology for removals were preliminary to substantive measures of restitution. Although this view was accepted by all State and Territory Parliaments, the Howard government's (1997–2008) view that such was not justified because a Parliament could not accept 'guilt' for the policies of another, meant that the issue was one of significant public controversy until the government's defeat in 2007.

Apology is symbolically important. Its practical significance is that it carries a commitment to restitution and to ensure that the unjust practice for which the apology was made does not resume. It is also a 'very powerful instrument of recognition – refusal to offer one withholds that recognition with new sharpness' (Warner, cited in Mitzsal, 2003, p. 13). This point was accepted by the newly elected Rudd government (2007–10) and in moving a Motion of Apology, Rudd (2008) told the House of Representatives that:

> The time has now come for the nation to turn a new page in Australia's history by righting the wrongs of the past and so moving forward with confidence to the future.
>
> We apologise for the laws and policies of successive Parliaments and governments that have inflicted profound grief, suffering and loss on these our fellow Australians...
>
> Let us resolve over the next five years to have every Indigenous four-year-old in a remote Aboriginal community enrolled and attending a proper early childhood education centre...and engaged in proper preliteracy and prenumeracy programs...Let us resolve [also] to use this systemic approach...to provide proper primary and preventive healthcare for the same children, to begin the task of rolling back the obscenity that we find today in infant mortality rates in remote Indigenous communities – up to four times higher than in other communities.

Developments toward self-determination have followed the apology. However, their adequacy and inconsistency with other policy measures are contested and this book examines the tensions of perspectives and aspirations that remain, and which help explain the bleak contemporary indigenous population profile, where indigenous Australians die younger than other citizens, often from preventable causes, and are less well educated. They are also more likely to be unemployed or imprisoned (Australian Institute of Health and Welfare, 2015), and there is no single policy or theoretical approach to diminish these examples of colonial legacy. Nevertheless, there are broad principles of citizenship and belonging that this book examines for their likely contributions to self-determination which would, for Anderson (2014), mean that by 2030:

- there would be true reconciliation – treaty, constitutional recognition, resulting in an Australian society in which Aboriginal and Torres Strait Islander people and cultures have pride of place;
- there would be real community control in our community controlled sector;
- there would be significant improvement in health outcomes and life expectancy;
- there would be real cultural equity, and no racism;
- Aboriginal knowledge would be part of the mainstream, part of the norm: 'Nunga streaming' not 'mainstreaming';
- Aboriginal models of health would be brought to the fore and privileged, for example, spirituality;
- there would be informed choices and control concerning education and employment;
- diversity and difference would be celebrated;
- there would be seamless integration of Aboriginal values which would become part of the landscape;
- there would be no 'othering';
- there would be Aboriginal representation at all levels of government and society;
- Aboriginal people would be influencing decisions, across all dimensions of society, not just fiscal approach;
- on a broader scale across society we would have a broader approach, it wouldn't just be about money, there would be a return to values and ethics (individual and community), less focus on consumerism and capitalism, and sustainable and ecological ways of living.

The post, rather than neocolonial image, that Anderson (2014) anticipates is one where a representative indigenous woman would reach the age of 29 years with the following characteristics:

- she has higher education qualifications, and is technically, socially and culturally savvy;
- she is mentally and socially in touch with community and family;
- she is a non-smoker, with a good BMI and no drinking problem;

- she is in a stable relationship;
- she has choice and control over her own fertility, childcare and employment;
- she is world-aware but with a sense of individual purpose;
- she is well-travelled and has global visions;
- she is economically independent;
- she is grounded in mixed cultures;
- she builds on family history for positive outcomes. (Brands, 2014, pp. 12–13)

'On the other hand', Anderson (2014) says, 'we can imagine an Australia which turns its back on diversity, which increases the divide between rich and poor, and which sees little or no real improvement in the health and wellbeing of its First Peoples'. Under these circumstances the life of a representative 29-year old indigenous woman in 2030 is likely to be distinguished by experiences of:

- family breakdown/violence
- an abusive relationship
- having been a school dropout
- substance abuse
- imprisonment
- housing crisis
- her children being at risk/social service involvement
- stress/mental illness
- chronic disease
- premature death
- her family and community deeply affected by her loss. (Brands, 2014, p. 13)

In New Zealand, Maori comprise a sizeable and growing proportion of the national population (15 per cent). Maori politics is distinguished by a concern for constructing political institutions congruent with cultural priorities and with the political capacity to engage the nation-state in serious dialogue on the nature of shared political authority. The claim to shared sovereignty is grounded in the Treaty of Waitangi and supported by developments at both the common law and international law. The Treaty provides a marked contrast with the circumstances of Australian colonisation. Although there remains disagreement about whether or not the Treaty involved Maori ceding sovereignty to the British Crown and what ought to be its application in contemporary politics and public policy, it was, without Australian parallel, an agreement for British settlement to occur.

The contrast helps to explain the very different ways in which indigenous/state relationships have developed in each context. While successive New Zealand governments have insisted that the Treaty was, in fact, a cession of sovereignty, a generally representative and consistent Maori interpretation, upheld by the Waitangi Tribunal, is that: 'The rangatira [chiefs] consented to the treaty on the basis that they and the Governor were to be equals, though they were to have different roles and different spheres of influence' (Waitangi Tribunal, 2014).

Tensions over the Treaty's application and meaning have distinguished New Zealand politics since 1840, even though important developments towards self-determination have occurred since the introduction of guaranteed Maori parliamentary representation in 1867. However, it was not until the 1970s that self-determining measures became significant and sustained as language revitalisation, Treaty settlements and the partial restoration of the Maori economic base reflected the potential for differentiated citizenship to influence public policy arrangements. While these developments are significant, they have not fully set aside colonial legacy and there remains important scope for indigeneity, as a politics of potential, to increase its public influence. The Treaty provides contemporary New Zealand politics with an important moral, jurisprudential and political framework for conceptualising reconciliation as 'belonging together differently'.

Since 1996 Maori have enjoyed at least proportionate representation in parliament, linguistic and cultural revival is well established and economic security is enhanced by increasing personal incomes (Statistics New Zealand, 2013). There is a strong foundation for differentiated citizenship to reflect what Durie (2003) calls the 'dual aims of Maori development': 'Facilitating Maori access to New Zealand society and economy on the one hand; and enhancing Maori lives, Maori society and Maori knowledge on the other' (pp. 90–1). In other words, 'Maori want to retain a distinct identity that comes from a unique heritage, common journeys, a familiar environment, and a set of shared aspirations' (p. 98), where:

> development can not be prescribed from outside. Direct Maori involvement in planning, policy formulation and priority setting makes it more likely that the direction of development will be consistent with Maori aspirations. It may also mean that the goals of development will be

rejected if they have been set without reference to Maori. (pp. 309–10)

Treaty settlements have played a particular role in the pursuit of Durie's 'dual aims' of development and have weakened the dependence on the state promoted by earlier policy paradigms. For example, O'Regan (2014) explains that from the Ngai Tahu iwi's perspective:

> we are, relatively, wealthy with net assets of close to $1 billion (and rising) with a tribally managed superannuation scheme of more than 19,000 members and $35.3 million of funds under management. We are a significant force in the tourism, fishing and farming industries. We are major property developers and investors. We own a number of major government properties within our traditional southern territory which are leased back on commercial terms. Since our settlements in 1998 we have distributed approximately $300 million of funds back into our tribal structure, communities and to individuals.

Beyond the economic, significant changes to public sector social service delivery arrangements, beginning in the 1980s, created opportunities for Maori participation as contractors to the state in the provision of services such as primary healthcare and schooling (Boston et al, 1996). The number of schools teaching partly or wholly in the Maori language and according to Maori epistemologies significantly increased during the 1980s and 1990s, in particular.

Differentiated terms of 'belonging' secure Maori participation in the national sovereign and, because that sovereignty is dispersed, assures Maori capacity to influence its possibilities and constraints. Differentiation strengthens customary rights and in New Zealand, for example, 'the explicit incorporation of tikanga Maori concepts [Maori customary concepts] into formal state law [which] has not been uncommon in the years since 1991' (Williams, 2005, p. 381). Williams cites a number of examples, including changes to the *Adoption Act 1955* to have regard to Maori familial customs. There are also customary concepts in the *Resource Management Act 1991*, while *Te Ture Whenua Maori Act 1993* [Maori Land Act] 'makes provision for a more collective control of Maori freehold land interests' (Williams, 2005, p. 382). For some Maori, these legislative developments bring a new dimension to citizenship because: 'The defining characteristic of indigenous peoples is...not necessarily premised on colonisation, sovereignty, or a prior claim to settlement, but on a long-standing relationship with land, forests, waterways, oceans, and the air' (Durie, 2005, p. 137). However, as in Australia, indigeneity provides no panacea for the creation of a genuinely non-colonial politics, but it does propose foundational principles for considering the right to self-determination.

British colonial authority was established in Fiji by a Deed of Cession in 1874. By 1970, political independence had been restored. However, in the intervening period, the British importation of Indian indentured labour had changed the country's demographic characteristics and the now majority Indo-Fijian population retained significant political authority under the constitutional arrangements established for Fijian self-government (Lal, 2006).

Political instability has distinguished post-independence Fiji, with three coups and a putsch highlighting the extent of political division. Instability stems from the fact that Fiji is not a postcolonial state in the term's ordinary sense. While the colonial power withdrew in 1970, the Indo-Fijian population was numerically and materially dominant and assumed neocolonial characteristics and influences, while also retaining many of the characteristics of a displaced colonised population. Fijian politics was distinguished by the same constant tension between post-settler and indigenous citizens that distinguished Australia and New Zealand in their very different demographic, cultural and socio-political circumstances.

Since independence from Britain in 1970, national constitutions have strictly protected indigenous Fijian rights, meaning that ethnic difference is not the sole cause of contemporary political unrest. The coups were motivated by class politics and it was only afterwards that alliances of convenience were created with indigeneity to seek popular legitimacy. It was in this context that the 1987 Constitution required that a native person hold the office of Prime Minister; a requirement based on a particularly narrow view of the relationship between that office and fuller political authority. As the *Fiji Post* (2001) noted, the country had had a non-indigenous Prime Minister for only one of the last 30 years. Timoci Bavadra, whose government was the first to be forcibly removed in 1987, was an ethnic Fijian while the limited policy success for indigenous people of the indigenous-led Rabuka (1992–99) and Qarase (2000–01 and 2001–06) governments powerfully illustrates the absence of any causal link between an indigenous Prime Minister and indigenous self-determination.

Liberal democracy disperses authority among the executive, parliament and judiciary, and no Prime Minister has authority to the point of being unconditionally free and powerful. Prime Ministerial authority is hindered by a multitude of constraints on national sovereignty so that when indigenous peoples, in whatever jurisdiction, speak of reclaiming sovereignty it is not the all-encompassing commanding construct that many imagine. It is not a final and absolute authority. Nor is it 'natural or inevitable or immutable' (Jackson, 1999, p. 10). Fiji's inward-looking politics is preoccupied with power, without broadly developed perceptions of how, and to what end, power ought to be exercised. Fraenkel and Firth (2006) argue that 'the central question of Fiji politics since independence remains unresolved: Who should rule and for whom' (p. 6)? The three constitutions, three coups and putsch since independence have failed to resolve this foundational political question partly because of sustained Fijian incapacity to admit the relative and relational nature of sovereignty, and the ways it is shaped by international considerations and its distribution within the domestic polity.

Fijian political behaviour is influenced by a multitude of factors. Religion, class, occupation, education, gender and place of residence combine with ethnic identity to shape political aspirations and values. Fijian politics is not a simple binary with the indigenous on one side and Indo-Fijians on the other. Intra-ethnic conflict, and class and rural/urban divisions are also relevant as the central political problem 'is not really about having a Fijian head of government, but rather which Fijian leader would be acceptable to a particular group of Fijians at any given time' (Lal, 2012, p. 13). So it was that a coup followed the Qarase government's democratic return to office after the 2006 general election. The government had prevailed over the army's active intervention in the election campaign, where military intimidation was blatant and unapologetic (Alley, 2010). It was clear that sovereignty was not the preserve of the Fijian people, even though the intervention was to counter established instances of racism and corruption in the administration of government. Dissonance between the Fijian people and national sovereignty is not only an outcome of three coups (1987 and 2006) and a putsch (2000), but was evident in 2006, as the Qarase government was re-elected according to due constitutional process, but with 'little sense of the electorate's ownership of the election as a genuinely national contest'. (p. 147). Or as Alley (2010) continues: 'the contest was an engagement more to do with holding the line by electing what was mistrusted least – the communally based party devil that voters knew – rather than an exercise endorsing or mandating a policy programme taking the country into the future' (p. 147). Yet, in postcolonial jurisdictions with majority indigenous populations, such as Fiji, indigeneity is constrained, both morally and practically, where it fails to consider the relative and relational character of political power. Indigeneity's strategic utility is also compromised when it fails to balance its concern for the correction of perceived power imbalances, with the liberal rights of individual citizenship, and the pragmatic truth that national political stability is inevitably preliminary to collective self-determination.

In 2014 Bainimarama retained office after an election based on universal suffrage. However, his selective and self-serving interpretation of democracy continues to prevent the concept's stable and secure development. There is not scope for a robust, yet politically safe, contestation of ideas or for indigenous peoples' *particular* political status to be settled. It is this inability to think about the political complexities of indigenous rights and responsibilities in an ordered and coherent fashion that most compromises the realisation of a genuine, substantive and politically workable self-determination.

Though this book's focus is one of contemporary secular political relationships, claims and philosophies, a public theology of reconciliation has set their tone and context and is introduced in Chapter One for its foundational significance. The chapter establishes the context for the remaining chapters to consider what reconciliation means as a secular policy goal grounded in human equality, where indigenous peoples are agents of their own affairs with an equal claim to the capacity to exercise that agency. Indigenous ideas about reconciliation as secular politics stem from a broader politics of indigeneity, explained in Chapter Two as a political theory concerned with the terms of indigenous belonging to the nation state.

Chapter Three explains how citizenship's structure determines the nature of indigenous belonging to the national political community. It contrasts the ideological presumptions that underlie citizenship and shows liberal democracy's potential to privilege *either* an emancipatory *or* an exclusive account of indigenous belonging. Chapter Four extends the argument for group rights, through differentiated liberal citizenship, as preliminary to the protections of the individual rights and liberties of the indigenous person. The argument proceeds from the view that individual identity is culturally contextualised and, for indigenous peoples, politically contextualised by colonialism itself. The chapter proposes differentiated citizenship as a model from which contemporary Fijian politics might draw stability and cohesion as preliminary to greater levels of indigenous self-determination.

Chapter Five shows that indigenous self-determination is as much a product of extra-state political and economic relationships as a product of those occurring within the state. The chapter shows that the global political order creates opportunities for greater self-determination in modern times even though, historically, it was globalisation that rationalised and gave effect to the oppressive colonial project. As well as creating new economic opportunities, contemporary globalisation is creating new intellectual spaces for worldwide indigenous cooperation leading to the United Nations' *Declaration on the Rights of Indigenous Peoples* (2007a) as the most important among a number of international legal instruments from which indigenous peoples in Australia and New Zealand have been able to constrain state power. These experiences do, however, expose a significant weakness in contemporary international law's applicability to indigenous/state relationships in other jurisdictions; the *Declaration*'s uncertain applicability to Fiji, for example, on the grounds that its indigenous population is a majority. The chapter shows that because contemporary Fijian politics is so strongly contextualised by colonial experience the *Declaration* could, in fact, make a significant contribution to stability and cohesion by proposing indigeneity's pragmatic limits as well as its possibilities.

Chapter Six is a case study in indigenous Australian economic development as differentiated citizenship. The cultural aspirations that underlie indigenous approaches to economic development distinguish it from the presumptions that more commonly influence state policy. Indigenous policy actors tend to favour economic development approaches that are closely associated with and responsive to aspirations for cultural development, social stability, employment, health and educational opportunities. The chapter shows that 'culture counts' (Bishop and Glynn, 1999) in economic development and lays the foundation for Chapters Seven and Eight to consider further the possibilities and constraints on economic development as differentiated citizenship in New Zealand and Fiji. Indeed, Chapter Seven begins with the proposition that citizenship is, itself, a determinant of economic opportunities. Citizenship's potential to recognise culture in policy development and in people's participation in the education and labour markets sits alongside its potential to admit the Maori use of natural resources for their own culturally framed purposes. Differentiated citizenship is a constituent of economic agency; the chapter shows how and why, before Chapter Eight shows the significance of differentiated citizenship's absence in Fiji where military sovereignty means that there is not a public sovereignty in which that country's indigenous population might seek both proportionate and distinctive shares to support economic and other aspirations. In these ways, Chapter Eight provides a contrast with Australia and New Zealand where economic development is well understood as an essential constituent of indigenous claims to self-determination.

Note

1   This book develops and expands extensively on work previously published in different form as D. O'Sullivan, 2014, Indigeneity, ethnicity and the state: Australia, Fiji and New Zealand. *Nationalism and Ethnic Politics*, 20, 1, 26–42; D. O'Sullivan, 2014, Reconciliation as public theology: Christian thought in comparative indigenous politics. *International Journal of Public Theology*, 8, 5–24; D. O'Sullivan, 2012, Globalization and the politics of indigeneity, *Globalizations*, 9, 5, 637–50; and D. O'Sullivan, 2010, Democracy, power and indigeneity. *Australian Journal of Politics and History*, 57, 1, 86–101.

ONE

Reconciliation

Introduction

Although in very different ways, reconciliation is a political/theological nexus of foundational significance to indigenous politics in all three of Australia, Fiji and New Zealand. Christian public theology extends reconciliation beyond its primary sacramental interest in relationships between God and penitent to the construction of 'socially just' public relationships for the settlement of intra-national conflict. Theologically, reconciliation brings public relationships into what Hally (1998) calls 'the Christ narrative of passion, death and resurrection' in which the perpetrators of injustice repent and seek forgiveness (p. 2). It is relevant to secular politics because it conceptualises unjust secular political decisions as the product of social sin, which occurs because political decisions, 'whether they are good or bad, are the result of [hu]man's actions' (Sacred Congregation for the Doctrine of the Faith, 1984, IV, 15). Phillips' (2005) observation for Australia is equally true of Fiji and New Zealand, that public reconciliation has 'several distinctly Christian resonances and ambiguities, including the difficult relation of justice and forgiveness' (p. 11).

This chapter demonstrates the role of Christian churches in reconciliation's development from a solely religious precept to one of secular political priority deeply intertwined with the politics of indigeneity as it is introduced in Chapter Two. The remaining chapters are then able to show that effective indigenous political expression in Australia and New Zealand has developed, partly, from that integration of theoretical precepts to provide a framework for expressing indigenous claims on the state.

Reconciliation: towards a politics of possibility

Prior to the 1990s, 'general apathy, with intermittent stirrings of a troubled conscience' (Stockton, 1988, p. 202) best describes Church responses to indigenous public policies of un-Christian intent. By the late twentieth century Australian churches were taking a more forthright interest in the religious implications of secular politics setting aside the rights of indigenous peoples. Their public advocacy for reconciliation was internationally supported by the World Council of Churches and the Holy See. In 1986, Pope John Paul II's (1996) address to Indigenous Australians in Alice Springs set the tone for subsequent Christian intellectual engagement with secular perspectives, particularly on indigenous land rights and apologies to the stolen generations. John Paul argued, to some secular derision, that:

> The establishment of a new society for Aboriginal people cannot go forward without just and mutually recognised agreements with regard to these human problems, even though their causes lie in the past. (p. 70)

> Let it not be said that the fair and equitable recognition of Aboriginal rights to land is discrimination. To call for the acknowledgement of the land rights of people who have never surrendered those rights is not discrimination. (p. 69)

John Paul's pontificate was distinguished by the conviction that where concrete political circumstances had religious implications, especially in relation to human dignity, it became a requirement of religious mission to influence secular policy choices; political developments during the 1990s provided the context for this to occur. In particular, the High Court's *Mabo* judgment, in 1992, contributed to an evolving public narrative of reconciliation by dismissing the legal validity of *terra nullius* as the basis on which government could proceed (Reynolds, 1996). The judgment gave context, authority and political momentum to the work of the Council for Aboriginal Reconciliation, established by the government in 1991, in recognition of prior indigenous occupancy, 'dispossession and dispersal', and the absence of any earlier formal attempt at reconciliation (Council for Aboriginal Reconciliation, 2003). Yet, as a mark of the depth of philosophical disagreement over reconciliation's wisdom and efficacy, the Howard government's (1996–2007) *Native Title Amendment Bill* restricted indigenous access to land for spiritual purposes which is preliminary to their religious freedom. For the churches, the tense public debate over land rights highlighted the case for a national reconciliation movement. Indeed, reconciliation's place in secular political discourse was especially strengthened by measures such as the *National Report of the Royal Commission into Aboriginal Deaths in Custody* (Johnston, 1991) and the report, *Bringing Them Home: National Inquiry into the Separation of Aboriginal and Torres Strait Islander Children from their Families* (Dodson and Wilson, 1997). Indeed, reconciliation was explicit in *Bringing Them Home*'s recommendation that:

> churches and other non-government agencies which played a role in the administration of the laws and policies under which Indigenous children were forcibly removed acknowledge that role and in consultation with the Aboriginal and Torres Strait Islander Commission make such formal apologies and participate in such commemorations as may be determined. (Dodson and Wilson, 1997, 6)

Policy advocacy was among the ways in which the churches accepted this recommendation, and reconciliation acquired momentum as secular politics. However, the Australian community struggled philosophically to discern a response to the Report's further recommendations that 'all Australian Parliaments':

1. officially acknowledge the responsibility of their predecessors for the laws, policies and practices of forcible removal,
2. negotiate with the Aboriginal and Torres Strait Islander Commission a form of words for official apologies to Indigenous individuals, families and communities and extend those apologies with wide and culturally appropriate publicity, and
3. make appropriate reparation as detailed in the following recommendations. (Dodson and Wilson, 1997, 5a)

While the state parliaments quickly accepted the recommendation to offer apologies, it was not for 11 years that the Commonwealth Parliament did the same to recognise the relationship between apology and substantive policy measures to improve indigenous people's living conditions, material opportunities and equal deliberative capacity in public affairs.

Like reconciliation, justice is the subject of philosophical disagreement; it is neither constant nor absolute. It is not politically neutral even though it might claim to be the outcome of philosophical objectivity. Conceptions of justice evolve as the political order continuously re-balances competing claims on the state. What is especially important, however, is that indigeneity holds that it is only through a process of substantive reconciliation of indigenous rights with the claims of the state, that the state itself can secure moral legitimacy (Tully, 1999; Maaka and Fleras, 2005). From this perspective, indigenous peoples ought to be able to extract policy concessions from governments and think about ways of re-ordering the institutions and practices that curtail indigenous freedom (Maaka and Fleras, 2005).

Apologies meet the symbolic requirements of sorrow, while reparation involves the perpetrator correcting, as far as possible, the ongoing impact of the initial transgression. As Dance (1998) notes: 'Saying sorry…commits us to working in a creative partnership with the indigenous people of Australia in overcoming the tragic aftermath of this pain and loss' (p. 1). Sorrow, then, makes reparation and restitution inescapable pre-conditions for future political relationships of trust, and for providing members of the stolen generations with the financial capacity to respond to the psychological and economic consequences of familial deprivation. Although the National Inquiry recommended reparation, including financial compensation, this has not been provided in any substantive way, meaning that the full conditions of reconciliation remain elusive and the central problem in contemporary indigenous Australian politics remains 'the extent to which Aboriginal people really are permitted to define their own vision of the good life and require other Australians to let them live it' (Clarke, 2006). Yet, it is also true that a new public narrative calling for the radical reshaping of indigenous/state relationships is incrementally emerging. Indigenous voices and perspectives have been admitted into mainstream public discourse through, for example, the *Mabo* (The High Court of Australia, 1992) and *Wik* (The Hight Court of Australia, 1996) decisions of the High Court, and the deaths in custody and stolen generations' Royal Commissions. *Mabo*, for example, challenged the basic assumptions and foundations of a racially exclusive state. Justice Brennan observed that the law would:

> perpetuate an injustice if it were to continue to embrace the enlarged notion of terra nullius and to persist in characterising the indigenous inhabitants of the Australian colonies as people too low in the scale of social organization to be acknowledged as possessing rights and interests in land. (*Mabo and Others v. Queensland* (No. 2), 1992)

Courts can take a broader view of justice than parliaments which tend to 'recoil from the prospect of inherent sovereign rights that supersede the sovereignty of the State as the exclusive repository of authority and entitlement' (Tully, 1999, p. 223). It is in this context of on-going political and legal paradoxes that reconciliation has emerged as a political discourse capable of positioning reparative justice at the forefront of indigenous state relationships. Just as in New Zealand, reparation and reconciliation reflect a form of 'transitional justice' in which 'indigenous and western worldviews confront each other in fundamental ways' and where indigeneity's goals 'transcend those of the reparations system' itself (Hill and Bönisch-Brednich, 2007, p. 163).

Conversely, however, as Justice Brennan explained in the *Mabo* decision:

> In discharging its duty to declare the common law of Australia, this court is not free to adopt rules that accord with contemporary notions of justice and human rights if their adoption would fracture the skeleton of principle which gives the body of our law its shape and consistency. (*Mabo and Others v. Queensland* (No. 2), 1992, 29:11)

Even the Australian *Wik* judgment which gave greater legal meaning to indigenous land rights left no doubt about whose interests must prevail in the event of conflict. Where pastoral land leases were at odds with native title it was to be the native title rights that would yield (The High Court of Australia, 1996). What this showed, as did the foreshore and seabed legislation in New Zealand in 2004, is the liberal state's difficulty with the expression of equal citizenship of the one polity in specific indigenous context. It showed the limits of egalitarian justice and the government's unease with growing Maori political assertiveness.

Reconciliation is diminished and the depths of the affront to human dignity understated when apologies are not accompanied by reparative and restitutive measures. Indeed, a disregard for the gravity of the separation policy's impact on indigenous families was the obvious implication of the Prime Minister John Howard's refusal to say 'sorry'. Howard's position was a politically expedient appeal to those without empathy for the people removed from their families. His view was that saying 'sorry' was an admission of personal culpability for past events over which he and his government had no influence: 'I don't believe that current generations of Australians should be seen as responsible for deeds over which they had no control and in which they had no involvement' (Howard, 2000). His view contrasted with the theological basis to sorrow, which does not imply personal guilt, but a 'grave moral responsibility', 'to dispel the ideologies, ignorance and biases in which racist attitudes may still fester and largely be hidden from conscious awareness' (Prowse, 1995, p. 118).

Although the contemporary Australian state has accepted the propriety of saying 'sorry', it remains uncertain and perhaps even indifferent towards reconciliation's presumption that 'sorrow' requires contrition, as a meaningful policy attempt to correct the consequences of the injustice for which sorrow has been expressed, and to resolve not to repeat those transgressions of justice in public policy. However, contrition is among reconciliation's essential elements; and has broad contemporary public policy significance. The book will demonstrate that significance in the chapters to follow and will propose a liberal politics of indigeneity distinguished, especially, by differentiated citizenship as a foundation for reconciliation. In this context, it is significant that the Uniting Church, among others, endorsed in 2012 proposals to amend the Commonwealth Constitution to recognise indigenous first occupancy and remove powers of racial discrimination, as 'concrete steps' towards reconciliation (Uniting Church in Australia, 2012). These are measures that recognise the inherent dignity of the human person and legitimise human equality as a just and important founding principle in law and politics.

Contrition and the Treaty of Waitangi as practical reconciliation

Contrition is, in contrast with Australia, integral to reconciliation as it is played out through Treaty of Waitangi settlements, among other measures, in contemporary New Zealand politics. The Treaty has provided the historical, legal and political contexts for government expressions of sorrow under procedures established in 1975 and amended in 1985 for the investigation and settlement of Maori grievances against the Crown. While the Treaty is not a panacea for reconciliation as it has provided neither recognition to Maori claims in full, nor gained uncontested public acceptance as a legitimate influence over contemporary public policy (O'Sullivan, 2007), it does allow policy to proceed on the assumption that to varying degrees, the Crown ought to offer measures of contrition for transgressions against Maori rights and that different peoples ought to be able to live within the one polity with as much freedom and autonomy as possible. In addition, the Treaty presumes that Maori ought to be able to participate in shared public affairs with reference to cultural preferences and priorities.

The Treaty is an important instrument in Maori politics. As McHugh (2005) notes, instances of political disagreement between Maori and the Crown can usually be traced to Maori perceptions of the Crown acting without regard for its terms, and in response to political pressure from public resistance to reparation and restitution. Indeed, in 2004, the Leader of the Opposition National Party, Don Brash, attracted widespread support for his claim that Maori policy was distinguished by measures giving Maori a 'birthright to the upper hand' over other citizens (Brash, 2004). In the same year, a Court of Appeal decision upholding customary title to the foreshore and seabed intensified public suspicion, as the government encouraged a popular belief that the decision jeopardised public access to the national coastline for recreational purposes. The litigants in the case confirmed that restricting access was not their intention and there was authoritative independent legal advice that such was not the decision's effect (O'Sullivan, 2007). The ensuing public debate was deeply polarising and, in response, the Anglican and Roman Catholic Bishops jointly intervened to emphasise the point in procedural justice that the Treaty requires the Crown 'to act in good faith towards Maori, which must mean honest dialogue with Maori when their rights to property are at stake' (Anglican and Catholic Bishops, 2004). Indeed, honest dialogue is essential to a society in which peoples are able to 'live together differently' (Maaka and Fleras, 2005), reconciled in the ways that they address historic disagreements as well as contemporary disagreements on the terms of different peoples' participation in national public life. 'Living together differently' requires agreement on the principle that different peoples are free to live as autonomously as possible within their own communities, both as the object of the politics of indigeneity and as a mark of reconciliation. The fact that Brash's view did not enjoy prevailing influence in the long term and the subsequent repeal of the *Foreshore and Seabed Act 2004* showed that although contested, reconciliation does retain influence, and provides intellectual rationale for the politics of indigeneity that is introduced in the next chapter.

The Treaty provides much of the framework for contemporary relationships between the Crown and iwi (Maori tribes) and is central to contemporary Maori politics; this centrality remains, in spite of the Treaty's persistent breaches by the Crown, and populist resistance to correcting that history of broken promises. The Treaty provides the context for reconciliation as public theology; it does so in recognition of missionary encouragement to the Chiefs to sign the document in 1840, and in recognition of its contemporary potential to provide a framework for just political relationships. Indeed, as Orange (1987) notes, it was Anglican missionaries who translated the Treaty from English to Maori and presented it to the Maori Chiefs in the biblical language of covenant. This missionary intervention was instrumental in convincing the Chiefs that the Crown's intentions were honourable in seeking their acquiescence to an agreement that would, in fact, quickly be taken as a secession of absolute political authority (Orange, 1987). It is for this reason that land alienation and its consequent economic, social and cultural deprivation are the subject of many settlements for breaches of the Treaty under the *Treaty of Waitangi Amendment Act 1985* (New Zealand Government, 1985). The Waikato (New Zealand Government, 1995) and Ngai Tahu (New Zealand Government, 1998) tribal settlements are the two largest examples, providing both symbolic and substantive expressions of reconciliation. Treaty settlements are a secular parallel to reconciliation as a theological precept; they make atonement, without presuming personal guilt, and offer restitution and a commitment to avoid repeated transgressions of justice. Treaty settlements have increased collective wealth to raise new possibilities for the terms of belonging together differently (Maaka and Fleras, 2005). The Treaty brings clarity to the question of who ought to apologise to whom and for what, although even in religious discourse, the term reconciliation is not as widely used in New Zealand as it is in Australia to reflect its relatively less controversial status at the highest levels of government. The Minister for Treaty Negotiations puts it thus:

> All components of a settlement are valuable – the historical, cultural, financial and commercial parts of a comprehensive settlement all represent different ways of addressing grievances and breaches of the Treaty of Waitangi and its principles. Comprehensive settlements are the most effective way of repairing relationships. (Finlayson, 2009)

Settlements accept restitution and the legitimacy of public 'sorrow'. Settlement Acts of Parliament explicitly and simultaneously attend to the symbolic and the practical. For example, the Waikato apology was for the military invasion in 1863. It sought 'on behalf of all New Zealanders to atone for these acknowledged injustices, so far as that is now possible, and... to begin the process of healing and to enter a new age... of co-operation' (New Zealand Government, 1995, Part I, s. 6(6)). The Ngai Tahu settlement admitted that the Crown had 'acted unconscionably and in repeated breach of the Treaty of Waitangi' (New Zealand Government, 1998). In 2014, the Tūhoe settlement was especially concerned with atonement as a foundation for future just political relationships. The Minister for Treaty Negotiations explained that:

> Through this apology and settlement the Crown hopes to honestly confront the past and seeks to atone for its wrongs. The Crown hopes to build afresh its relationship with Tūhoe and that this new relationship will endure for current and future generations.
>
> Let these words guide our way to a greenstone door – *tatau pounamu* – which looks back on the past and closes it, which looks forward to the future and opens it. (Finlayson, 2009)

Following the settlement Tūhoe is negotiating further measures of self-determination including to take responsibility from the Crown for tribal housing, schooling, healthcare and welfare benefits. Tūhoe maintains that 'we can design a system where there is a transition from benefits to wages and salaries' (Kruger in *New Zealand Herald*, 18 November 2015) and that it 'could get better results… because of the knowledge, proximity and influence with the potential beneficiaries' (Moore et al., 2014, p. 33).

Treaty settlements contribute to increased tribal political authority and, in turn, increase the possibilities for shared public sovereignty. Their significance is, therefore, much broader than governments attending to a 'duty' to 'do justice' to Maori because reconciliation means that Maori are not 'subjects' of the Crown but equal participants in the definition of political relationships where Maori may 'do justice' to themselves. Shared sovereignty means that rights to self-determination are not 'granted' by biculturalism's 'Pakeha state' (O'Sullivan, 2007) but enjoyed as inherent rights of first occupancy that have not been justly extinguished.

From this perspective, Maaka and Fleras (2005) imagine indigenous peoples as 'sovereign in their own right yet sharing sovereignty with society at large' (p. 5). Corporate and individual membership of the common political community can then be expressed in different ways, while retaining equal legitimacy. In this way, unbridled majoritarian democracy is mediated by an assured indigenous political voice. The effect is that rather than simply asserting that it is right, a majority must subject its claims to public contest; to an informed and inclusive citizenry because 'the test of whether a claim on the public is just, or a mere expression of self-interest, is best made when persons making it must confront the opinion of others who have explicitly different, though not necessarily conflicting, experiences, priorities, and needs' (Young, 1989, p. 263). Indeed, 'deep conflicts can be resolved publicly only if political liberalism is revised in two ways: if the political conception of justice is made more dynamic and if public reason is made "plural" and not "singular"' (Bohman, 1995, p. 254). This book contributes to reconciliation by showing the merits of a liberal political theory equipped to mediate tensions between indigenous peoples' 'particular' and collective rights and those of the whole political community where 'an intercultural dialogue [occurs] in which the culturally diverse sovereign citizens of contemporary societies negotiate agreements on their forms of association over time in accordance with the three conventions of mutual recognition, consent and cultural continuity' (Tully, 1995, p. 30).

Opportunities for self-determination are broadened when one thinks about sovereignty as a relative and relational construct capable of evolution in form, purpose and distribution. Exclusive state sovereignty positions Maori beyond the political, while reconciliation responds to 'the paradox of sovereignty [producing] sites of contestation that allow political actors to challenge unjust legal exclusions and produce new political possibilities' (Dahl, 2016, p. 2).

Reconciliation's assumption of human equality allows the book to respond to Dahl's (2016) view that, as liberalism cannot give theoretical account to 'conquest', it must position indigenous peoples 'as paternalistic wards of the state unable to make political claims of their own' (p. 3). This perspective is inconsistent with the Maori experience of reconciliation through Treaty settlements which have changed the nature of Crown sovereignty as Maori are increasingly able to assert a distinctive space in the national democratic whole. Indeed the Treaty, with the affirmation of the United Nations' *Declaration on the Rights of Indigenous Peoples* (2007a), suggests that space must be found to minimise the risk of self-determination being a right 'trumped by the interests of the nation-state' (Mörkenstam, 2015, p. 644). The risk is further mitigated by the strengthening of the Maori economy (discussed in Chapter Seven) to which reconciliation has contributed.

Maori economic integration with the national economy also makes it difficult to define the interests of the state as distinct and always in conflict with Maori interests. Although there remains a 'profound question of whether a State built upon the taking of another people's lands, lives and power can ever really be just' (Independent Iwi Working Group on Constitutional Transformation Matike Mai Aotearoa, 2016, p. 29), justice is not absolute and reconciliation cannot guarantee its pervasive presence, but it can support it, and set it as an aspiration that must always be pursued and as suggesting principles upon which relationships ought to be constructed. On the other hand, there are limits to reconciliation and these, too, are the concern of a relationally just politics of indigeneity. Reconciliation, as it is played out in contemporary Fijian politics, well illustrates the point.

The limits to reconciliation: Fiji

Reconciliation requires attention to the limits of indigenous political claims. These limits are seldom tested in Australia or New Zealand, but in Fiji, the bounds of possibility and moral legitimacy are tested by an openly nationalist and exclusive politics that does not position its objective of political self-determination in relation to the rights of others or as an outcome of inter-ethnic relationships of common purpose.

Paramountcy starkly illustrates the moral limits to indigeneity, which are never seriously tested in Australasia because demographic characteristics prevent a focus on political goals beyond those that can be negotiated with the wider polity. Paramountcy can, for example, depend on occasioning injustice to others and rejecting the relative and relational character of indigenous self-determination. One widely held perspective is that paramountcy demands ethnic Indian exclusion from the national polity as preliminary to fair and reasonable political organisation. An alternative position is that Indians may properly enjoy the right to vote and be elected to parliament, but ought to be excluded from the offices of President and Prime Minister. A third alternative is that all citizens reasonably enjoy full membership of a liberal democracy with paramountcy meaning the protection of indigenous cultures and their guaranteed participation in public affairs. There is an obvious pragmatic, as well as moral imperative, to the construction of an inclusive community marked by the capacity to protect indigenous cultural priorities and authority over traditional resources. However, the self-serving politicisation of reconciliation in Fiji has undermined peoples' capacity to 'live together differently' in mutually advantageous, peaceful interdependence where self-determination is also the product of peoples' relationships with one another, and not simply the outcome of just institutional relationships. It is also contextually relevant that since the first coup in 1987, the state has been subservient to military rule. The inverse of the normative relationship between the military and liberal democratic government prevailed even when elected parliaments provided constitutionally appointed governments. The fragility of the relationship meant that governments were vulnerable and, in practice, accountable to the military leadership in more substantive ways than they were accountable to parliament and the people. Indeed, as Norton (2007) explains: 'The army now conceives itself to be the most important part of the state, as much in the protection of domestic order and governance as in matters of external defence. In this, it rejected paramountcy as the central argument in the Fijian politics of indigeneity' (p. 417).

The coup, in 2006, was motivated especially by military objection to two legislative proposals of the Qarase government. The first, *The Promotion of Reconciliation, Tolerance and Unity Bill 2005* (Attorney General's Chambers, 2005) was according to the government, inspired by a desire for national reconciliation after a civilian overthrow of the government in 2000. The Bill affronted military sensitivities because one of its alleged purposes was to be the release of putsch leaders from imprisonment, among them people who had been involved in an unsuccessful mutiny against Bainimarama. While the Bill was before Parliament, Bainimarama's position was that the army ought to prevent it from passing 'or get rid of the Government if it is passed. We can recover without this Government, we cannot recover from this Bill' (Bainimarama, 2005).

The Department of National Reconciliation and Unity, had been established to promote, among other things, 'greater unity within the indigenous Fijian community through various programs and activities at village, tikina [regional], provincial and national levels' (Lal, 2006, p. 248). However, at the same time, exclusive conceptions of indigeneity were used to marginalise urban and non-aristocratic indigenous Fijians which naturally undermined collective nationhood and political order. Disconnection occurred through the difficulties that urban indigenous peoples experience in gaining access to land and other natural resources and because aristocratic authority is privileged to restrict indigenous 'commoners' ability to participate in collective decision making (Naidu, 2009).

The second legislative measure, the *Qoliqoli Bill 2006*, affronted commercial interests by proposing the transfer of ownership in the foreshore from the state to traditional indigenous owners. The Fiji Law Society objected that: 'the state is in fact transferring... [its] right of sovereignty within these qoliqoli areas' (Radio New Zealand International, 2006). On one hand, the *Qoliqoli Bill* could be interpreted as an attempt to share public sovereignty, but on the other, Fijian politics is distinguished by deeply unsettled notions of public authority and the absence of a substantive relationship between the state and citizenship means that one cannot engage in principled discussion about the just distribution of public power and authority. A more promising approach, privileging human rights over violent and intimidatory claims to political power, would be one that provides indigenous Fijians with international legal precepts on which to make claims on the state, while also recognising the rights of others. The balancing and mediating influence of the United Nations' *Declaration on the Rights of Indigenous Peoples* (2007a) would, potentially, make a significant contribution to working out the principled exercise of popular sovereignty in contemporary Fiji. Its uncertain applicability to Fiji is a marked deficiency in international law's contribution to Fijian domestic stability.

The *Promotion of Reconciliation, Tolerance and Unity Bill 2005* co-opted reconciliation in support of a fervently nationalist indigenous politics. Its appeal to forgiveness resonated with the predominantly Methodist indigenous population, but its weak emphasis on the parallel requirement for contrition distorted reconciliation because contrition acquires substantive political effect only through an implicit resolve to desist from wrongdoing. Indeed, in 2006 Bainimarama told the *Fiji Sun* that the Qarase government: 'continuously brings in racist policies and programs to justify its existence to the indigenous community'. In a pointed rejection of communal sovereignty the military chief went on to say that the 'military is willing to return and complete for this nation the responsibilities we gave this government in 2000 and 2001'.

Laisenia Qarase's was certainly a nationalist government pursuing policies of 'Fijian advancement'. But its affirmative action policies were 'characterised more by play-offs among indigenous elites than a concern to raise standards for ordinary Fijians' (Lawson, 2004, p. 536). Even as the political developments that precipitated the coup were played out in 2006, Bainimarama (2006) remarked that 'Qarase is trying to weaken the army by trying to remove me… If he succeeds there will be no one to monitor them, and imagine how corrupt it is going to be.' The government responded with the traditional Westminster democratic view that the military had no role as constitutional or moral guardian of the state. Its relationship with the government of the day was necessarily subservient. However, immediately after the coup the Chief Justice's partisan political alignment with the military regime and the subsequent dismissal of politically neutral judges confirmed that there was to be no wider domestic check on the military. As self-appointed guardian of the Constitution, the military left itself with physical power over domestic affairs but with its moral legitimacy under international scrutiny. Reconciliation is, thus, preliminary to the political stability that sustainable indigenous self-determination presumes. However, the Methodist Church, which counts approximately 80 per cent of the Fijian indigenous population among its membership (about a third of the national population) (McCarthy, 2011), maintained an overt and unapologetically nationalist involvement in the election campaign, preceding the coup in 2006. The church lacked the political independence necessary to preach a convincing religious message capable of transcending ethnic and denominational differences. Later, the Roman Catholic Church, the country's second largest, with 13 per cent of the indigenous population among its adherents, curiously expressed its claimed interest in multi-racial democracy through an alliance with the military government that is presently explained. The result was that both churches, with their overwhelmingly indigenous congregations, chose to interpret reconciliation in isolation from internationally developed public theologies that are helping other jurisdictions to establish a 'discursive, democratic space' (Muldoon, 2003, p. 182) in which historical difference can be worked out and the terms of future political relationships established. Christianity's close alignment with indigenous Fijian culture and politics makes this an important distinction. In Australia and New Zealand, reconciliation provides a theoretically coherent set of principles to engage with a stable political order to contest and influence public conceptions of justice.

The Methodist injunction to its members, through a secular newspaper advertisement, to vote for the United Fiji Party (SDL), superficially co-opted religious precept to direct peoples' voting, but was not accompanied by a coherent theological or political account of reconciliation, and its contribution to the Christian nation, that the SDL would apparently assure:

> PARLIAMENT IS THE SUPREME LAW MAKING BODY OF THIS NATION.
> It is God's Will that the Laws of this Land are based on the Laws of God!
> IT IS THEREFORE THE DUTY OF ALL CITIZENS OF THIS NATION TO ELECT A GOD-FEARING AND PROVEN PRIME MINISTER
> whose party will make righteous laws
> ...
> Healthy Nation Building should be founded on God's Law which reflects the higher eternal values of the Kingdom of God
> LOVE JUSTICE PEACE

RECONCILIATION UNITY. (Newland, 2007, pp. 300–1)

The proposed 'righteous laws' to which the advertisement referred and which the church had actively supported were the *Promotion of Reconciliation Tolerance and Unity Bill 2005* and the *Qoliqoli Bill 2006*. These proposed laws were widely understood as 'attempts to marginalise the Indian community' (Prasad, 2009, p. 211) and assert indigenous paramountcy; the general idea that non-indigenous rights must necessarily be subservient to the indigenous.

The advertisement showed that while Australasian indigenous politics draws on reconciliation to present its argument for a political order based on 'living together differently', the Fijian political tension between indigenous paramountcy and universal political equality persists because there is no theoretical or practical account, in public life, that rationalises or sets out the terms for 'living together differently'. The strong international body of Christian public theology on the subject of reconciliation is not drawn upon by the churches in their engagement with the public realm. Instead, the Methodist construction of indigeneity occurs within the context of an exclusive Christian state, where the non-indigenous, non-Christian, Indian guests do not enjoy the same rights to land ownership and political participation that are the paramount rights of native Fijians. Christianity's mission, then, was not to influence the state's attention to justice, but to control it towards a particular construction of indigenous political rights, in a context where Indigenous Fijians already dominated national politics and where there had always been recourse to the political system to protect and promote native interests. What was missing was a fuller understanding of liberal democracy and its implications for cultural strength and economic power in a nation where land is substantially Fijian-owned (Horscroft, 2002, p. 4). As the *Fiji Post* has suggested:

> we are the most privileged and most protected indigenous community in the world. We have had 30 years of indigenous Prime-Ministership for Fijians; we have had all the permanent secretaries…but what have we done? We have 84% of the land. But I would say that Fijians are the poorest community not because of the other communities but because they have not been led by the people who care about Fijian people. (*Fiji Post*, 2001)

Just as the Methodist Church was unwilling to adopt reconciliation as a metaphor for peaceful coexistence, the Fijian Roman Catholic Church aligned itself with the military regime which, in 2007, established a Council for the People's Charter for Change and Progress to set out the terms for a return to democratic political arrangements. The regime invited Petero Mataca, Archbishop of Suva, to co-chair the Council with Bainimarama. Many Fijian Catholics interpreted Mataca's acceptance as tacit endorsement of the regime. However, the Archbishop's view was that:

> some people in Fiji who courageously upheld the rule of law and democracy since 1987 have a different view of the latest coup in the belief that democracy was abused and circumvented long before the military ousted the Qarase government…the Church believes in a democratic framework that upholds human dignity and equality, rights and responsibilities, the common good and the protection of the minorities and the vulnerable must be absolute. (*Catholic News*, 2007)

In accepting the appointment, however, Mataca aligned his church to a regime whose affronts to human rights were well known and whose very existence was a denial of political freedom. His justification was put by the Archdiocesan Vicar-General, who suggested that the Charter 'was formulated by civil societies, not by the interim administration [military regime]' and that the Archbishop accepted the appointment 'out of fear that the 1997 Constitution would be abrogated', which would, the Vicar-General stated, 'take the country back to the dark ages' (Newland, 2007, p. 205). Mataca described the Charter as a Covenant which, as Newland (2007) points out, suggests 'a more intense relationship between the state and the Roman Catholic Church' (p. 205), which in the contemporary political context, diminished the Archbishop's authority to support the obligation upon every person to claim their human rights as 'marks' of their dignity and to recognise those rights in others. In other words, the church cannot abandon humanity, since human 'destiny… is so closely and unbreakably linked with Christ' (John Paul II, 2001). Yet, simultaneously, the church's stated concern for multicultural democracy becomes hypocritical when set alongside its failure to distance itself from the regime's well-documented and sustained disregard for human dignity and political freedoms.

Conclusion

Reconciliation is a theologically grounded concept that has entered secular indigenous policy debate, across three jurisdictions, in markedly different ways. In Australia and New Zealand, where secular politics is becoming incrementally more sympathetic to indigenous claims, reconciliation envisages a political order distinguished by relationships of 'non-dominance involving interdependent people who work through differences in a non-coercive spirit of relative yet relational autonomy' (Fleras, 2000, p. 113). The influence of these philosophical presumptions is evident in measures such as increased attention to land rights, indigenous health and wellbeing, the stolen generations (in Australia) and Crown settlements to iwi (Maori tribes) for breaches of the Treaty of Waitangi (in New Zealand). By contrast, in the Fijian context, what is lacking is a coherent account of reconciliation of the sort that has assisted New Zealand Maori especially, but also Indigenous Australians, to reconfigure, incrementally, the terms of their belonging to the nation state. Their ability to use and develop theories of reconciliation has influenced these indigenous people's political engagement with their respective states, and has strengthened indigeneity as a theoretical construct capable of framing and articulating indigenous claims. It is preliminary to a liberal theory of indigeneity grounded in inclusive differentiated liberal citizenship. In this context, reconciliation transcends its intellectual foundations in Christian public theology to become the central political point in contemporary indigenous politics. The following chapters extend reconciliation from religious discourse to its practical significance as an indigenous framed politics of indigeneity, juxtaposed with liberal democratic citizenship, as the prevailing political arrangement in Australia and New Zealand.

Liberal democratic citizenship is also the arrangement that the international community seeks to impose on Fiji and that may, in turn, provide that jurisdiction with a stronger foundation for the coherent articulation and recognition of the rights of indigenous peoples as they are set out at international law. It is in this context that the book draws on the politics of indigeneity to distinguish the claims of first occupancy from simple ethnic identity politics, illustrating that relative political marginalisation in Australasia is not so much a function of minority status but of indigeneity itself. Its concern for collective rights in the nation state is not grounded in need or disadvantage, nor on claims to reparative justice, but on 'ancestral occupation' (Fleras, 2000, p. 129), and the development of political relationships 'of non-dominance involving interdependent people who work through differences in a non-coercive spirit of relative yet relational autonomy' (Fleras, 2000, p. 113).

TWO

The politics of indigeneity

Introduction

Indigeneity is a developing theory of justice and political strategy used by indigenous peoples to craft their own terms of belonging to the nation state as 'first peoples' (Ivison et al., 2000; Maaka and Fleras, 2005; O'Sullivan, 2005; Shaw, 2008; Tully, 1999). It claims extant political rights to challenge traditional assumptions of state power and authority. Its aim is to create political space for substantive and sustainable reconciliation through self-determination and a particular indigenous share in the sovereign authority of the modern state itself (Maaka and Fleras, 2005; O'Sullivan, 2007; Shaw, 2008). A foundational assumption is that, if culture is preliminary to individual liberty, it must necessarily concern normative liberal theory, as 'fairness demands more than [Rawlsian] "neutrality"' (Scott, 2003, p. 93). While liberalism is not always associated with protecting indigenous people's culturally framed liberty against the state, it does enjoy that potential. Indigenous rights are necessarily framed as group rights, which provide context and meaning to individual liberty; which does not always and necessarily set group rights aside. The politics of indigeneity is a discourse of both resistance and transformation presenting 'a fundamental challenge to the prevailing social and political order'. It requires that colonial ideas about political arrangement, authority and power make way for political spaces of indigenous autonomy (Fleras, 2000, p. 200). Its effectiveness requires some juxtaposing of traditional notions of independent authority with western political theory, to craft new bases for political engagement. In this way political theory may contribute to the possibilities for working out principled relationships for living together differently in the one national jurisdiction.

The politics of indigeneity responds to the proposition that while liberal citizenship might tend towards homogeneity in public life it is also reasonable for 'cultural pluralists [to] demand a degree of differentiation not present in almost any developed democracy' (Fleras, 2000, p. 373). The chapter explores the bases on which one might find a shared framework for working out the kinds of recognition that are fair and reasonable for meeting the principal test of liberal acceptability, which is, whether or not group rights 'undermine the integrative function of citizenship' (Fleras, 2000, p. 373).

Indigeneity

The politics of indigeneity is, potentially, a politics of reconciliation that seeks just political relationships between indigenous peoples and the state by having the state correct the consequences of affronts to indigenous human rights and dignity and agreeing to the terms of indigenous and non-indigenous peoples 'belonging together differently' (Maaka and Fleras, 2005). It distinguishes the claims of prior occupancy from simple ethnic identity politics to illustrate that relative political marginalisation in Australasia is not so much a function of minority status but of indigeneity itself. The politics of indigeneity confronts the political and legal assumptions of the contemporary state by looking to the cultural foundations of the past as a basis for setting forward-looking political priorities (Simpson, 2000). The politics of indigeneity recognises political possibilities in liberalism's privileging of the freedom of association, and argues that liberal freedoms may be exercised through and contextualised by culture.

The proposition that 'culture counts' (Bishop and Glynn, 1999): 'Is compatible with a form of universalism that counts the culture and cultural context valued by individuals as among their basic interests' (Taylor and Gutmann, 1994, p. 3) even though, for the politics of indigeneity, cultural rights are inherent to indigenous being and do not proceed from a 'conjunction between "culture" and "disadvantage"' (Scott, 2003, p. 94). Language, land and ways of being belong equally to all indigenous persons. One needs, then, to develop a normative liberal theory of indigeneity to consider what is justly claimed by indigenous peoples and to describe the ways in which these claims might be recognised.

The rights to culture, language and identity are essential to the substantive indigenous exercise of both individual and collective citizenship rights. The term 'cultural integrity' summarises indigenous claims, as not simply claims of ethnic minorities, but as appeals to extant rights, giving rise to a distinctive jurisprudence, especially in New Zealand, where the Treaty of Waitangi has assumed the moral and political authority to which the United Nations' *Declaration on the Rights of Indigenous Peoples* (2007a) aspires in other jurisdictions.

Group rights are claimed as an indication that people do not see the state as their sole, or even principal, point of identity. Collective interests and the possibility that particular grievances can arise by virtue of group membership, alone, means that a theory of justice inattentive to group rights is necessarily inattentive to the circumstances in which some people's individual rights are located. From this perspective, one could admit that group rights matter but that there is no consequent need 'to depart from the liberal language of *individual* rights to do justice to them' (Kukathas, 1992, p. 107). For Kukathas (1992), liberalism is inherently equipped to ensure that 'no one should be forced to accept any particular ideal of the good life' (p. 108). While this may be true in purely theoretical terms, practice positions the argument as one of romantic idealism. The sum expression of a majority groups' individual liberty naturally tends towards the exclusion of minority voices. Culture, history and socio-political circumstances contextualise the ways in which and purposes for which indigenous people seek to protect their personal liberty. There are different perspectives on what liberty is for and while liberal acceptance of plural rights and interests is always democratically possible, it is never assured.

The politics of indigeneity's concern for the recognition of difference based on prior occupancy, means that liberal democracy aims to secure freedom and liberty, but sees protection of group rights as preliminary to these wider goals. They are preliminary because freedom requires access to language, customary use of land and resources, and culturally cognisant schooling and healthcare, for example. National sovereignty cannot be reasonably shared without recognition of culturally framed and exercised rights, which in turn, demands public recognition of indigenous peoples as members of distinct communities with continuing claims on the nation state. The claims can be summarised as a right to be different in some senses and the same in others – to speak a different language but to enjoy the same employment opportunities; to elect members of parliament in different ways but to expect the same opportunities to participate in public decision-making; and to own land according to custom while enjoying the same protection of property rights as other land holders.

For indigeneity, difference is not just a matter of ideas and the personal merits of one candidate for public office over another. It is fundamentally concerned with what Phillips (1995) calls a 'politics of presence'. The politics of presence recognises that people themselves can be as important as their ideas in influencing individual voting preferences. This is not to say that indigenous voters will, as a matter of course, support an indigenous candidate for public office, but to say that among the diversity of indigenous political positions there are likely to be commonalities of culture, background and experiences tending towards a collective desire for presence in legislative bodies.

Certainly there are commonalities among citizens which allow non-indigenous people to represent indigenous voters on many issues, but where political positions arise from unique group experiences then representation from within the group becomes an essential guard against exclusion. It is on this basis that the politics of presence argues that the politics of ideas alone is ill-equipped to deal with the nature of exclusion: 'when difference is considered in terms of intellectual diversity it doesn't matter who represents the range of ideas' (Phillips, 1996, p. 6). However, when questions of land and other cultural rights, the nature of indigenous schooling or policies to improve indigenous health are under consideration the politics of presence becomes essential to a representative deliberative process.

Indigeneity challenges the proper competence of the state to define political agendas and establish political entitlements and obligations without reference to indigenous perspectives. It tries to make sovereignty inclusive and neither absolute nor incontestable. Indigeneity relies on engagement with other people and other discourses to draw out the national commonalities that provide the polity with cohesion and stability. But, at the same time, it proposes that the state ought to recognise the unique political status of people whose cultures and geopolitical presence pre-dates the creation of the state itself (O'Sullivan, 2007). At some point in history, indigenous groups enjoyed undisturbed sovereignty over the lands and resources that circumstances now require them to share with others. At the very least the forceful dispossession of indigenous communities might place a moral obligation on nation states to protect, as far as possible, traditional values, lifestyles, lands and resources. Citizenship is, therefore, best conceptualised and constructed to create opportunities for the translation of broad principles of self-determination into tangible political arrangements and policy outcomes. Inclusive citizenship makes substantive and equal political participation the preserve of *all* the people not simply the Executive, parliament or military.

The search for shared sovereignties remains even as the nature of the reclamation of power and authority differs between Australia and New Zealand, on the basis of different iwi (tribes) and nations making distinctive claims against the state, on the basis of New Zealand indigeneity's recourse to moral, political and jurisprudential authority in the Treaty of Waitangi, while indigenous Australia looks to the common law and the moral authority of reconciliation. Differences in the broader population's willingness to admit a distinctive, rather than just proportionate indigenous voice in national politics is also significant. Yet, in spite of these cultural, political and contextual differences, the claim to particular political authority under similar national political arrangements means that there is sufficient cross-jurisdictional commonality for the Australasian experiences to show, collectively, that when indigeneity, as both political theory and political strategy, is juxtaposed with western liberal ideas of government and governance it proposes the sharing of national sovereignty to recognise the right of *all* people to political participation in government without compromising the concern for a specific, not simply proportionate, indigenous share in the distribution of public resources, power and authority (Ivison, 2002). It is from this juxtaposition of ideas that the book is concerned with reconciliation as secular politics.

Indigeneity and egalitarian justice

The politics of indigeneity is a legal and political 'site of critical enquiry' (Byrd and Heyer, 2008) which 'contests the exclusive sovereignty of the State to pass and enforce laws, define agendas, establish priorities, articulate patterns of entitlement, or demand compliance by decree if not by consent' (Tully, 1999, p. 223). It envisages inclusive sovereignty 'grounded in the right of all citizens to shape the society in which they live' (Clarke, 2006) and is supported by international law's erosion of 'the traditional idea of sovereignty as the unconditional prerogative of the State' (Lenzerini, 2005). Indigeneity maintains that at the very least, individual liberty does not require the suppression of group rights. Indeed, for indigenous peoples, individual liberty cannot occur without cultural, linguistic and resource rights. No individual is not, also, a member of a group. For these reasons, liberal egalitarianism alone is a limited and limiting response to the claims indigenous peoples make as citizens. Yet its retention of favour in Australian indigenous policy discourse and its claim for ascendency over indigeneity and biculturalism in New Zealand means that it continues to have marked policy influence.

Rights of indigeneity are advanced to protect the broader and substantive right to self-determination that belongs, at international law, to *all* peoples. In particular, the United Nations' *Declaration on the Rights of Indigenous Peoples* (2007a) affirms 'the fundamental importance of the right of self-determination of all peoples, by virtue of which they freely determine their political status and freely pursue their economic, social and cultural development' and proposes that 'the recognition of the rights of indigenous peoples in this Declaration will enhance harmonious and cooperative relations between the State and indigenous peoples, based on principles of justice, democracy, respect for human rights, non-discrimination and good faith' (Preamble).

The *Declaration* positions indigeneity beyond identity politics to recognise that justice cannot be understood 'irrespective of issues about whose ancestors were here first, irrespective of any history of injustice that may have attached to the process by which these people came to be side by side in that territory' (Waldron, 2002, p. 1). History is a determinant of political agency and the group right to self-determination is diminished if its relationship with social, cultural, economic and political circumstances is not fully admitted. Nor can group rights be confined to the private sphere because the good life is expressed principally through culture, a necessarily public as well as private construct. As Kymlicka (1996) points out, culture's centrality to the politics of indigeneity counters an alternative liberal position that holds that 'ethnic identity, like religion is something which people should be free to express in their private life, but which is not the concern of the state... it is not the place of public agencies to attach legal identities or disabilities to cultural membership or ethnic identity' (p. 3). However, indigenous Australians did not consent to British settlement and Maori consent was on the understanding that pre-existing rights would be protected (Treaty of Waitangi, 1840). This makes their positions 'fundamentally different from that of voluntary immigrant minorities' (Short, 2003, p. 491), and it makes their claims transcend Waldron's (2002) 'principle of proximity' which holds that 'people have a paramount duty to come to terms with, and to deal justly with, those with whom they are, in Kant's phrase, 'unavoidably side by side' in a given territory, 'irrespective of cultural or national affinity' (p. 1). For example, the right to education in one's own language is an expression of self-determination that distinguishes indigenous claims. It is a right admitted at international law (United Nations, 2007a), broadly accepted in New Zealand (New Zealand Government, 1998) yet sharply contested in Australia where, for example, as Minister of Education, the former Prime Minister (2010–13), Julia Gillard, has argued against bilingual schooling for indigenous people (Gillard, in Robinson, 2008), even as difference in language and culture is integral to indigenous peoples' construction of postcolonial nationhoods.

Educational opportunities in indigenous languages ought to be admitted into a just theory of liberal citizenship because language is central to personal freedom and one of the necessary means through which equal participation in society is assured. In Australia, some choice in schooling is ordinarily accepted as a mark of citizenship; the right to religious or philosophically grounded alternatives to public schooling is usually exercised without elite objection. Yet, in 2008 Gillard insisted that schooling in the Northern Territory would be in the English language alone. The possibilities of bilingual schooling and the relevance of a child's own language to identity and cultural and cognitive development was overlooked.

> English is the language of further learning and English is the language of work, and if we want our kids who are growing up today right across the Northern Territory, right across the nation, to have a chance to do an undergraduate degree, do a postgraduate degree, go out and get a good job, then people need to read and write English. (Gillard, in Robinson, 2008)

The minister's position was ideological rather than pedagogic and missed deeper issues of school effectiveness, most especially teacher quality. The language of instruction is incidental to teaching quality; which is what most accounts for variations in achievement (Hattie, 1999).

The incident highlighted a key question in curriculum design and pedagogy: 'whose knowledge counts' (Savage et al, 2014, p. 89)? Further, Sarra (2014) rhetorically asks 'who has the greater influence over the perception of who Aboriginal people are and how we behave' (p. 79)? His answer, 'mainstream Australia', draws attention to powerful neocolonial influences ensuring that authentic 'culture' does not, in fact, 'count' in education, that discrimination prevails in the labour and housing markets and that prejudice is all pervasive. If the 'ways of being' Aboriginal, Maori or Taukei are framed by others there is no cultural foundation to self-determination. It is to this reality that measures such as Sarra's (2014) 'strong, young, black, powerful people' aspires, in the same fashion of Bishop et al's (2010) aspiration for Maori to 'achieve as Maori' in their schooling. These indigenous developed conceptions of schooling assume people's capacity to transcend victimhood and neocolonial stereotypes through differentiated citizenship, which is introduced in Chapter Three as a framework for translating reconciliation into practical politics, and provides for public decisions to be made as the outcome of genuinely deliberative processes to which all citizens believe that they have had fair and substantive opportunity to contribute. The chapter shows, once again, that political position is not simply a product of numeric strength, but a function of how postcolonial societies conceptualise and construct citizenship.

The status accorded indigenous languages has implications for a society's capacity to construct an inclusive national polity. Its centrality to human being makes the absence of linguistic recognition a powerful means of political exclusion. The denial of normative privilege to indigenous languages, in public life, helps to explain Moreton-Robinson's (2000) argument that citizenship rights are actually distinct from indigenous rights, where citizenship constitutes an individual right to welfare, while indigenous rights demand the right to independent nationhood. Moreton-Robinson's position contrasts with a singular undifferentiated understanding of nationhood where the term is conflated with the 'nation state' to explain Watson's (2009) use of 'the term *state* to identify the colonial relationship between Aboriginal peoples and the repository of colonial power', as the Australian state has rarely, if ever, intended or had the political will to empower Aboriginal people's laws and cultures. For example, the statutory recognition of Aboriginal land rights is vulnerable to veto clauses that are invoked in the 'national interest' (Watson 2009, p. 35), and Watson's (2009) conflictual view is supported by legislation such as the *Aboriginal Land Rights (NT) Act 1976* which distinguishes the Aboriginal interest in land from the national interest, and privileges the latter in the event of conflict.

In Australasia, state initiatives 'for accommodating indigeneity as a basis for renewal and reform tend to digress into political discourses that miscalculate the magnitude and intensity of transformational politics' (Fleras, 1999, p. 188). Biculturalism is a New Zealand example, which established Maori and Pakeha [New Zealanders of European descent] as oppositional forces, and confuses Pakeha for the 'Crown' in whom it vests sole sovereignty. While the Treaty of Waitangi secures the territorial and political integrity of the state; its legitimation of Crown sovereignty explicitly and distinctively includes Maori in the sovereign whole. In this way biculturalism's positioning of the Crown as 'Pakeha' in a binary relationship with Maori as a distinct and separate group is challenged by a relative, relational and inclusive understanding of inter-ethnic political relationships (O'Sullivan, 2007). Specifically, the Treaty positions Maori within the sovereign whole to ensure that political power is contested and continually re-balanced by the influence of Maori claims on and against the state. Sovereignty is not institutionally fixed and must be 'detached from the state' because: 'As a relational concept, the one thing sovereignty cannot have is an exclusive and exclusionary character' (Latham, 2000, p. 107).

The colonial placement of Maori as the political 'other' undermines equal citizenship and a distinct share in national sovereignty. Indigeneity cannot privilege biculturalism as Waldron (2002) suggests, because it locates Maori in junior partnership with the state and assumes that Maori and Pakeha are absolutely and always distinct; the significance of overlapping relationships through intermarriage and wider social and economic interdependence is understated (O'Sullivan, 2007; Nana et al, 2011). Indeed, biculturalism is an example of 'political theorists operat[ing] with the fallacious notion that cultures were internally homogenous, immobile, self enclosed, seamless and so on' (Scott, 2003, p. 101). It is Maori insistence that these characteristics do not describe their societies that has diminished biculturalism's influence in favour of a more assertive and effective self-determination, that this book will describe, to show that the relationship between culture and political recognition is not an essentialist one. Indigenous societies are not culturally monolithic, nor are they monolithic in their expectations of political systems.

In Australia health policy, for example, has understated indigeneity's purpose by reducing policy objectives to a goal of 'closing the [statistical] gap' in life expectancy between indigenous and other citizens. It is a well justified objective in egalitarian terms, but limited in its development of indigenous agency or the recognition it accords relationships between health and culture. It is, as Pholi et al. (2009) point out, illustrative of 'a substantial imbalance in power and control over the Indigenous affairs agenda…which is the "gap" that must be addressed for the health and wellbeing of Indigenous Australians to improve' (p. 1) as a mark of reconciliation. However, a more expansive contextualisation of indigenous political claims is possible with reference to Kant's (1970) doctrine of freedom, which holds that:

> no-one can or ought to decide what the highest degree may be at which mankind may have to stop progressing, and hence how wide a gap may still of necessity remain between the idea and its execution. For this will depend on freedom, which can transcend any limit we care to impose. (p. 1)

New Zealand's recognition of a Maori right to education in their own language and, to some extent, according to preferred pedagogies, occur with reference to the Treaty of Waitangi which provides jurisprudential, moral and political context to distinctive Maori development above and beyond whatever claims liberal egalitarianism might support. For example, the Treaty obliges the state in legislation dealing with matters as diverse as environmental management, broadcasting and health as well as being incorporated into general principles of governance:

> The Treaty signified a partnership between Pakeha and Maori requiring each to act towards the other reasonably and with the utmost good faith. The relationship between the Treaty partners creates responsibilities analogous to fiduciary duties. The duty of the Crown is not merely passive but extends to active protection of Maori people and their use of their lands and waters to the fullest extent practicable. (High Court of New Zealand, 1987, p. 642)

Indigeneity is distinguished from minority ethnic politics by its claim to a specific, rather than simply proportionate share, in national sovereignty. It counters Waldron's proposition that 'the general duty of a government to do justice to all people living in a territory is [not] trumped by any special duty it owes to those of the inhabitants who can claim indigenous descent' (Waldron, 2002). While injustices are not necessarily 'more egregious...just because they were perpetrated against *tangata whenua* [indigenous peoples]' (Kenrick, 2006, p. 19) their particular nature and impact demands contextualised and differentiated responses. Differentiated citizenship is, then, required to recognise that indigeneity cannot make its claims purely on the egalitarian grounds available to the ethnic minority politics of identity. Instead, indigeneity's purpose is to re-frame what it means to 'belong' to a common political community; to challenge the conflation of nationhood with the state to prevent difference from being seen as conferring counterliberal privileges rather than admitting fair and reasonable rights. From one perspective, these special privileges impede national political and social cohesion by accommodating the greed of one group over the legitimate wants of all others.

For Brash (2004), there needed to be 'one law for all' unable to admit a proper policy concern for group-defined cultural imperatives or aspirations. The 'one law for all' discourse denied deeply held differences in the ways people perceive political status and relationships to marginalise some people's conceptions of justice. The possibility that political systems can be designed for the simultaneous recognition of difference and commonality was illegitimised on the grounds that ethnicity makes claims beyond universal citizenship (Rata, 2005, pp. 279–80). It is, instead, more complex values, aspirations and experiences that distinguish Maori politics and to which a liberal theory of indigeneity might respond. For example, Maori vote from the Maori electoral roll as a deliberate statement of identity. They similarly participate in Maori civil society and seek recourse to the Treaty of Waitangi and international legal instruments to settle claims grounded in common interests and experiences. Gender, class, occupation and income may influence personal political identities but, for indigenous peoples across jurisdictions, colonialism is a distinguishing experience that ensures that ethnicity matters.

For some people, it is principally by virtue of ethnicity that they are excluded from the full opportunities that liberal citizenship claims to provide. Their indigeneity is significant because it is only by the historical occupation of their territories that the modern state has emerged. In this context, indigenous histories and experiences are relevant to the contemporary state's moral legitimacy (Young, 1989). As Young (1989) continues: 'We cannot develop political principles by starting with the assumption of a completely just society, however, but must begin from within the general historical and social conditions in which we exist' (p. 261). It is unreasonable to presume that race could or even should be eliminated from institutional arrangements in favour of a liberal democracy of the kind that Waldron proposes, where the right to common citizenship, alone, guarantees all people's fair and reasonable deliberative engagement. Waldron (2004) argues that these ideal attributes of citizenship are guaranteed by the concept's presumption that all citizens must engage with one another justly which, in turn, sets aside the consequences of any historic injustice. However, as Waldron (1992) himself has elsewhere argued: 'Everything that is done has to be done somewhere. No one is free to perform an action, unless there is somewhere he is free to perform it' (p. 302)

In Australia, an 'assimilationist nationalism' (Brett, 2005, p. 25), emphasised during John Howard's Prime Ministership (1996–2007), conceptualised the rights of indigeneity as indistinguishable from those of common individual citizenship, to make family, not the tribe or indigenous nation, the only relevant sub-national identity. The assumption was that all citizens are equally capable of participating and finding political identity in a single national homogenous community. As Taylor (1999) explains the position:

> You, like the rest of us, are free by virtue of the fact that we are ruling ourselves in common and are not being ruled by some agency that need take no account of us. Your freedom consists in the fact that you have a guaranteed voice in the sovereign, that you can be heard, and that you have some part in making the decision. You enjoy this freedom by virtue of a law that franchises all of us, and so we enjoy this together. Your freedom is realised and defended by this law, and this whether or not you win or lose in any

particular decision. This law defines a community of those whose freedom it realises and defends together. It defines a collective agency, a people, whose acting together by the law preserves their freedom. (p. 267)

In other words, the universal human duty to do well to one's neighbour can set aside the conditions where 'some individuals and groups are denied the status of full partners in social interaction simply as a consequence of institutional patterns of cultural value in whose construction they have not equally participated and which disparage their distinctive characteristics or the distinctive characteristics assigned to them' (Fraser, 2003, p. 29).

Egalitarianism, alone, restricts indigenous claims to the individual rights of liberal citizenship to diminish the philosophical centrality of culture, language, collective resource management and recourse to restorative justice. Collective identity is not an essential egalitarian concern which means that it imposes no obligation on the state to recognise indigenous development as distinct peoples.

Indigeneity's limits

Fiji's self-inflicted instability requires wide ranging and multi-faceted explanation. But at the core is a haphazard, incoherent indigenous conception of power and authority. Nor does Fijian politics enjoy a coherent philosophical rationale capable of admitting political authority's relative and relational character or considering the moral or pragmatic limits of indigenous claims, which is why the entrenched opportunities for parliamentary dominance and the institutionalisation of bodies such as the Great Council of Chiefs into the system of national governance did not increase the meaningful political authority of Fiji's indigenous peoples. Indeed, as Ratuva notes:

The more the state becomes a vehicle for structuring educational and economic opportunities according to ethnicity, the more reliant are emergent elites on ethnically exclusive ideologies and practices, in a state characterised by a complex juxtaposition of ideologies and practices, which are both contradictory and accommodating. (Ratuva, 2002, p. 56)

There is not a considered position on what is or ought to be the relationship between indigeneity and the state, leaving the Council's abolition by decree of the self-appointed Prime Minister in 2012, and his FijiFirst party's victory at the general election in 2014, as examples of the 'ebbing of a long-standing ideology of traditionalism' as a distinguishing point in the Fijian politics of indigeneity (Lawson and Hagan Lawson, 2015, p. 1). Fiji could, instead, have provided a model for peaceful co-existence in which the rights of indigeneity were paramount and the interests and aspirations of others respected, even to the point of enjoying the right to vote and participate fully in government. Instead, a fervently nationalist indigeneity coupled with unwavering military claims on national sovereignty has prevented the development of a political order capable of supporting security and cohesion. Even when parliaments, not the military, have provided governments the idea of popular sovereignty has been largely illusory.

Indigenous self-determination depends on civilian rule's stability and sustainability; the subordination of the military to a freely-chosen government, but at the same time, recognition that effective military sovereignty is not the single barrier to peaceful multiracial co-existence. This also depends on indigeneity forging unity among indigenous Fijians to strengthen a sense of extra-tribal nationhood in a country where collective numeric majority does not eliminate negative colonial legacy nor diminish indigenous claims to certain political authority. It is in this context, especially, that the question Fleras (1999) poses for Australia, Canada and New Zealand is equally applicable to Fiji: 'Is sovereignty indivisible or can it be shared without undermining integrity and cohesion?' (p. 190). However, Fiji lacks a political process for thinking about this question, and consequently, for recognising the limits to indigeneity implicit in Horscroft's (2002, p. 59) assertion that:

> linking Indigenous cultural rights to political control (including coups) undermines potential to forge consensus in Fiji's polity. Culture and language concerns are dismissed with the aggressive paramountcy claims of those who represent them. They could instead bridge the political divide by claiming legitimacy in liberal minority-rights paradigms. Therein, ethnic groups are entitled to protection because the cultural frameworks within which people make meaning are *prerequisites* for members to enjoy equal opportunities to live meaningful lives (Thompson 1997: 789; Kymlicka and Straehle 1999: 72). Equality requires recognition and protection of cultural groups: it cannot legitimately be deployed to undermine them.

Indigeneity is an insightful theoretical construct for the study of contemporary Fijian politics simply because native Fijians cite prior occupancy as a basis for their political claims. Fiji's distinct colonial history means that constitutional arrangements made in isolation from the relationship between colonial history and its contemporary legacy will always be unjust. Special efforts are required to bring a rights-based discourse to the Fijian construction of a fair and widely accepted national sovereignty. However, the United Nation's reductionist definition of indigenous peoples to include only those of non-dominant status deprives international law and politics of an important avenue for rationalising the limits to indigeneity in a society where postcolonial stability is elusive because questions about where indigenous power ought to lie in relation to that of more recent settlers remain sharply contested. This argument is developed in Chapter Five's substantive consideration of the *Declaration* and in Chapter Eight's consideration of the economic consequences of Fiji lacking a framework for differentiated citizenship in ways that the *Declaration* might establish.

Conclusion

Indigenous political claims are distinguished from the rights and claims of ethnic minorities by the historical deprivation of sovereignty and wider neocolonial context. Indigeneity's claims do not 'trump' the claims of others, but the unique circumstances in which they are made mean that the egalitarian principles of distributive justice cannot, on their own, provide a useful philosophical framework for thinking about the contemporary rights and obligations of indigenous peoples. Access to culture, language and traditional resources are preliminary to consideration of the ways in which indigenous peoples can exercise the rights of citizenship individually as well as collectively. The right to development as distinct peoples is among indigeneity's principal objectives and essential to fuller political freedoms. The conflation of indigeneity with the rights of ethnic minorities understates the significance of history and political context to the contemporary circumstances of indigenous life.

In Australia and New Zealand indigeneity is concerned with the inclusive construction of citizenship and sovereignty to include first occupants among the national 'sovereign' whole. It is simultaneously interested in securing rights to language, culture and resources as foundational to development as distinct self-determining peoples. In this way, indigenous peoples claim a specific rather than a simply proportionate share in national political authority. The extent to which indigenous peoples may assume authority over their own affairs is, however, deeply contested. In both jurisdictions paradoxical legal and political developments incrementally provide greater scope for indigenous authority and freedom but at the same time the state pursues opportunities to re-assert its own authority as guardian of an absolute indivisible non-indigenous sovereignty. Although Fijian indigeneity is marred by a series of missed political opportunities and marked by constant testing of the moral limits to indigenous claims it remains instructive to draw comparisons with a jurisdiction where the impact of historical deprivations of authority continue to shape national political arrangements more than 40 years after the withdrawal of the colonial power. Contemporary Fijian politics is not so much concerned with managing inter-ethnic political disagreements, but with working out the extent to which rights of prior occupancy ought to influence the distribution of power and authority so that a 'people' can be constructed in whom national sovereignty might be vested. It is in this context that the following chapter shows indigeneity's engagement with liberal democratic ideas to ask questions about where power ought to lie and how it ought to be shared in relation to political inclusion and national sovereignty.

THREE

Liberal democracy and differentiated citizenship

Introduction

Citizenship defines the terms of belonging to the modern state. It is an ideological and power laden concept which can exacerbate, exaggerate or mediate tensions over the distribution of power and authority. Reductionist conceptions of citizenship mean that it does not always affirm indigenous human dignity, equality or personal sovereignty (Alfred, 2009; Moreton-Robinson, 2004; Moreton-Robinson, 2005). Nor does it routinely contribute to the maintenance of a political order in which government is truly by the consent of the people, and in which indigenous peoples participate actively and on their own terms. The state is rarely seen as 'theirs' and citizenship is not perceived as a universal construct, capable of definition and expression in one absolute and just form. Its positioning of people vis-à-vis the state provides insight into wider dynamics of power and authority, and helps to explain why Aristotle's proposition that the citizen is 'he who has power to take part in the deliberative or judicial administration of any state' (Hindess, 2000, p. 94) does not always reflect contemporary indigenous political experience. It may also explain the view of Sitiveni Rabuka, who led the military removal of two Fijian governments in 1987, that democracy is a 'foreign flower unsuited to Fijian soil' (Lal, 2002, p. 148) and the position that one cannot justify recourse to liberal ideas, when democratic citizenship is not an indigenous Fijian concept, and when Fijians had little say in the mass Indian migration which dramatically re-shaped the local political order? Even the British Cabinet had accepted, at the time of independence, that Fijian dominance was just, provided that there were 'adequate safeguards for all other communities' (Emery in Norton, 2004, p. 163).

An alternative position to Rabuka's is that there is, in fact, considerable potential for a liberal theory of indigeneity, proceeding from differentiated citizenship, to develop the right to difference in cultural expression, but sameness in political opportunities; difference in forms of land tenure, but sameness in capacity to make decisions about how land will be used; difference in the way one is taught at school, but sameness in terms of educational quality. Indeed, a liberal theory of indigeneity constitutes a politics of distinctiveness, necessarily dependent on group rights – such as the rights to land, language and culture – as inescapable constituents of individual liberty. Individual autonomy is contextualised, conditioned, and given substantive meaning and value with reference to culture and the inter-relationships that people, themselves, decide are important. In contrast, liberal theory's limitations in dealing with the politics of indigeneity arise because its foundational thinkers 'assumed that all citizens primarily defined themselves as individuals and that they agreed on the values of choice and autonomy as well as on the content and prioritisation of their basic interests' (Parekh, 1997, p. 54). The inconsistency between this theoretical assumption and indigenous peoples' often collective political and cultural perspectives suggests broadened liberal focus to set out just terms for the development of political relationships in a plural society as developments in sociological theory emphasise the 'centrality of culture for an adequate understanding of citizenship' (Delanty, 2000, p. 61). Attention to relationships between culture and citizenship is also among the 'striking developments in recent political discourse' (Delanty, 2000, p. 60).

Indigeneity, democracy and difference

Rabuka insisted that liberal democracy undermined the inherent right to paramountcy that first occupancy accorded native Fijians. The argument was apparently so strong that it justified the violent removal of two governments, the setting aside of Fiji's Constitution, and the transfer of sovereignty from the people to the military. Democracy was positioned as a negative colonial legacy. But neither the military nor George Speight, who led a putsch removing the Chaudhry government in 2000 could advance a coherent alternative notion of power or admit a relationship between stable government and indigenous self-determination. The effect was that indigeneity's principal purpose of making the state responsive to indigenous aspirations became unattainable.

Rabuka's logic suggests that, if liberal democracy was a 'foreign flower' which interfered with inherent indigenous political rights, it would also be unsuited to other post- or neocolonial societies. Liberal democracy, indeed, remains deeply contested for indigenous peoples. Similarly, sovereignty makes presumptions about the sources of public authority, and by whom, or what, it is exercised and limited. Conceptions of sovereignty 'are neither natural nor neutral'. They reproduce a space for politics that is enabled by and rests upon the production, naturalisation and marginalisation of certain forms of 'difference' (Shaw, 2008, p. 8). However, the proposition that public sovereignty constrains indigenous sovereignty means that indigenous peoples tend not to look, within the liberal paradigm, for the greater political voice that, as this chapter shows, is participatory parity's presumption. Yet, where indigenous populations constitute the majority, liberal democracy distinguished by differentiated citizenship may in fact guarantee the necessary space for indigenous political authority to resurface. These alternative perspectives share the view that extant indigenous political rights properly influence governments and that internal decolonisation requires re-balancing political authority. But they differ in their preparedness to juxtapose indigeneity with prevailing international ideas about state governance. Liberal democracy's limits and opportunities are shaped by competing attempts to define and direct it towards different priorities and interests. This contestation of power is the principal common characteristic of indigenous politics across jurisdictions. A principled representative, liberal democratic order shaped and influenced by indigeneity and functioning as differentiated citizenship may not, in fact, be a noxious foreign flower but rather a medium for returning the balance of power to the native Fijian people and for guaranteeing the substantive participation of minority indigenous populations in their national politics. Its potential occurs through differentiated citizenship. Alternatively, if liberal democracy is indeed an unsuited flower, the central liberal problem remains: how should societies govern themselves in order to create peaceful relationships among people with different perceptions of the common good? How might reconciliation be achieved?

The fundamental questions for both indigeneity and liberal democracy are who belongs and on what terms? Societies do exclude. They do so as a means of protecting what dominant groups hold in common. But populist anti-indigenous sentiment still arises in Australasia in the absence of any clearly thought-out position on the legitimacy of the majority imposing its will on the minority. A medieval understanding of a majority being 'more likely to be substantively right than a minority' (Mansbridge, 1996, p. 53) often prevails in resistance to indigenous claims. This is, however, a simplistic and divisive approach to power which is better shared according to the common good and deeper principles of justice.

There are grounds in justice for protection against unbridled majoritarian rule because democracies can in fact 'produce outcomes…

that are substantively unjust' (Mansbridge, 1996, p. 57) to suggest that everybody ought to be included in the political life of the state. No one group should always and necessarily find itself on the losing side. Yet liberal citizenship, with democracy an essential constituent, remains potentially, the modern state's principal cohesive force; the instrument through which individuals are brought in to a positive relationship with the state, as members of a common political entity (Cairns, 2000). It is only through recourse to the state's legal and political institutions that indigenous peoples are able to position their claims for self-determination and autonomy. Liberal democracy is potentially emancipatory and, if it is to offer protection against the misuse of political power, it must make group interests an important concern of the political system itself. Liberal democracy potentially protects and fosters active political participation, although through differentiated arrangements, as an alternative to systemic assumptions of political and cultural homogeneity. In this context, indigenous peoples may position their claims to propose that state sovereignty is not, in practical terms, the absolute authority that Hobbes (1998) imagined, but a relative and relational construct dispersed among public actors and institutions, as a foundation for 'belonging together differently' (Maaka and Fleras, 2005, p. 43); a political outcome potentially consistent with both citizenship and indigeneity. In turn, it is citizenship and indigeneity that provide theoretical foundations for relationships based on democratic 'participatory parity' (Fraser, 2003), requiring that all members of the community can interact 'with one another as peers', so that it is actually possible for all people to contribute equally to public decisions.

While indigenous Australian alienation from the body politic suggests some truth in Moreton-Robinson's (2004, p. 79) argument that 'whiteness' is 'the definitive marker of citizenship; and a form of property born of social status', differentiated citizenship opens possibilities for setting aside her distinction of the 'collective rights of indigenous people' from the 'individual rights of citizenship' (p. 63) in favour of more broadly constructed inclusive appreciations of citizenship and its institutions. From this latter perspective, indigeneity proposes the 'reinvention' of the relationship between 'coloniser and colonised' (Johnson, 2008), with citizenship the essential political construct through which 'reinvention' can occur, as the United Nations' (2007a) *Declaration on the Rights of Indigenous Peoples* imagines:

> Indigenous peoples have the right to maintain and strengthen their distinct political, legal, economic, social and cultural institutions, while retaining their right to participate

fully, if they so choose, in the political, economic, social and cultural life of the State. (Article 5)

Colonial oppression helps to contextualise the contemporary politics of indigeneity. However, it is not the point that defines or justifies claims to language, culture or natural resources. Nor is it the point that raises a claim to particular expressions of citizenship. Instead, the politics of indigeneity claims that these are extant rights prior to those arising from restorative or restitutive justice. Maori do not claim guaranteed representation in parliament because they are oppressed, but because they are Maori. One needs, then, to look beyond Young's (1989) rationale for differentiated citizenship, as a response to 'oppression', but as a response to prior occupancy. Although: 'Nothing [in international law] gives an indigenous people superior or paramount rights in taking part in the government of their country' (Reeves et al, 1996), this does not negate claims to a *particular* as well as a *proportionate* share in public authority. For example, in New Zealand in 2016, the question of the structural arrangements necessary to secure substantive Maori deliberative voice is particularly important in ways that the Waitangi Tribunal's *Te Paparahi o te Raki Inquiry* (2014) can help to illustrate. In this case, the Tribunal found that Maori had not ceded sovereignty, but in acquiescing to the Treaty, were accepting a form of sovereign authority consistent with a modern argument for differentiated citizenship as it is set out in the following chapters. For the Tribunal:

- The rangatira [chiefs] who signed te Tiriti o Waitangi in February 1840 did not cede their sovereignty to Britain. That is, they did not cede authority to make and enforce law over their people or their territories.
- The rangatira agreed to share power and authority with Britain. They agreed to the Governor having authority to control British subjects in New Zealand, and thereby keep the peace and protect Māori interests.
- The rangatira consented to the treaty on the basis that they and the Governor were to be equals, though they were to have different roles and different spheres of influence. The detail of how this relationship would work in practice, especially where the Māori and European populations intermingled, remained to be negotiated over time on a case-by-case basis.
- The rangatira agreed to enter land transactions with the Crown, and the Crown promised to investigate pre-treaty land transactions and to return any land that had not been properly acquired from Māori.

- The rangatira appear to have agreed that the Crown would protect them from foreign threats and represent them in international affairs, where that was necessary. (Waitangi Tribunal, 2014)

While the finding is not binding and is contested by the Crown (Finlayson, 2014b) it does raise questions about the nature and distribution of sovereignty and how people might 'belong together differently'. Sovereignty transcends national constitutional and political arrangements because it is continually re-shaped by international political and economic factors that, at the very least, privilege the idea that the state is merely the agent of the people's sovereignty, rather than sovereign itself. In New Zealand, Maori political participation is fostered by a stable political environment in which indigeneity and its aspirations are potentially aligned with prevailing liberal democratic expectations of government to accommodate the specific, as well as proportionate, sharing of public sovereignty. So it is that indigeneity, citizenship and participatory parity intersect to allow 'belonging together differently', to recognise that If sovereignty belongs to the people it must, in the interests of cohesion, order and justice, belong to *all* the people, and answer questions of power and authority from an inclusive and emancipatory conception of Crown, sovereignty and state.

The claims to particular and proportionate shares in the sovereignty of the nation-state arise from deeper philosophical reasoning than the laws of a benevolent state, to draw moral authority from the argument that disenfranchisement is an inevitable outcome of deprivation of 'the lands ancestrally occupied by [indigenous peoples] as entities actually owning the attributes of sovereignty pursuant to international law' (Lenzerini, 2005). Citizenship is not, then, simply the embodiment of rights. It is also concerned with the fair distribution of public opportunities. 'It concerns the learning of a capacity for action and for responsibility but, essentially it is about the learning of the self and of the relationship of self and other' (Delanty, 2000, p. 64).

Indigeneity, citizenship and 'belonging together' differently

Access to rights such as land, language and culture are often preliminary to the indigenous person's capacity to enjoy the individual liberties that universal citizenship proposes. 'Belonging together differently' imagines an indigenous corporate citizenship interested in those human rights that can only be collectively enjoyed, while participatory parity is 'a normative criterion by which the validity of the claims and reforms of others can be evaluated' (Blunden, 2004). It is one of the possibilities that liberal political theory offers for working out the aspirations of 'postcolonial liberalism' to do as Ivison proposes: articulate 'a space within liberal democracies and liberal thought in which…Aboriginal perspectives and philosophies cannot only be heard, but given equal opportunity to shape (reshape) the forms of power and government acting on them', as 'liberal practices and institutions have the greatest chance of being endorsed and supported, and resulting in political arrangements which are just, when they emerge out of and combine with the complexity of local environments and frameworks, and most importantly, with the dynamic forces therein' (Ivison, 2002, p. 2).

The expansive conception of citizenship that the politics of indigeneity advances is one that admits differentiated modes of belonging to both national and indigenous political communities, where differentiated citizenship contributes to 'mainstreaming indigeneity' to reflect 'moves towards participatory governance, but also…a commitment to indigenous models of self-determining autonomy' (Maaka and Fleras 2009b, p. 1).

'Belonging together differently' responds to Barry's (1990) suggestion that state welfare has not promoted active citizenship and challenges Marshall's (1963) construction of citizenship as one that privileges 'passive' entitlements with no corresponding expectation that the citizen also deliberates for the common good. Instead, citizenship is potentially a 'social construction' of much wider significance than codifying individual rights and responsibilities (Turner, 1993). Indigenous understandings of citizenship are concerned with more than the simple rights of the welfare state because the question, for indigeneity, is not so much one of whether citizenship *can* provide, but one of the ways in which it *needs* to provide, 'a common experience, identity and allegiance for the members of society' (Kymlicka and Norman, 1994, p. 355). Instead, plural societies might aspire to common acceptance of the *range* of possibilities not a *particular* possibility for the exercise of citizenship. What scope might there be for the liberal toleration of difference?

'Citizenship is intimately linked to ideas of individual entitlement on the one hand and of attachment to a particular community on the other' (Kymlicka and Norman, 1994, p. 352). However, it is its capacity to satisfy multiple and simultaneous attachments that determines its potential as a cohesive force through which people are drawn to a common polity in their differences, as well as in their similarities. Citizenship's cohesive significance can be measured by the strength of people's 'desire to participate in the political process in order to promote the public good and hold political authorities accountable' (Kymlicka and Norman, 1994, p. 353). It is democratically important that indigenous people see the state as theirs and see themselves as legitimate and meaningful shareholders in national public sovereignty. So citizenship theory must do more than explain social obligations. It needs to provide an account of the ways in which the capacity to meet these obligations is distributed. Obligations are culturally determined, so it might be that a plural society does not require common agreement on what those obligations contain, but simply agreement on how differences of perspective can be mediated to avoid one group's conception of just obligations being imposed on others.

Citizenship's full possibilities do not develop from public benevolence, nor simply from the just intersection of rights and responsibilities, but from personal capacity.

> Consider the many ways that public policy relies on responsible personal lifestyle decisions: the state will be unable to provide adequate health care if citizens do not act responsibly with respect to their own health, in terms of a healthy diet, exercise, and the consumption of liquor and tobacco; the state will be unable to meet the needs of children, the elderly, or the disabled if citizens do not agree to share this responsibility by providing some care for their relatives; the state cannot protect the environment if citizens are unwilling to reduce, reuse, and recycle in their own homes; the ability of the government to regulate the economy can be undermined if citizens borrow immoderate amounts or demand excessive wage increases; attempts to create a fairer society will flounder if citizens are chronically intolerant of difference and generally lacking in what Rawls calls a sense of justice. (Rawls, 1971, in Kymlicka and Norman, 1994, p. 360)

> [Participation is] the means whereby individuals may become accustomed to perform the duties of citizenship. Political participation enlarges the minds of individuals, familiarises them with interests which lie beyond the immediacy of personal circumstance and environment, and encourages them to acknowledge that public concerns are the proper ones to which they should pay attention. (Oldfield, 1990, p. 184)

[Participation] includes the willingness to listen seriously to a range of views which, given the diversity of liberal societies, will include ideas the listener is bound to find strange and even obnoxious. The virtue of political discourse also includes the willingness to set forth one's own views intelligibly and candidly as the basis for a politics of persuasion rather than manipulation or coercion. (Galston and Galston, 1991, p. 227)

Macedo (1997) describes a liberal virtue of 'public reasonableness' where citizens cannot simply make demands, but must provide 'public reasons'; that is reasons that can be publicly understood. While this virtue of 'public reasonableness' restricts indigenous recourse to tradition, it also requires that objections to Maori claims on the state are grounded in reason rather than prejudice. As Kymlicka and Norman (1994) observe, the search for that balance creates an intellectual tension, for 'the liberal commitment to liberty or neutrality or individualism renders the concept of civic virtue unintelligible' (p. 365). For example, Treaty settlements have facilitated more focused Maori attention on self-defined aspirations. They have weakened the 'deficit lens' through which Maori economic engagement was traditionally viewed and have raised expectations of what is achievable. They have broadened perceptions of relationships among economy, culture and self-determination, even as culture's policy acceptance in areas such as health and education has helped to position indigeneity as an important employment attribute (Coleman et al, 2005). Maori language revitalisation is economically significant in the creative industries where art, music and popular culture illustrate the relationship between cultural and economic development (New Zealand Institute of Economic Research, 2003).

When indigeneity is juxtaposed with a conception of liberal political theory recognisant of group rights and identity it potentially re-casts citizenship to make it inclusive and emancipatory. Indeed, the former Maori party Member of Parliament, Tariana Turia, makes indigeneity central to citizenship: 'We will claim our indigeneity and we will speak of it, regardless of whether people want to see us as "one people"' (Turia, 2006). A liberal theory of indigeneity cannot proceed from the view that cultural groups are akin only to 'private associations' (Kukathas, 1992, p. 115) and for Turia, Maori 'belonging' is *both* equal *and* distinctive and the rights of individual citizenship are not owed at the expense of those arising from collective experience and identity. Just political arrangements are not the concern only of an imagined 'culture-free' individual. 'Indigeneity's claims do not "trump" the claims of others, but the unique circumstances in which they are made mean that the egalitarian principles of distributive justice cannot, on their own, provide a useful philosophical framework for thinking about the contemporary rights and obligations of indigenous peoples' (O'Sullivan, 2014, p. 39). Alternatively, indigeneity is a politics of distinctiveness concerned with the substantive liberties of *all* not just *some* members of the national political community. This requires responsiveness to differences as well as the upholding of commonalities. Liberal democracy's essential tenets include the mediation of difference, so that commonalities are not used to set aside distinctiveness and its contribution to personal political identities and the terms on which people seek 'belonging' to the nation state. In New Zealand, differentiated terms of 'belonging' secure Maori participation in the national sovereign and, because that sovereignty is dispersed, assures Maori capacity to influence its possibilities and constraints.

Indigeneity, however, does recognise that liberalism can, alternatively, presume the subsuming of ethnic diversity into a single homogenous community and the condition that the 'we are one people' argument most fears is one where 'giving everyone the opportunity to speak and make meaningful contributions to public debate and deliberation requires expanding the range of acceptable reasons and interpretations' (Bohman, 1995, p. 266). On the other hand, differentiated citizenship can transcend 'recognition', as a simple claim to negate the effects of 'otherness' through a 'democratic model that permits maximum cultural contestation' (Benhabib, 1996, p. x). Citizenship's theoretical development from van Gunsteren's (1978) description of a concept that had 'gone out of fashion among political thinkers' (p. 9) occurs alongside its jurisprudential development from the comparatively empty category of 'subjecthood' that, for example, the Treaty of Waitangi had promised.

Differentiated citizenship presumes indigenous peoples' autonomy over their own affairs and some say over the ways in which they will contribute to national political decision-making. It allows justice to be conceptualised as a constituent of 'belonging', where people must still ground their substantive political claims in justice and expose them to democratic contest; but they are increasingly able to challenge the position that citizenship should constrain rather than promote their political expression. This need not require interpreting Benhabib's argument that 'democratic equality' can be constructed 'to create impartial institutions in the public sphere and civil society' (Benhabib, 1996, p. 8) as one that necessitates all aspects of difference being reconciled. Instead, extant rights and those aspects of 'otherness' that indigenous people wish to retain, raise the possibility that institutional arrangements based on 'relative and relational autonomy', provide more secure and substantive political space for indigenous peoples to work out the nature and form of their citizenship.

The ways in which citizenship is constructed determines whether public decisions are the outcome of a genuinely deliberative process to which all citizens believe that they have had the opportunity to contribute, or whether the concept is a tool to contain and control indigenous aspirations. Nevertheless, indigeneity creates space for citizenship to provide a conceptual framework for thinking about power and authority, and as Hindess observes: 'Insofar as it helps us... to campaign against the arbitrary impositions of governments and their mistreatment of weak minority groups, then the language of citizenship is well worth preserving, in spite of its substantial limitations' (Hindess, 2000, p. 73).

Institutional indifference to indigenous cultural claims makes self-determination, rather than accommodation, a generally more attractive policy proposition. The contrast is between 'the former kind of identity/difference politics [which] focuses on the negotiation, contestation and representation of difference within the public sphere of liberal democracies [and]...[t]he politics of ethno-nationalism [which] seek to redefine the constituents of the body politic, and aim at creating new politically sovereign bodies' (Benhabib, 1996, p. 3). Maaka and Fleras (2005) propose a model of this kind for Canada and New Zealand, to illustrate 'how much difference is compatible with the ideal of the rule of law under fair and equal conditions' (Maaka and Fleras, 2005, p. 3). They imagine a relationship where indigenous people are 'sovereign in their own right, yet shar[e] sovereignty with society at large' (Maaka and Fleras, 2005, p. 5). This proposition allows corporate indigenous membership of the polity to stand alongside individual membership, with each category allowing different expressions of civic rights and responsibilities. If citizenship's pragmatic utility is to overcome political inequalities while providing a philosophical base for the critique of exclusionary public policy then there is almost certainly no such thing as 'an inclusive undifferentiated citizenship' (Cairns, 2003).

Participatory parity and differentiated citizenship

Participatory parity is a 'radical-democratic interpretation' that 'assumes that the distribution of resources allows participants independence and voice. It also requires that institutionalised patterns of cultural value express equal respect for all participants and ensure equal opportunity for achieving social esteem' because 'an adequate understanding of justice' must consider recognition as well as distribution (Fraser, 2003, p. 36). On its own, egalitarian justice is insufficient to admit first occupancy, culture, or broader colonial legacy, as factors that differentiate appeals to justice.

Participatory parity is concerned with distributing political authority in ways that allow each person equitable opportunities to participate in public affairs. It presumes that all citizens are owed a 'parity of esteem' to protect Aristotle's (1988) ideal of the citizen as 'he who deliberates', which is important because deliberation contributes 'to the formation of values and priorities' which is, in turn, what gives substantive meaning to the notion of political community (Sen, 1999, p. 153). 'In the absence of a Philosopher King who reads transcendent normative verities, the only ground for a claim that a policy or decision is just is that it has been arrived at by a public which has truly promoted the free expression of all' (Young, 1989, p. 263).

A just process for the determination of community values is required to bring 'people as close to good functioning as their natural circumstances permit' (Nussbaum, 1987, p. 36) as politics is 'not simply the allotment of commodities, but [concerned with] making people able to function in certain human ways' (Nussbaum, 1987, p. 1). Participatory parity is, then, concerned with *all* citizens being able to influence 'the conditions under which and the practices through which authority is constituted and legitimated, and what these constitutions and legitimations enable and disable' (Shaw, 2008, p. 1). Political authority *within* the state is, therefore, important and relies on a form of public sovereignty that admits distinct cultural perspectives and relationships between colonial experiences and contemporary political claims. This first tier of liberal citizenship requires culture's admission into the common polity alongside the second tier's proposition that the 'right to lands, territories and natural resources is the basis for collective survival and thus inextricably linked to their right to self-determination' (Daes, 2008, p. 8).

Ratuva (2005) argues that simultaneously recognising 'communal identity and individual democratic rights' can, in fact, preserve social and political order because political contradictions are balanced by accommodation. Differentiated citizenship works in this context as 'the state becomes the site for both contradiction and accommodation as different communal identities, compete, negotiate, compromise, or sometimes converge' (p. 2).

Differentiated citizenship shows that: 'Democratic equality and deliberative practices are quite compatible with cultural experimentation and with new legal and institutional designs that accommodate cultural pluralism' (Benhabib, 1996, p. x). Indeed: 'In participatory democratic institutions citizens develop and exercise capacities of reasoning, discussion, and socializing that otherwise lie dormant, and they move out of their private existence to address others and face them with respect and concern for justice' (Young, 1989, p. 252).

Parity of participation is 'a normative criterion by which the validity of the claims and reforms of others can be evaluated' (Blunden, 2004). Therefore, as well as providing a basis on which indigenous people can make claims against the state, it also provides a philosophical rationale for testing the limits of those claims: 'the test of whether a claim on the public is just, or a mere expression of self-interest, is best made when persons making it must confront the opinion of others who have explicitly different, though not necessarily conflicting, experiences, priorities, and needs' (Young, 1989, p. 263).

Participatory parity responds to liberal political theory's appeal to freedom and equality. Indeed, as Kymlicka observes, indigenous rights can only be secured when they are understood as an inescapable component of liberal theory rather than as a competitive counterliberal force (Bennett, 2005). Specifically, indigeneity's principal claim, the claim to self-determination, seeks precisely the liberal objectives of freedom, autonomy and liberty, and any liberal account of justice which sets aside these precursors to personal freedom necessarily diminishes indigenous peoples' access to substantive citizenship (Bennett, 2005).

Liberal democracy citizenship and the politics of inclusion

Liberal democracy and indigeneity emphasise separate but intertwining conceptions of power. Liberal democracy serves indigeneity by potentially providing a way of mediating power relationships and reconciling indigenous nationalism with the harmonious sharing of national sovereignty which, short of expelling non-indigenous populations, is the only means which indigenous peoples have of securing self-determination. At the same time, liberal democracy is served by indigeneity's constant reminder that it ought to be interested in the liberty and representation of *all* not just *some* people. Liberal democracy is ideally all-encompassing and inclusive. However, in this context 'Rawls has not adequately recorded the problem of "irreconcilable values"' (Bohman, 1995, p. 254). The question for liberalism is how it might promote agreement among citizens who are not, in fact, free and equal in substantive terms. For indigenous politics, liberalism's underlying weakness is its search for common public positions as the outcome of a singular public reason. It is from that perspective that liberalism draws its capacity to exclude, and, 'deep conflicts can be resolved publicly only if political liberalism is revised in two ways: if the political conception of justice is made more dynamic and if public reason is made "plural" and not "singular"' (Bohman, 1995, p. 254). However, it is not sufficient to expect that: 'The achievement of consensus in public deliberation depends on the discussion being guided by an ideal of impartiality' (Bohman, 1995, p. 266). People bring deeply held and diverse perspectives to public decision-making. While commonalities between indigenous and non-indigenous peoples are important, these are not the questions to which a liberal theory of indigeneity must turn its attention. It is the political system's capacity to mediate difference, not its ability to recognise commonalities that tests its capacity for fairness in the consideration of indigenous interests. Although there are limits to liberty and tolerance, a just political order is one where different conceptions of the good life are admitted; where different values and understandings are positively upheld through measures that accommodate plurality in the distribution of public sovereignty. In short, political stability requires agreement on the ways in which points of conflict are settled; but it need not presume that agreement on substantive points is always necessary.

Indigeneity's concern with collective rights means that it is also inevitably interested in correcting the effects of colonisation as a serious violation of individual liberty. Indigeneity gives theoretical expression to the recognition of differences based on first occupancy. Its interpretations of political rights evolve in response to its theoretical and political interactions with other discourses; its potency is a function of its engagement with liberal democracy as the prevailing internationally accepted framework of state governance. Together liberal democracy and indigeneity create opportunities for indigenous peoples to articulate their own conceptions of justice. Liberal democracy can then be crafted towards its inclusive potential, based on the foundation it provides for differentiated citizenship as a model for reconciliation.

Indigeneity is also concerned with differentiation from the wider polity, but this does not inevitably or necessarily require political separation. Instead 'one of the interesting consequences of the encounter between liberalism and its colonial past and present might be a more context-sensitive and multilayered approach to questions of justice, identity, democracy and sovereignty. The result would be a political theory open to new modes of cultural and political belonging' (Ivison et al., 2000, p. 21).

Such a theory can accord with indigenous aspirations because there need not necessarily be any inconsistency between collective group rights and the sovereignty of the entire polity. Kymlicka (2000) argues that the paradigm shift from democracy 'suppressing to accommodating' minority ethnic groups in the United States of America has 'actually played a vital role in consolidating and deepening democracy' (p. 227). There is a parallel with indigenous contexts which adds to the rationales for guaranteed indigenous parliamentary representation in Australia, New Zealand and Fiji, for example. In these jurisdictions, emphasis on individual rights in isolation from the collective offers no real prospect for securing comprehensive individual freedom or the certainty of equal individual influence over the polity. Democracy's concern with liberty is its particular strength even though such a concern can never remain unqualified and unconstrained. Liberty, as Held (1989) puts it, is 'limited' (p. 185). The limits, set out in Held's model of democratic autonomy, are however, more likely to constrain the activities of the more powerful political actors in societies where indigenous peoples seek a non-colonial politics. According to Held (1989), one person's liberty cannot be at the expense of another's (1989, p. 185). All people are entitled to security 'in their capacity of being citizens' (Arendt in Held, 1989, p. 187).

Held (1995) outlines four democratic criteria which would, if applied consistently and universally, make states more responsive to indigenous aspirations. Democracy, he argues, should provide for:

> Protection from the arbitrary use of political authority and coercive power...
>
> The involvement of citizens in the determination of the conditions of their association through the provision of their consent in the maintenance and legitimation of regulative institutions...
>
> The creation of the best circumstances for citizens to develop their nature and express their diverse qualities...
>
> The expansion of economic opportunity to maximise the availability of resources... (p. 150)

These criteria arise because 'the capability of persons to determine and justify their own actions, with their ability to determine among alternative political programmes is the 'core of the modern liberal democratic project' (Held, 1995, p. 150). In practice, then, democracy at least offers indigeneity a political voice and recourse to judicial consideration of points of dispute with the legislative and executive branches of government.

Liberal democracy can limit elite powers of exclusion. Its basic premise is that government of the people ought to be by and for the people. But at the same time the concept can be more narrowly interpreted to restrict the terms of indigenous engagement in public decision-making. Restriction can occur to the point that for minority indigenous groups, assimilation into a culturally homogenous community is positioned as an essential and necessary precondition for full democratic participation. Tensions between indigeneity and democracy surface where the community is not, in fact, a culturally homogenous whole. Homogeneity simplifies the aspiration for democratic popular sovereignty 'to form an entity and have a personality'. Yet democracy does not 'unfailingly [lead] to exclusion' (Taylor, 1999, pp. 143, 146). Its exclusive capacity is not merely accidental, but nor is exclusion an essential and necessary constituent.

Democratic autonomy is enhanced, if as Benhabib (1996) proposes, 'the institutions and culture of liberal democracies are sufficiently complex, supple, and decentred so as to allow the expression of difference without fracturing the identity of the body politic or subverting existing forms of political sovereignty' (p. 5). But here, too, there are limits, as Benhabib herself acknowledges. The 'claims of culture' are conditional upon their consistency with wider norms of respect, equality and reciprocity (p. 5). Certain Fijian claims to exclude non-Fijians from national government fail this test. Military authority as the keeper of political morality at the exclusion of a freely chosen parliament is similarly wanting.

Benhabib (2002) is also reasonably concerned that the rights of culture ought not to take precedence over the rights of the individual. Recent decisions of the Australian judiciary accepting alleged cultural practices as mitigating factors in cases of non-consensual sexual association of adult men with teenage girls arouse liberal democratic concerns. Setting aside the fact that the 'cultural practice' was contested within the community itself, and that the complainants found no connection between the neocolonial court's interpretation of culture and their own self-determination, the case does 'enable us to see most clearly the moral and political choices involved in advocating the preservation of traditional cultural identities over and above individual rights' (p. xii). The distinction clarifies cultural rights in liberal terms, which holds that customary rights should be recognised only to enhance personal citizenship rights, not to limit the recourse to protection that victims of violence may seek (Kymlicka, 1995). It does not logically follow that liberal states should allow one party in a contested internal dispute over customary practices to impose illiberal values on selected citizens.

For Kymlicka, land and linguistic rights and differentiated opportunities for political participation are external protections of culture, intended to secure fair and reasonable political outcomes. They are justified to protect indigenous people from the probable negative aspects of engagement with wider society. Yet at the same time, Kymlicka argues liberals 'ought to reject internal restrictions which limit the right of group members to question and revise traditional authorities and practices' (Kymlicka, 1999, p. 37). When cultural precepts are clear, broadly accepted and important to the ways in which people choose to live, it is a matter of political recognition to admit them into the policy process.

The question for indigeneity is whether it views culture as a relic demanding preservation and never subject to internal let alone external questioning, or whether culture is a reference point and social context in which individual being is given identity – a context in which security and self-worth are provided. In this latter case cultural identities are subservient to the personal rights of group members and culture is worth preserving for its capacity to give substantive context to indigenous freedom. Liberal democracy similarly requires that culture ought not to be protected where it affronts the dignity and self-determination of its members. Kymlicka (1995) distinguishes 'external protections' and 'internal restrictions' to clarify the cultural rights that might be claimed without disturbing the principles of liberal democratic order. For Kymlicka, external protections could include land or linguistic rights and distinct opportunities for political participation justified by the intention to 'protect a particular ethnic or national group from the destabilizing impact of the decisions of the larger society' (p. 37).

External protections can be accepted by liberals if they are concerned with fairness and just political outcomes. Liberal political theory developed to respond to religious diversity. It follows that it ought to be able to consider the political and constitutional implications of ethnic diversity. Its purpose is to manage rather than to mask differences and to consider, not automatically dismiss conflicting ideas. 'Men have different views on the empirical end of happiness, and what it consists of, so that as far as happiness is concerned, their will cannot be brought under any common principle, nor thus under an external law harmonizing with the freedom of everyone' (Kant, 1970, pp. 73–4).

Conclusion

Liberal democracy's relationship with indigeneity is paradoxical. It neither accommodates absolutely nor rejects entirely the general claims of indigeneity. There is a democratic parallel with indigeneity's concern for personal and collective freedom. Although contested, there is certainly a potential theoretical convergence between these two concepts of power and authority. The principal argument for differentiated citizenship is that liberal democracy alone does not guarantee the elimination of injustice, nor does it guarantee that indigenous political aspiration will not be marginalised by its own decision-making processes. But because liberal democracy recognises the legitimacy of conflicting ideas and aspirations it potentially offers institutional means for the airing of grievances, hopes and aspirations, and indeed for proposing the constitutive elements of a more just political order, none of which was possible in the pre-democratic colonial environments of Australia or New Zealand. Nor is such possible in contemporary Fiji where the ideal of national sovereignty belonging to the people have been set aside. In jurisdictions where sovereignty is held to reside with the people there is at least political space to propose an inclusive conception of sovereign political order. Contemporary Fijian politics well demonstrates that liberal democracy better provides theoretical and institutional opportunities for thorough deliberation and resolution of contested priorities than does any currently developed alternative regime. Indeed, self-determination cannot be reduced to the simplistic wish to overthrow governments on the assumption that control of the machinery of government necessarily equates to universal indigenous authority. At the same time while citizenship presumes commonalities within the one polity, if it does so at the considered exclusion of some groups of people, division and tension inevitably arise; 'a framework for belonging together differently' cannot develop and one has 'needless conformity in an age of diversity' (Maaka and Fleras, 2005, p. 43). The objection that differentiation leaves citizenship without the capacity 'to cultivate a sense of community and common sense of purpose' (Heater, 2004, p. 295) presumes that it would actually contain those attributes in an undifferentiated form. It is, instead, undifferentiated citizenship's exclusivity that explains indigenous alienation from the common polity, and the idea that the right to differentiated citizenship would extinguish if 'oppression' was no longer present denies self-determination's purpose and legitimacy. 'Belonging together differently' requires an approach to politics concerned not so much with who gets what, but with how and by whom questions of distribution are considered.

In Australia and New Zealand, indigenous claims to differentiated citizenship are inconsequential to the substantive rights of others, yet there remains significant popular resistance to public recognition of those claims to a particular form of belonging to the one state (O'Sullivan, 2007). While there are also significant examples of the public recognition of rights grounded in indigeneity, which are presently discussed, tension does emerge as these claims to inherent political rights compete with liberal notions of undifferentiated national citizenship. Even in New Zealand, where the level of integration between Maori and non-Maori is relatively high, one cannot speak of the simple common identity or cultural foundation that liberal citizenship often assumes, which is why citizenship can be proposed as a constraint on the claim to distinct indigenous shares in postcolonial political authority (O'Sullivan, 2007), to support a non-Maori expectation that policy ought to uphold a general public suspicion of Maori values and prevent their intrusion into the public domain.

FOUR

Liberal democratic inclusion

Introduction

Recognising differences does not counter liberalism's sacrosanct protection of individual rights. Individual identity must come from somewhere. It is heavily shaped by culture and derives meaning from communal relationships. Differences in political identities contribute to the differences in ideas that democracy requires for its own effectiveness. The ideas that compete for popular ascendancy are not confined to abstract philosophical positions and 'The unity of society and the allegiance of its citizens to their common institutions rest not on their espousing one rational conception of the good, but on an agreement as to what is just for free and equal moral persons with different and opposing conceptions of the good' (Rawls, 1971, p. 160).

The degree to which difference and diversity ought to co-exist is contested, however. Public attitudes to differentiation and diversity influence the opportunities and practices of indigenous civil society. The tension is an intellectual contest between liberal democracy's capacity for inclusion and its practical tendency towards exclusion. It is also a tension between the policy outcomes that might proceed from each possibility.

The chapter assesses examples of democratic inclusion and exclusion in Australia and New Zealand, for the political values they reflect about differentiated citizenship, before proposing the concept as one that might contribute stability and coherence to Fijian politics as foundational conditions for the greater self-determination that indigenous Fijians seek.

'Belonging together differently'

Although the previous chapter described circumstances where liberalism reasonably limits the claims of culture, there remain alternative positions which actually remove culture from the individual and therefore undermine freedom and equality, for example, the denial of collective representation in parliaments and local governments, especially as indigenous peoples argue for such representation as an important constituent of self-determination.

The former Australian Prime Minister, John Howard (1996–2007), for example, developed a powerful assimilationist narrative to counter growing demands for indigenous self-determination. The line in an election campaign theme song: 'Son, you're Australian; that's enough for anyone to be' (Brett, 2005, p. 25) became a simple theme of his Prime Ministership. He was untroubled by the intellectual conflict between socially conservative emphases on homogeneity and liberal emphases on freedom. Reconciliation and assimilation became the opposite sides of a nationally polarising debate which contrasted limiting with expansive democratic interpretations. Underlying the assimilationist narrative was a normative racism as 'cultural artefact' (James, 1997, p. 57). But even so, it is not true that the modern state is necessarily 'a compulsory association which organises domination'. Liberal democracy, in fact, constrains the capacity of postcolonial states to dominate and, while the state does monopolise coercive power (Weber, 1984, p. 37), coercion is not always and necessarily negative for indigenous peoples; for example, guaranteed Maori representation in the New Zealand Parliament and the enactment of settlements to grievances under the Treaty of Waitangi, when a simple majority vote is unlikely to have allowed either. Similarly, while self-determination had been official Australian government policy in the 1970s and 1980s, when attention to land rights had begun and the Keating government (1991–96) responded favourably to the *Mabo* decision in 1992, it remains that in more recent Australian history the coercive power of the judicial system (most significantly through the *Wik* decision) also imposed incremental developments in indigenous legal rights. These judicial developments were especially significant as they occurred under the generally unsympathetic Howard government (1996–2007). There is pragmatic truth in the general observation that: 'While the state is the burden individuals have to bear to secure their own ends, it is also the basis on which it is possible to safeguard their claims to equal rights and liberties' (Held, 1995, p. 145). The limiting factor is that liberal democracy only safeguards the right to make these claims: it does not guarantee a political order that will ensure indigenous perceptions of equality and liberty.

In Australian Federal elections, there is presently no electoral incentive for mainstream political parties to court indigenous votes. There are simply not enough of them to make an appreciable difference. Indigenous voters, therefore, have a lesser opportunity to hold influence or control over political decisions (Ivanitz, 2002).

They have recourse only to moral persuasion not electoral strength in pressuring political parties to treat seriously their concerns. Political parties are not immune to moral argument but they are more certainly attentive to electoral pragmatism, courting the votes of those who count over those who do not. Indigenous peoples require a guaranteed voice and vote in Parliament to enjoy the full rights of citizenship. It is a reasonable and fair expectation that they might, as a matter of course, sit in the Executive and participate in national affairs at the highest level, remembering especially that policy failure, which is the 'most significant feature of the relationship between governments and indigenous Australians' (Cook, 2004, p. 239), is always a likely outcome of indigenous political exclusion.

Guaranteed representation overcomes the otherwise inevitable distance between the Executive and the indigenous peoples for whom policy is made. Ivanitz, however, argues that: 'demands for the formulation and implementation of policy relevant to the needs and circumstances of indigenous people are based on claims to special political status, group rights and cultural uniqueness, all of which tend to contradict core values of liberal democracy' (Ivanitz, 2002, p.130).

On the other hand, there is, as Ivanitz (2002) notes, a distinction between 'formal' political equality and 'substantive' political equality (p. 130). While formal equality may satisfy some liberal democrats, it is substantive political equality that better corresponds with the claims of indigeneity. Liberal democracy gives indigenous peoples the reasonable expectation that they will engage in government as participants and not merely as interest groups, even though interest group status does remain simultaneously important.

Interest groups facilitate the robust yet ordered contestation of ideas that are the outcome of different human identities. Indigenous interest groups are also important 'because no democracy ever reaches the point at which justice is simply done, democracies need to recognise and foster enclaves of resistance' (Mansbridge, 1996, p. 58). What Mouffe (2006) calls the 'antagonistic dimension of the political' (p. 90) is essential in allowing indigenous peoples to make their political claims. One of the ways in which substantive political equality can be realised is through guaranteed indigenous representatives in state legislatures. A special measure of this kind gives substantive effect to the group claim to participation in national decision-making. Active participation in the political life of the community fosters a positive conception of citizenship and stable political order. Yet at present, the Australian Commonwealth Parliament includes just five indigenous members, making it difficult to speak of a genuinely representative institution, as the *Declaration on the Rights of Indigenous Peoples* imagines.

Maori, in contrast, are guaranteed seven directly elected members of the 120-seat legislature while, in practice, additional members are elected from general constituencies and party lists. Maori are guaranteed representation on District Health Boards which are required to give particular and specific attention to Maori health needs, and city and district councils increasingly choose to guarantee Maori representation. However, there also remain strong public objections to such 'privileged' representation which is an example of the constraints that liberal democracy can, but does not necessarily, have to impose on Maori deliberative agency. The translation of differentiated citizenship from an abstract theoretical construct to a practical and tangible political arrangement is difficult. While, in 2001, the Bay of Plenty Regional Council became the first local authority to guarantee Maori representation through the establishment of Maori constituencies, similar proposals have met significant resistance in the New Plymouth District. The Council's decision to guarantee Maori representation was overturned by an 83 per cent vote against the proposal in a public referendum in 2016. The referendum debate was distinguished by violent personal hostility towards the Mayor (Radio New Zealand, 2016). In contrast, liberal reforms to the public sector, beginning in the 1980s, created space for an assertive Maori corporate citizenship supported by the inherently non paternalistic principles of freedom, choice and responsibility. These principles were allowed to develop among important sites of indigenous transformation, such as schooling and primary healthcare, where Maori could develop services, at least to some extent, within a Maori worldview and cultural framework. The number of schools teaching partly or wholly in the Maori language and according to Maori epistemologies significantly increased during the 1980s and 1990s.

Objections to these examples of differentiated citizenship are often motivated by undemocratic insecurities and prejudices which position cultural homogeneity as the social ideal from which political life ought to stem. But Mouffe's (2006) argument that 'a democratic society cannot treat those who put its basic institutions into question as legitimate adversaries' (p. 20) exposes the limits of democracy for indigeneity; and offers some context to Rabuka's exception to democracy providing a fair and reasonable model of government for Fiji. Indigeneity inevitably calls into question the legitimacy of the basic institutions of a liberal democratic society: in particular, the legislature and judicial system. Yet in Australia and New Zealand there is an indigenous sense of realism preventing any attempts to destabilise these institutions and even in Fiji sufficient pragmatism guided the coups and putsch so that parliamentary reform rather than revolution was the political objective.

Liberal democracy, then, requires national reconciliation; not to the point where the legitimacy of political difference is called into question as Mouffe (2006) fears, but where reconciliation is concerned with recognising objective and demonstrable wrongs, for example, the removal of indigenous Australian children from their families, or the confiscation of Maori land. Recognising objective wrongs requires consensus, but when societies come to consider the nature and form of recompense, there remains space for the plurality and contestation of ideas which Mouffe argues are essential to democratic politics.

Democratic inclusion, democratic exclusion

Australia's democratic stability is conducive to broad conceptions of liberty. Yet democracy is widely interpreted as unbridled majoritarian rule giving the minority indigenous population no moral claim to particular recognition. Exclusion remains the legacy of a colonial political order over which indigenous peoples had no influence or connection. In 2009, for example, arguments about the propriety and form of a national indigenous representative body were couched in exclusive assumptions of state power and regulation. The government, not indigenous people, led policy debate on a replacement for the Aboriginal and Torres Strait Islander Commission (ATSIC) which was the primary national representative indigenous body for 14 years until it was abolished in 2005. ATSIC developed an important advocacy role and provided health services to indigenous communities. Its potential to contribute to indigenous self-determination was significant, but inevitably constrained by its statutory rather than community foundation. In gaining non-government organisation (NGO) accreditation at the United Nations, ATSIC had provided an alternative to government positioning of indigenous affairs and its political voice increasingly diverged from prevailing government policy direction. Sanders (2004), among others, argued that ATSIC should not have been abolished until an alternative 'representative arrangement' was 'negotiated' with indigenous Australians (p. 1). This view supposed that governments, not indigenous communities, should determine how they are represented to government. Independent political expression is constrained when governments develop then 'negotiate' the terms of some citizens' political engagement. Yet democracy potentially empowers groups of citizens to pursue their common interests, balanced only by the right of other groups to do the same. An independent civil society is an essential accompaniment to free elections and political parties in protecting against tyranny and in ensuring that the full plurality of political perspectives can be expressed, and one finds an important contrast with New Zealand where, during the 1990s, the Prime Minister, Jim Bolger, argued for the creation of a national representative Maori advisory body. The proposal did not succeed because Maori tribes saw the initiative as more concerned with meeting the needs of government than with advancing their own interests. Iwi have, instead, developed their own representative models. For example, members of the Tainui tribal confederation elect representatives to a parliament, Te Kauhanganui, which manges its own affairs and assets in its own way for its own self-determining purposes. It is a model that allows indigenous people to set their own public agenda and avoid the centralisation of power that inevitably accompanies state control over the nature of representation.

The abolition of the ATSIC did, however, create an opening for indigenous Australians to make a definite statement of self-determination by strengthening their own representative organisations. In 2008, the Australian Aboriginal and Torres Strait Islander Social Justice Commissioner, who is independent of the Executive, initiated discussion on the establishment of a new national representative body. The Commissioner's discussion paper raised the possibility of the body not being a government entity but did not commit itself to that course of action, even though it noted the importance of such a body being able to work credibly with each tier of government – implying that independence from the Commonwealth would be desirable. The paper made the significant observation that although not a government entity it ought to have the advantage of 'privileged access to government', even as this had not been the ATSIC experience. Privileged access, if it were to occur, could come at a very high cost for a body that requires independence to establish its own authority and to provide an unhindered indigenous public voice.

A further perspective considered by the Commissioner is that an indigenous representative body might have a formal role in Senate Estimates committees because their 'ability to call the government and bureaucracy to account is something that many Indigenous peoples would like to emulate' (Calma, 2008, p. 99). Given the constraints of contemporary Australian politics this could provide a more inclusive and accountable democratic form. But on the other hand, it masks one of the most fundamental failures of Australian democracy — that there has on only three occasions in 116 years been an indigenous senator able to speak and vote as of right on an Estimates Committee. The membership of indigenous senators, Neville Bonner (1971–83), Aden Ridgeway (1999–2005), Nova Peris (2014–16), Jackie Lambie (2014–), Pat Dodson (2016–) and Malarndirri McCarthy (2016–), does not mitigate against arguments for guaranteed indigenous parliamentary representation. Nor does the appointment of Ken Wyatt, an indigenous member of the House of Representatives, as the first indigenous minister in 2016. Indeed, it strengthens the arguments by highlighting the institutional barriers to indigenous representation. It is in this context that the proposal to recognise indigenous first occupancy in the Preamble to the Commonwealth Constitution might purposefully consider Tully's (1995) proposition that constitutions develop as 'an intercultural dialogue in which the culturally diverse sovereign citizens of contemporary societies negotiate agreements on their forms of association over time in accordance with the three conventions of mutual recognition, consent and cultural continuity' (p. 30). Tully's is an aspiration beyond prevailing ideas in the contemporary Australian debate over the terms and purpose of indigenous constitutional recognition. However, the debate may still lay an important foundation for that aspiration to enter longer-term public discourse.

Liberal democracy can encourage conformity but it can also protect difference depending on how its fundamental purpose is understood and how its institutions and processes are ordered. The democratic ideal of a strong civil society creates space for indigenous political expression and a forum for the contestation of ideas. When civil society functions well across the entire political community a significant check on power is established. This means that a national representative indigenous body could be expected to enhance democracy. But, as the ATSIC experience so pointedly illustrates, it needs to stand apart from the state if substantive independence capable of contributing to checks on power is to be assured. The essential problem is that the body, the National Congress of Australia's First Peoples, became reliant on public funding which was discontinued in 2016 on the grounds that it was allegedly not sufficiently representative of indigenous peoples. Its status was better described as an advocate, or lobby group, for its own perception of indigenous interests, rather than as a broadly representative institution.

The inevitable price of independence, however, is that it becomes impossible to accept state financial support for operational expenses in a context of ideological uncertainty and policy tension where objections to indigenous peoples' policy agency remains influential. Measures such as the Northern Territory Emergency Response (the 'Intervention') and the Council of Australian Governments' policy Closing the Gap in Indigenous Disadvantage further illustrate this point.

The Intervention responded to allegations of sustained and widespread sexual abuse and violence across the Territory's indigenous communities. The desperate dysfunction of these communities was a product of the inability to curb alcohol and substance abuse and confront entrenched violence against women and children. State paternalism and policy failure also impeded indigenous women's efforts, especially, to bring safety and stability to these communities.

Poverty, poor housing, health and education also seriously curtail the freedoms that democracy is intended to foster. The democratic principle of state rule by the peoples' consent has never applied substantively to indigenous Australians who have never had formal representation in any of the country's parliaments, nor been able to organise a collective independent political voice. On the other hand, liberal democratic justification for the Howard Government's intervention into indigenous communities could, perhaps, be found in Bentham's view that:

> Tied to the advocacy of a 'minimal state', whose scope and power need to be strictly limited, there is a strong commitment to certain types of state intervention: for instance, intervention to regulate the behaviour of the disobedient, and to reshape social relations and institutions if, in the event of the failure of *laissez faire*, the greatest happiness of the greatest number is not achieved. (Held, 1995)

The Intervention sequestered welfare payments without requiring evidence that an individual's entitlement was being misappropriated. Although the practice was later extended to other communities, race was initially sufficient to deny beneficiaries the minimal self-responsibility that their circumstances allowed, while negligent and violent parents in white communities could continue untroubled: protected by race. Yet the Intervention's motivation was allegedly to protect the innocent. It contrasted with the philosophies behind recent criminal trials where judges had ruled that moral culpability for sexual violence was diminished if the actions were sanctioned in customary law (Cunneen, 1992). The 'Intervention's' openly conditional illustration of some people's citizenship, like the Social Responsibility Agreements (SRAs) introduced by the Howard government (1996–2007), raises questions about what it means for indigenous people to enjoy common national citizenship. By way of example, the Mulan Agreement in Western Australia, in 2005, stipulated that to gain access to regular health checks for poverty related diseases – trachoma, skin infections and worm infestations – the Mulan indigenous community would have to ensure, among other things, that its members would wash their faces twice daily (Lawrence and Gibson, 2007). Race became a legitimate discriminator between two levels of the rights and responsibilities of citizenship mediated by 'colonial visions of place and culture' (Lawrence and Gibson, 2007, p. 650) in a counter-liberal project to restrict indigenous peoples' capacity for power and control over their own lives. Citizenship was not the protector of freedom that liberal democracy proposes.

The SRAs labelled indigenous peoples as '"failed" or "ungovernable" citizens', unable to 'be governed through their capacities and freedoms', and 'in need of subjection to specific governmental demands' (Lawrence and Gibson 2007, p. 662). In some ways the '"authoritarian" or "despotic" side of liberalism' is accentuated (Lawrence and Gibson, 2007, p. 652), as the SRAs compromised the indigenous person's fundamental rights to equal shares in the sovereignty of the nation state. The 'Intervention' which remains among indigenous policy's key measures, extends these same themes, while Closing the Gap illustrates policy conflict over the extent to which indigenous agency ought to be admitted.

Closing the Gap is a significant Federal, State and Territory government policy partnership aimed at closing statistically measurable 'gaps' between indigenous and other population groups across seven inter-related policy areas: early childhood education, schooling, health, economic participation, healthy homes, safe communities, governance and leadership (Macklin, 2009, p. 8). Although consistent, with liberal egalitarian aspirations, the policy was widely critiqued by indigenous peoples for its emphasis on sameness as common citizenship's proper outcome (O'Sullivan, 2014). It left outstanding the political question of whether citizenship demands homogenous public policy or whether space can properly be found for indigenous cultural expression, and the lack of cultural recognition in Closing the Gap's initial development provides further insights into the uncertain status of indigenous peoples' deliberative agency.

Closing the Gap continued the policy theme of restricting indigenous autonomy. If individual autonomy is to be upheld, government interference in people's lives ought to be minimal and truly aimed at enhancing self-determining capacity, in contrast with the historical intrusion which is indefensible in liberal terms. There is consequently an active but tightly focused role for governments which is at odds with conventional liberal ideas about limited government. However, in 2017, there is evidence of incremental shifts in policy values, which give practical expression to the concept of differentiated citizenship. These developments, presently discussed, respond to Closing the Gap's intellectual forerunner 'Close the Gap' to show the scope that exists for cultural and political recognition through inclusive and differentiated arrangements.

Differentiated citizenship: from theory to practice

Customary rights are used to enhance participatory parity and their statutory recognition is a distinguishing characteristic of differentiated citizenship. In New Zealand, for example, indigeneity remains institutionalised into the liberal state's political structures, even though its influence is conditioned by democratic constrains on absolute political voice.

In Australia the *National Aboriginal and Torres Strait Islander Health Plan* provides a less far-reaching but, still, potentially important development in 'belonging together differently'. The Plan, published in 2013, was the Commonwealth's first acknowledgement of indigenous objections to Closing the Gap. The Plan's significance arises from its explicit acceptance of the merits of indigenous engagement in its development. According to the Commonwealth it was 'a collaborative effort after extensive consultation with Aboriginal and Torres Strait Islander people and their representatives' (Commonwealth of Australia, 2013, p. 1). It recognised indigenous expectations of 'health equality and a human rights approach, Aboriginal and Torres Strait Islander community control and engagement, partnership and accountability' (Commonwealth of Australia, 2013, p. 7). The Plan reflected a development towards policy alignment with the indigenous developed 'Close the Gap', which proposed a 'human rights' policy approach focused on addressing disadvantage in health, with the full political determinants of disadvantage being addressed, including, for example, the unavailability of sufficiently robust data to inform policy making and evaluation, ensuring appropriate policy benchmarks for evaluation and inter-governmental cooperation and indigenous deliberation in the policy process (Calma, 2005). Further, the Australian Indigenous Doctors' Association (2008) argues that Closing the Gap should focus more deliberately on:

- land, culture and connectedness;
- a strength-based, healing approach, which incorporates kinship care and builds on the resilience of Aboriginal and Torres Strait Islander people;
- genuine partnership with indigenous people;
- learning from existing good practice in indigenous health;
- valuing existing indigenous health expertise and engaging the indigenous health workforce.

These goals are consistent with Dodson's (1994) appreciation of self-determination as integral to substantive indigenous citizenship:

> Time and again indigenous peoples expressed the view that the right to self-determination is the pillar on which all other rights rest. It is of such profound nature that the integrity of all other rights depends on its observance. We [indigenous peoples] hold that it is a right that has operated since time immemorial amongst our people, but it is the right that is at the centre of the abuses we have suffered in the face of invasion and colonisation. The dominant theme of our lives since colonisation has been that we have been deprived of the very basic right to determine our future, to choose how we would live, to follow our own laws. When you understand that, you understand why the right to self-determination is at the heart of our aspirations. (p. 44)

Self-determination is the practice of differentiated citizenship. It proceeds from relational justice and is important to the policy process in the way that Pat Anderson, Chair of the Lowitja Institute for Indigenous Health Research, proposed in suggesting that there are three elements of 'respect' required for improvements in indigenous health outcomes to occur.

> The first is respect for rights – positive change must be built upon the recognition of our rights as people and as First Nations. The second is respect for the evidence – rights alone are not enough, they need to be combined with what we know works. The last is respect for each other – we need to Close the Gap in respect between Aboriginal and non-Aboriginal Australia, so that we are seen not just as a 'problem' that needs 'solving' but where our unique cultures, histories and abilities are recognised and welcomed. (Anderson, 2012)

Respect, as relational justice, underlies two-tiered citizenship, as a theoretical model, for admitting substantive indigenous political authority in to the modern state. It is more significant than what Watson (2009) describes as negotiating 'between the cracks of the sovereign power of the state' (p. 15) where sovereignty is absolute and indivisible. Instead, differentiated citizenship understands sovereignty as dispersed, necessarily shared, and reflective of multiple possibilities for the exercise of political power. While such a characterisation of political power may not routinely reflect contemporary indigenous experience it is a more promising aspiration than one that understands state and indigenous sovereignty as oppositional and strictly independent of one another. The Congress of Australia's First Peoples, similarly, refers to the *Declaration on the Rights of Indigenous Peoples* to explain the share in political authority that it claims. For the Congress, the *Declaration* 'enshrines our right to be different as Peoples and affirms the minimum standards for the survival, dignity, security and well-being of Indigenous peoples worldwide' (The National Congress of Australia's First Peoples, 2013).

Fijian indigeneity and the possibilities of differentiated citizenship

The New Zealand and Australian examples show that political influence requires coherent and effective theories of power. It is their absence, in Fiji, that adds to that country's instructiveness as a site of comparative political inquiry to show that relative population size is not the principal determinant of indigenous political agency. Relative capacity to influence and share in the exercise of political authority is a function of how postcolonial societies conceptualise and construct citizenship.

Ratuva (2002) argues that modern Fijian political history is characterised by 'a complex juxtaposition of ideologies and practices, which are both contradictory and accommodating' (p. 2). The first of these was the Native Policy, instituted by the first British Governor in 1876. On the one hand, the policy privileged the indigenous population to entrench expectations of political paramountcy, while on the other, it restricted indigenous economic activity to the subsistence sector with considerable authority and patronage vested in 'chiefs and colonial state officials' (Ratuva, 2002, p. 8). The outcome was a differentiated citizenship of illiberal character, which failed to preserve indigenous autonomy or recognise autonomy as relative and relational and dependent on the development of a wider national identity inclusive of the substantial Indo-Fijian population. The Native Policy 'helped to reproduce ethnicity as the dominant political ideology' (Ratuva, 2002, p. 8), whereas two-tiered liberal citizenship potentially admits extant rights, but within a shared national political community. A liberal politics of indigeneity, grounded in differentiated citizenship, might, for example, seek inalienable protections of language and culture, economic opportunities and self-governance in respect of their own affairs, but would not rely on the denial of rights to non-indigenous Fijians to secure these protections.

Fiji's relationship with liberal democracy has been largely experimental. It is a relationship proposed since independence in 1970, but interrupted by coups and subsequent military rule in 1987 and 2006. The putsch in 2000 claimed differentiated indigenous political status as a legitimate path to entrenched privilege. The claim transcended the cultural and political recognition claimed by indigenous people in Australia and New Zealand and highlighted Fijian indigeneity's isolationist approach to politics, which denies the interdependence from which groups draw the ability to function to the fullness of human potential. The ability to negotiate relationships with others is 'at the very core of, what it means to be a self-determined people' (Scott, 1996, p. 819), and the ability to understand the 'complex ways by which ethnicity is produced and reproduced' is also important if citizenship is to reconcile both the 'real and imagined' points of instability in Fijian politics (Dakuvula, 2004). However, Fijian politics is not distinguished by the ideal that:

> The responsible citizen is concerned not merely with interests but with justice, with acknowledging that each other person's interest and point of view is as good as his or her own, and that the needs and interests of everyone must be voiced and be heard by the others, who must acknowledge, respect, and address those needs and interests. (Young, 1989, p. 263)

The equality of all persons is an important moral foundation to citizenship. Just as indigenous peoples ought not accept subjugation, it is unreasonable that they would themselves seek to dominate others. The denial of rights to others is not a just or logical basis on which to defend one's own. Excluding Indo-Fijians from the public life of the community removes any prospect of the kind of political dialogue required to bring order, cohesion and stability to the state. Instability persists because the nature of citizenship remains contested.

'Fundamental rules and institutions in Fiji are accepted up to a point, but not if they threaten vested interests too directly or they deliver the wrong outcome' (Firth and Fraenkel, 2007, p. 21).

Effective military sovereignty has suppressed questions of differentiated political rights and possibilities. However, these are questions that must be settled if one is to expect the 2014 election to have broken the pattern of 'lurch[ing] from one coup crisis to the next' (Fraenkel, 2015, p. 161). The breadth with which the military's responsibility to ensure 'the security, defence and well-being of Fiji and all Fijians' might be interpreted also stresses the importance of a coherent and broadly accepted account of citizenship and its limits.

There is considerable indigenous support for Bainimarama's disruption of the old chiefly order (Ratuva, 2015a). However, relationships between traditional power and broader national political power remain poorly understood. The relationship is also one of scholarly contest. Carens (1992) justifies the Fijian Great Council of Chiefs having an institutionalised role in national politics on the grounds that indigenous Fijians endorse its political status and that it is part of a 'systematic effort to protect a traditional way of life and to enable it to evolve over time' (p. 201). Lawson (2015) argues, in contrast, that this objective was never realised and that Fijian culture was actually undermined by institutionalised deference to chiefly authority. The system, she continues, served chiefly interests above those of ordinary Fijians and impeded the development of national democratic institutions. The suggestion is, then, that rather than democracy being antithetical to indigenous Fijian self-determination it is a guard against the misuse of traditional authority by chiefly interests. However, political stability may not lie in disrupting that order in favour of a form of citizenship where indigeneity does not matter at all, but in a differentiated model of liberal citizenship where people make their own choices about the relative importance of the old and the new for the ways in which they participate in public affairs if, indeed, such an absolute distinction is the one that people wish to make. 'Indigenous Fijians are with Bainimarama now because that is where the power lies. They will shift their allegiance and loyalty to whoever exercises power in the future. That is the way it has always been in indigenous Fijian society. Pragmatism always trumped principle' (Lal, 2015, pp. 87–8).

Bainimarama's electoral success is attributable more to 'the remorseless power of incumbency' (Fraenkel, 2015, p. 151) than to a principled endorsement of non-racial liberal democracy. Indeed, many of the basic institutional tenets of liberal democracy that minority indigenous populations have drawn upon in stable jurisdictions such as Australia and New Zealand to protect their interests are simply not available to indigenous Fijians. For example, neither an independent indigenous press nor an independent judiciary exists in that country, and human rights protections in the draft 2012 Constitution were removed by the government. The re-drafted document, under which the 2014 election was conducted, is precariously positioned after Bainimarama's insistence that 'the army would not tolerate an elected government rewriting the new constitution' (Marks, 2014). In contrast, the *Declaration on the Rights of Indigenous Peoples* proceeds on the assumption that 'the recognition of the rights of indigenous peoples…will enhance harmonious and cooperative relations between the State and indigenous peoples, based on principles of justice, democracy, respect for human rights, non-discrimination and good faith' (United Nations, 2007a, 3).

Fraenkel (2015) describes the 2014 election as being 'competitive authoritarian'. There were political parties setting out contrasting policy ideas. However, the proper presentation and contestation of those ideas was compromised by Bainimarama's constraints on the political process and the knowledge that true authority remained with the military and could be used at any time. However, it was clear that traditional divisions about indigenous people's *particular* status remained important, even as the institutional markers of difference had been removed from the 2013 Constitution: communal seats in Parliament, the Great Council of Chiefs and even, after the election, a government decree preventing the use of native languages in Parliament (Republic of Fiji, 2013b).

Bainimarama's paradoxical assumption that he alone is competent to define the multiracial equality that the military should impose makes no concession to people's general wish to participate in national governance. Nor does it defer in any way to international norms of justice, which have become all the more important as the country's own Human Rights Commission took a partisan position in support of the military intervention, and proposed that the military assume an ongoing role of political oversight once an elected parliament is re-constituted as has, indeed, occurred.

Norton's (2009) concession to a military role in a new ordered system of government would similarly formalise Bainimarama's claim to a military duty to exercise 'guardianship' of the political community by overseeing parliamentary government. This is especially so as Norton leaves unconsidered the question of to whom or what the military should account, and positions it over the Great Council of Chiefs (GCC) as the site where the indigenous 'conviction of their entitlement to power' (p. 103) is constitutionally protected.

To show the contrasting perspectives in contemporary Fijian politics, however, the purpose of undermining the GCC is to 'realise the army commander's view that [it] should primarily be an instrument of government, insulated from electoral and parliamentary politics, especially the influence of Fijian nationalist groups' (Norton, 2009, p.112). Any kind of political oversight, 'external to the people' is a formal transfer of sovereignty from the political community, which weakens systemic capacity to institutionalise checks and balances on the exercise of sovereignty. Political authority would then become the benevolent gift of a distant force answerable to no one and democracy itself would fit the fragile description proposed by the *Fiji Daily Post* (21 April 2007) shortly after the coup in 2006:

> Democracy remains an article of faith – always. That is, it stands by the faith citizens have in themselves to arrive at proper decisions affecting their common future, and the faith they have in each other respecting that faith and its processes and outcomes. This renders democracy precarious because anyone at any time with sufficient resources can knock it over and down. All it takes is 'bad faith.' That is, anyone can destroy democracy by simply losing faith in what it is by its very nature.

The resurrection of Fijian civil society and a free and independent press are essential precursors to accountable and democratic government. In the absence of a secure Parliament and certain judicial independence, interfering with civic and media freedoms removes the only remaining check on executive power. Civil freedoms are fundamental to the expression and protection of human rights and contribute to stable extra-parliamentary constraints on political power. Their vulnerability is a key factor in the nation's weak public sovereignty, compromised by normative political values that accept 'fundamental rules and institutions...up to a point, but not if they threaten vested interests too directly or they deliver the "wrong" outcome' (Firth and Fraenkel, 2007, p. xxi).

While the 2013 Fijian Constitution contains significant liberal democratic shortcomings, it does ensure that parties need to transcend ethnic differences to attract meaningful support, even as ethnic identity and ethnic ideology remain important determinants of voting behaviour. An appreciation of political authority in these terms is beyond the capacity of a singularly focused ethnic political party and the predominantly indigenous Social Democratic Liberal party's (SODELPA) long-term competitiveness means that it must consider 'the increasing relevance of socio-economic issues over cultural preservation' (Ratuva, 2015a, p. 148) not just to attract a greater proportion of the Indo-Fijian vote, but also to recognise meaningful and sustainable economic empowerment as an essential constituent of indigenous self-determination. In 2014, however, ethnic identity and ethnic ideology remained important determinants of voting behaviour. Bainimarama's FijiFirst party's appeal to common citizenship was especially popular among Indo-Fijian voters, while cultural protection was important for SODELPA. However, its 15 seats to FijiFirst's 32 reflected an ideological division in indigenous politics where SODELPAs cultural concerns were positioned against FijiFirst's focus on 'Taukei development and progress' (Ratuva, 2015a, p. 145) as if the two were incompatible alternatives. Contemporary Fijian politics is, then, unlikely to hold the long term 'potential…to sever Fiji's links to its failed race-obsessed past and point the country in a new direction' (Lal, 2015, p. 85).

It is especially important for the politics of indigeneity's influential capacity that it admits that self-determination's relative and relational character requires that the political claims that it understands as fair and reasonable are, pragmatically even if not morally, accepted as such by others. In the absence of normative cross-cultural conceptions of justice there is some political urgency about developing a language of justice through which competing groups can fairly position their claims. Breaking the pattern of crisis requires that a coherent politics of indigeneity is juxtaposed with the Indo-Fijian and international community's expectations of liberally just democratic arrangements. So it is, that if one understands '*citizenship as capacity* rather than *citizenship as rights*', one can better attend to indigenous 'ways of being present and effective' in the public sphere (Rowse, 2002, p. 86).

Demographic projections are that the indigenous population will reach two thirds of the total over the next ten years, but it is not expected that broader political freedoms will accrue to each and every indigenous citizen or that there will be a restoration of traditional chiefly power. It is the military, not Parliament nor any indigenous institution that has the constitutional responsibility of 'defender of the national interest' (Lal, 2015, p. 86).

Bainimarama's ban on active military political participation, during the 2014 election campaign, was one of short-term convenience and is inconsistent with the military's constitutionally prescribed duty to maintain 'the overall responsibility…to ensure at all times the security, defence and well-being of Fiji and all Fijians' (*Constitution of the Republic of Fiji*, 2013, s. 131(2)). Bainimarama's Cabinet comprises seven former military officers (Lal, 2015) so that: 'In the new scheme of things, it is the *turaga* (chiefs) who play second fiddle to the *bati* (Warriors). Once it was the other way around' (Lal, 2015, p. 87).

Instead, differentiated citizenship may help to address Fijian indigeneity's incapacity to make its claims in the liberal language conducive to international sympathy (Horscroft, 2002, p. 64), which insists that 'individuals or groups cannot simply assert that they want something; they must say that justice requires or allows that they have it' (Horscroft, 2002, p. 263). Unlike indigenous peoples in many other jurisdictions, native Fijians have, until the coup in 2006, enjoyed significant political privilege. However, as Habermas (1994) remarks, 'the institutions of constitutional freedom are only worth as much as a population makes of them' (p. 27). From this perspective, it is not ethnic difference itself that creates political conflict, because conflict is the outcome of political institutions' inability to mediate 'the relations of domination and oppression between groups' (Young, 2001, p. 407), to create the political and social conditions for 'living together differently'. One cannot set aside Norton's (2015) presumption that: 'Indigenous Fijian power in some institutional form would seem to be the necessary keystone in Fiji's political architecture' (p. 123). There are lessons from both Australia and New Zealand, affirmed by the *Declaration on the Rights of Indigenous Peoples* that would contribute to a theoretically coherent juxtaposition of a politics of indigeneity with liberal citizenship to create: 'A space within liberal democracies and liberal thought in which…Aboriginal perspectives and philosophies cannot only be heard, but given equal opportunity to shape (and reshape) the forms of power and government acting on them' (Ivison, 2002, p. 1).

The *Declaration* sets out extant rights of first occupancy as relative and relational, rather than isolationist and exclusive, as has been customary in the Fijian politics of indigeneity by insisting that: 'The provisions set forth in this Declaration shall be interpreted in accordance with the principles of justice, democracy, respect for human rights, equality, non-discrimination, good governance and good faith' (United Nations, 2007a, 46, 3).

The *Declaration* would assist a Fijian politics of indigeneity to develop Horscroft's (2002) proposal that there is not, in fact, a conflict between Fijian indigeneity's paramountcy and liberalism's individual supremacy. '[P]aramountcy and equality can form a foundation for an inclusive national policy that respects all its citizens and is attuned to the protection of Indigenous culture and socio-economic wellbeing'

(p. 2). That is, paramountcy is concerned with protecting indigenous land, resources, cultures and languages and the guaranteed participation of indigenous peoples in the political community, even to the extent of ensuring an indigenous majority in the House of Representatives. There is, however, an obtuse logic in the assumption that the rights of others must be subjugated for paramountcy to prevail, as Speight argued in 2000 when he suggested that Indo-Fijian rights ought to be protected but that did not require or justify their participation in national governance (Fry, 2000, p. 299). The corollary to the argument that Fijian independence ought not justify or require the domination of others is that native Fijians need not accept subjugation to allow others to protect their own freedom. Indigeneity need not claim privilege by taking rights from others, even though it does claim different rights on the basis of first occupancy.

Democracy is usually concerned with how territorial sovereignty is exercised. But for indigenous peoples a wider conception of sovereignty is advantageous; one which includes authority over resources, language and culture and the institutions which might safeguard these. 'In the absence of any alternative, Fijian people may discover the 'foreign flower' of democracy as a political saviour' (Lal, 2002, p. 166). Even for Fijian nationalists, democracy is only selectively a 'foreign flower'. Qarase, for example, has argued that democracy is unsuited to Fiji (Srebrnik, 2002, p. 210). Yet in 2006 he found no philosophical impediment to drawing on the concept to resist the military coup against his government. Mahendra Choudry, the country's only Indo-Fijian Prime Minister, whose government was removed in 2000, sought recourse to democracy in defence of his office, yet accepted a position in the military government after the 2006 coup.

For indigenous peoples, liberal democracy is indeed a 'foreign flower'. However, that foreign status does not, of itself, invalidate this prevailing internationally accepted theoretical basis to ordered and representative government. Liberal democracy is not, as a matter of course, unsuited to recognising indigenous claims. Indeed, for majority indigenous populations in jurisdictions such as Fiji it may even offer a path to reclaiming traditional authority. There are substantive differences between liberal democracy and indigeneity but areas of philosophical consistency do emerge where political systems allow the equal rights proposed by liberal democracy to be expressed with recognition of indigenous peoples' unique and historically grounded circumstances. Free societies are strengthened by the things they hold in common, but at the same time they need to find ways of accepting that indigenous peoples do not wish to be part of an imposed cultureless political community so often presented as a political ideal. Accepting difference can strengthen social cohesion by giving indigenous peoples grounds for believing that their value systems have a place in the public realm. Inclusive and participatory understandings of democracy can also contribute important foundations to indigenous self-determination and to the possibility of their belonging in their own terms to the nation state that has developed in the lands of their ancestors.

Conclusion

Citizenship sets the terms of belonging to the postcolonial state. It establishes the rules for the conduct of political relationships and sets out, often subtly, the criteria for participation and deliberation in the political community. It is often used to exclude and promote homogeneity as a political ideal. Yet when the politics of indigeneity is juxtaposed with liberal political theory's emancipatory potential, citizenship may become an inclusive construct capable of two-tiered differentiation, to allow the simultaneous recognition of indigenous peoples' rights as individual members of the state, and as members of corporate indigenous entities. Differentiated citizenship allows indigenous and non-indigenous members of the one political community to 'belong together differently' without either group imposing conditions on the other's membership, or unjustly manipulating the relative and relational character of political power, to the exclusion of others.

Citizenship gives practical articulation to ideas about public authority and individual rights and responsibilities. It is constantly re-shaped by legal as well as political discourses on the terms of indigenous peoples' association with the state and its non-indigenous members. As Patton (2005) points out, terms of association based on lesser legal status which has justified the expropriation of indigenous land and opportunities to exercise political voice, no longer hold unquestioned legal and political currency, but they continue to help to explain indigenous political inequality and show the relevance of history to contemporary politics. There is consequently a reparative argument for the re-conceptualisation of citizenship based on just terms of association. The theoretical intersection of indigeneity, differentiated citizenship and participatory parity provides ways of working out such terms.

FIVE

Indigeneity and contemporary globalisation

Introduction

Globalisation is a political paradox, an 'ambiguous' concern (MacDonald and Muldoon, 2006, p. 209), evoking sharply conflicting assessments of opportunity on the one hand, and neocolonial injustice on the other. Indigenous self-determination, through differentiated citizenship, is as much the product of global developments in extra-state political and economic relationships as it is the product of a group's place within the nation state. These developments support indigenous peoples' efforts to set aside colonial legacy. Yet it also remains that indigenous peoples' initial experiences of globalisation are with imperial expansion and the colonisation of their territories. Tendencies in contemporary scholarly discourse to position globalisation as continuing to oppress and marginalise are well argued (Friedman, 1999; Fenelon and Hall, 2008; Kelsey, 2005a; 2005b; Stewart-Harawira, 2005) but, as this book's remaining chapters show, there are alternative possibilities that indigenous peoples pursue to demonstrate that global capitalism need not always and necessarily compromise indigenous goals.

Indigenous economic agency is also enhanced where the globalisation of political and jurisprudential thought on the rights of indigeneity counters state assertions of absolute sovereignty often to reinforce the economic opportunities that globalisation can create to reduce indigenous dependence on the state. When states try to assert authority over the wishes of indigenous communities, one sees that it is not globalisation *per se* that affronts the rights of indigenous peoples, but its regulation by prejudice, historical legacy and state claims to overriding sovereignty. In contrast, globalisation is increasingly creating new space for worldwide indigenous political activism and cooperation. Indigeneity's growing influence within the United Nations has heightened international scrutiny of colonial and assimilationist conceptions of citizenship. Developments at international law provide a principled framework for thinking about both the possibilities and limits to indigenous rights in postcolonial societies. In globalisation's current phase of capital expansion and the universalisation of human rights, opportunities for indigenous peoples to reclaim personal agency are increasing and the barriers of prejudice and history that do remain are largely due to domestic considerations. Globalisation *per se* does not harm indigenous peoples; rather it is the regulation of its conduct and broader domestic public policy that exclude indigenous peoples from economic development that better explains their economic and political vulnerability. There is also significant political scope for indigenous peoples to examine international legal instruments to support their domestic claims on the nation state.

Globalisation as paradox

Globalisation provided the economic rationale for imperial expansion and for colonialism's sustained confrontational engagement with indigenous societies. Kelsey (2005a; 2005b) and Stewart-Harawira (2005) argue that contemporary globalisation, with its emphasis on rapid capitalist expansion, inevitably sets indigenous cultural priorities aside to make colonisation a continuing phenomenon. Fenelon and Hall (2008) suggest that indigenous peoples, 'by their very continued existence...pose a major challenge to neoliberal capitalism on the ground, politically and ideologically' (p. 1872), while Lauderdale (2008) proposes that globalisation fosters 'cultural assimilation' to inhibit local and global democracy' (p. 1837). According to Friedman (1999), 'liberation from one form of oppression [colonialism] can lead to another integrative process and new forms of class differentiation' (p. 1) to foster 'socio-economic depression and further cultural suppression' (Fenelon and Hall, 2008, p. 1874).

For Stewart-Harawira (2005), traditional indigenous societies are destabilised by the 'co-optation of tribal elites within a Western paradigm of corporatisation and co-modification' (p. 179). Similarly, in New Zealand, Friedman (1999) objects to a perceived Maori tribal 'movement from cultural identity to tribal property' focused on 'genealogical rights to means of production' (p. 9). These arguments juxtapose material accumulation with cultural identity as incompatible alternatives. Modern colonial practices in parts of Africa, Asia and Latin America provide supporting evidence, while indigenous experiences have sometimes been coopted into wider non-indigenous political campaigns of resistance. However, indigenous peoples are generally not 'interested in reforming the world [capitalist] system. They are more interested in autonomy and collective determination' (Lauderale, 2008, p. 1837). The salient point, then, becomes a deeper questioning of how engagement with international economic and political orders may enhance opportunities for autonomy, prosperity and collective self-determination. Specifically, the recent developments in international law and politics that globalisation has fostered emphasise the relative and relational autonomy that indigenous peoples seek over their traditional resources and provide context for indigenous claims to collective development. Sovereignty transcends national constitutional and political arrangements because it is continually re-shaped by international political and economic factors that, at the very least, privilege the idea that the state is merely the agent of the people's sovereignty, rather than sovereign itself. These developments also show the influence of domestic political considerations, rather than globalisation, in restraining indigenous attempts to re-configure sovereignty as a shared expression of political authority.

Economic participation is preliminary to the personal agency that cultural development requires. For many, the alternative to engagement with the global market is deprivation and welfare dependence, so that overstating a tension between cultural and economic imperatives can have a significant negative impact on people's wellbeing. While differences between capitalist and indigenous values and aspirations are widely admitted, the suggestion that these constitute 'a binding constraint to economic development' is not as simple as Jacobsen et al propose (2005, p. 2). Indeed, many indigenous actors argue that acceptance of capitalism's opportunities, rather than inevitable submission to its constraints, is pragmatically important and preliminary to realising the relationship between economic and cultural security.

Sovereignty's relational and relative character precludes indigenous assertions of self-determination in isolation from wider economic and political considerations. Therefore, alliances of common aspiration become preliminary to substantive self-determination involving 'relative yet relational autonomy between peoples, each of which is autonomous in their jurisdiction' (Maaka and Fleras, 2005, p. 97). A constant tension of both principle and politics allows indigenous peoples to assert a shared national sovereignty, with occasional and sometimes significant success. This is because: 'Public power is an expression of a political relationship, it would be a mistake to assume that sovereignty resides in a specific locus, whether that be the king, the people, or an institution such as parliament. Sovereignty ultimately inheres in the form which the political relationship takes' (Loughlin, 2003, p. 55).

Specifically, the recent developments in international law and politics that globalisation has fostered emphasise the relative and relational autonomy that indigenous peoples seek over their traditional resources and provide context for indigenous claims to collective development.

Collective economic development relies on political and economic alliances with the ultimate goal of eliminating obstacles to 'human freedom' (Sen, 1999, p. 12). It is integral to meaningful indigenous sovereignty and 'requires the removal of major sources of unfreedom: poverty as well as tyranny, poor economic opportunities as well as systemic social deprivation, neglect of public facilities as well as intolerance or overactivity of repressive states' (Sen, 1999, p. 3). Globalisation's imperial phase and its continuing legacy explain many of the contemporary barriers to indigenous freedom. However, at the same time, globalisation also ensures that the modern nation state is only ever 'partially sovereign' (Ingram, 2003, p. 387) and open to differentiated citizenship through economic opportunities.

Differentiated citizenship means that the global economy does not present a choice between isolable self-determination and assimilation, which helps to explain why contemporary indigenous discourses do not routinely accept Plaganyi's (2013) argument that 'market-based management options' must always and necessarily compromise indigenous values.

Differentiated citizenship's particular significance is that it may serve as a prerequisite for sustained and materially worthwhile economic opportunity for indigenous peoples. As this book argues, as one of its principal concerns, the proposition applies to indigenous Fijians as much as to the minority indigenous populations of Australia and New Zealand. This chapter's discussion of the relevance of the United Nations' *Declaration on the Rights of Indigenous Peoples* (2007a) to Australia and New Zealand helps to illustrate its potential contribution to ordered, stable and relative and relational self-determination in Fiji.

Differentiated citizenship is important in all three jurisdictions because economic development is not 'culture free' (Scambary, 2013). Indigenous peoples have the right 'to maintain and strengthen... distinct political, legal, economic, social and cultural institutions, while retaining their right to participate fully, if they so choose, in the political, economic, social and cultural life of the State' (United Nations, 2007a, Article 5).

The *Declaration on the Rights of Indigenous Peoples* also affirms that:

1. Indigenous peoples have the right, without discrimination, to the improvement of their economic and social conditions, including, inter alia, in the areas of education, employment, vocational training

and retraining, housing, sanitation, health and social security.

2. States shall take effective measures and, where appropriate, special measures to ensure continuing improvement of their economic and social conditions. Particular attention shall be paid to the rights and special needs of indigenous peoples. (United Nations, 2007a, Articles 21, 1 and 2)

Economic development's capacity to respond to different peoples' particular aspirations precludes uniform policy arrangements; a singular path to development means that some people will be prevented from living lives that they have reason to value (Sen, 1999), and the relationship between self-determination and economic development is one that 'requires *both* redistribution *and* recognition' (Fraser, 1995). Differentiated citizenship allows separate *and* integrated development to co-exist to circumvent the assimilationist tendencies that have, historically, impeded meaningful economic opportunities (Howitt, 2012). Co-existence preserves indigenous cultural integrity. It makes a particular response to the claim that human equality requires liberalism to privilege *sameness* over *difference*. It seeks the political space to advance distinct indigenous aspirations, where indigenous assets and natural resources constitute 'territories of difference' (Escobar, in Altman, 2011) and where there is 'the potential for economic development initiatives to align with the sociological and citizenship features of Indigenous communities' (Jacobsen et al, 2005, p. 1).

Economic opportunities and economic development policy are, then, constituents of the 'struggle for recognition' (Fraser, 2003, p. 68). Yet, it is as misleading to propose that indigenous peoples, always and everywhere, 'ascribe to the mainstreaming development goals of the state' as it is to presume that they 'lack aspirations and agency to pursue alternate forms of livelihood' (Altman, 2011). That presumption's effect would be to define indigenous opportunities with reference to others' accounts of what indigenous values constitute and deny differentiated citizenship's propriety and possibilities. Indigenous economic development is thus located amid the 'increasingly fraught' 'politics of policy reform' that Altman (2005) identifies. However, it is only differentiated citizenship that admits economic development's occurrence in distinct indigenous contexts where culture matters.

Globalisation and the political rights of indigenous peoples

Significant developments in international political and jurisprudential thought has flowed from the juxtaposition of liberal democratic ideas with the politics of indigeneity. These developments challenge the view that globalisation's focus on capital accumulation sets aside indigenous cultural priorities to undermine self-determining authority over lands and resources; to oppress and marginalise indigenous peoples (Friedman, 1999; Fenelon and Hall, 2008; Kelsey 2005a; 2005b; Stewart-Harawira, 2005). For example, the *Declaration on the Rights of Indigenous Peoples* 'sets out the individual and collective rights of the world's 370 million native peoples, calls for the maintenance and strengthening of their cultural identities, and emphasises their right to pursue development in keeping with their own needs and aspirations' (United Nations, 2007a). It is the culmination of more than 50 years' work on the development of international legal instruments to contextualise, codify and articulate a body of rights belonging to indigenous peoples. It follows the International Labor Organization's *Convention Concerning the Protection and Integration of Indigenous and other Tribal or Semi-Tribal Populations in Independent Countries* (No. 107), which was adopted in 1957. In 1989, its *Convention No. 169 on Indigenous and Tribal Peoples* was developed as 'both a reflection of the normative consensus concerning the content of indigenous peoples' rights under international law and a key catalyst of that consensus' (Rodriguez-Pinero, 2005, p. 7).

The *International Covenant on Civil and Political Rights* (United Nations, 1966) has addressed matters of cultural integrity, including indigenous rights to political participation, self-government, land, resources and family. *The International Convention on the Elimination of All Forms of Racial Discrimination* (United Nations, 1965) provides similar protections, while the *International Covenant on Economic, Social and Cultural Rights* (United Nations, 1966) is concerned with food and water, housing, education, health and the right 'to benefit from scientific, literary or artistic production' (Anaya, 2008, 12). The Conventions on *Biological Diversity* (United Nations, 1993) and the *Rights of the Child* (United Nations, 1989), along with the work of the United Nations' Committees on the Elimination of Discrimination against Women, the Committee on the Protection of the Rights of All Migrant Workers and Members of Their Families, and the *Vienna Declaration on Human Rights* (United Nations, 1993) add to a growing international discourse providing normative authority to indigenous people's domestic claims against the state.

The High Court of Australia's Mabo judgment, for example, relied very heavily on international law to establish that the common law ought not be 'locked into a racist past' (Hocking and Hocking, 1999, p. 196). Mabo drew on a decision of the International Court of Justice to find that '*terra nullius*' was inapplicable to the Australian context (*Mabo and Others v. Queensland*) (The High Court of Australia, 1992, 40). Justice Brennan explained that:

> The opening up of international remedies to individuals pursuant to Australia's accession to the Optional Protocol to the International Covenant on Civil and Political Rights... brings to bear on the common law the powerful influence of the Covenant and the international standards it imports. The common law does not necessarily conform with international law, but international law is a legitimate and important influence on the development of the common law, especially when international law declares the existence of universal human rights. A common law doctrine founded on unjust discrimination in the enjoyment of civil and political rights demands reconsideration. It is contrary both to international standards and to the fundamental values of our common law to entrench a discriminatory rule which, because of the supposed position on the scale of social organisation of the indigenous inhabitants of a settled colony, denies them a right to occupy their traditional lands. (The High Court of Australia, 1992, 42)

The Court was able to hear the *Mabo* case only by virtue of the Commonwealth *Racial Discrimination Act 1975*, enacted to allow Australia to ratify the *International Convention on the Elimination of All Forms of Racial Discrimination* (1965). The principles of non-discrimination also derive authority from the *United Nations Charter* (1945), the *Universal Declaration of Human Rights* (1948), the *International Covenant on Civil and Political Rights* (1966), and the *International Covenant on Economic, Social, and Cultural Rights* (1966) (Nettheim, 1998).

A series of legislative reforms followed the *Mabo* and *Wik* decisions and although, in 1998, parliament legislated to nullify certain provisions of the Keating government's (1991–96) *Native Title Act 1993*, the 1998 legislation was well removed from the 'bucketloads of extinguishment' of native title initially proposed by the deputy Prime Minister, Tim Fischer. The public discussion that preceded the legislation was a significant challenge to postcolonial exclusion of customary law from the relative distribution of power and authority. While their demands were compromised in a parliamentary process from which indigenous peoples were excluded, it remains that perhaps for the first time in colonial history the same parliamentary process did insist on a degree of customary recognition, demonstrating that *Mabo* and *Wik* had influenced the national geopolitical landscape. This influence was, in fact, the outcome of international legal developments shaping domestic discourses.

The *Declaration* supplements common citizenship rights by recognising that for indigenous peoples, 'the right to lands, territories and natural resources is the basis for their collective survival and thus inextricably linked to their right to self-determination' (Daes, 2008, p. 8). The *Declaration* must, however, be read as non-binding and in the context of existing human rights obligations, which are reasserted and codified to provide a framework for political recognition (United Nations, 2007). The *Declaration* reflects a gradual movement beyond international law's traditional focus on the state alone to acknowledge indigeneity as a legitimate focus of political identity. Indeed: 'The United Nations system was meant to be a system in which states were responsive to the needs of people and where people – as individuals and as part of groups – had a separate and legitimate role as part of the international community' (McCorquodale, 2006, p. 121).

For over 50 years, then, evolving international discourses have positioned the United Nations as a key participant in indigenous affairs, helping to bring international cohesion to their political aspirations. Indeed, Muehlebach (2001) proposes that 'no other global forum has ever enabled such a large group of activists and their organizations to fully articulate their problems on a regular…basis and to voice their opinion on how these problems should be solved' (p. 415). Xanthaki (2008) argues that:

> Although indigenous peoples have not been part of the creation of international law, they have refused to stand on its periphery and have been determined to become equal partners in its evolution. In a relatively short time they have managed to get their voices heard, have shifted attitudes and initiated a wave of intense international support for their claims. (p. 2)

Yet, even as it stands apart from the philosophical and ideological conflicts that states must mediate, the United Nations is also a site 'where intergovernmental efforts attempt to rein in indigeneity' (Soguk, 2007, p. 16). It was, for example, an overstatement of position for Australia, Canada, New Zealand, and the United States of America to vote against the *Declaration* on the grounds that an indigenous right to self-determination: 'could be misrepresented as conferring a unilateral right of self-determination and possible secession upon a specific subset of the national populace, thus threatening the political unity, territorial integrity and the stability of existing UN Member States' (Banks, 2007).

The focus on secession is inconsistent with normative international understandings of self-determination that indigenous peoples have themselves adopted. As Japan pointed out, the *Declaration*, in fact, affirmed the position that indigenous communities could not appeal to the right to self-determination to impair the political unity or territorial integrity of a state (United Nations, 2007). Or, as Young (1989) suggests, 'self-determination does not imply independence, but rather that peoples dwell together within political institutions that minimise domination among peoples' (p. 188). Yet, for the New Zealand government, the *Declaration* established two classes of citizenship with one group being accorded rights 'that take precedence over those of others'. New Zealand 'assumed that [under the *Declaration*] the rights of all individuals, which are enshrined in international law, are a secondary consideration' (Pearson, 2006). New Zealand instead proposed, but did not define, 'a *Declaration* that can become a tangible and on-going standard of achievement' (Pearson, 2006).

State assumptions of absolute and indivisible authority explain New Zealand's insistence that Articles 10 and 32 of the *Declaration* were incompatible with the state's 'constitutional and legal arrangements, the Treaty of Waitangi and the principle of governing for the good of all our citizens' (Banks, 2007) because they provide for 'free, prior and informed' indigenous consent to 'relocation from their lands or territories.' The Articles read that:

> Indigenous peoples shall not be forcibly removed from their lands or territories. No relocation shall take place without the free, prior and informed consent of the indigenous peoples concerned and after agreement on just and fair compensation and, where possible, with the option of return. (*United Nations Declaration on the Rights of Indigenous Peoples*, Article 10)

Indigenous peoples have the right to determine and develop priorities and strategies for the development or use of their lands or territories and other resources. (*United Nations Declaration on the Rights of Indigenous Peoples*, Article 32: 1)

States shall consult and cooperate in good faith with the indigenous peoples concerned through their own representative institutions in order to obtain their free and informed consent prior to the approval of any project affecting their lands or territories and other resources, particularly in connection with the development, utilization or exploitation of mineral, water or other resources. (*United Nations Declaration on the Rights of Indigenous Peoples*, Article 32: 2)

States shall provide effective mechanisms for just and fair redress for any such activities, and appropriate measures shall be taken to mitigate adverse environmental, economic, social, cultural or spiritual impact. (*United Nations Declaration on the Rights of Indigenous Peoples*, Article 32: 3)

Australia's objection was that 'free, prior and informed consent' would provide a right of veto to 'legitimate decisions of a democratic and representative government' (Hill, 2007). For indigenous Australians, the concept of representative government remains elusive and, rather than constituting a right of veto, the Articles balance political relationships by checking the absolute right of a Parliament, unrepresentative of indigenous perspectives, to make laws to override a considered indigenous position.

The argument that a right of 'veto' establishes additional citizenship rights for just one group of people ought to be evaluated with reference to liberalism's capacity to recognise group rights as preliminary to the protection of individual freedom. Similarly, 'global diversity is limited when it is built within the constraints of modern nation-states, which often view diversity as deviance if it does not conform to modern norms and definitions' (Lauderdale, 2008, p. 1836). Individual citizenship alone is insufficient to secure the legitimate cultural and economic rights of indigenous peoples. Group rights are emphasised because cultural rights can only be enjoyed in common with others and because economic deprivation is an outcome of injustices occasioned, principally, against groups of people not individuals. Where, for example, colonial practices have compromised the foundational liberal principle of unencumbered property rights it seems a reasonable concession for the modern state to seek 'free, prior, and informed consent' to developments over traditional lands, especially where continuing ownership has been recognised through a fair judicial process.

In a departure from its own well-established practice, New Zealand objected to the *Declaration*'s requirement to provide redress for land acquired without the consent of the indigenous peoples. New Zealand's own statement on the *Declaration* acknowledged that it had already settled claims over half the country's land mass (Banks, 2007), but Lightfoot's (2008) conditions for securing indigenous rights illustrate what New Zealand perhaps feared: 'Securing indigenous rights means that several critical changes in the international discourse must occur, including an alteration of the liberal international Westphalian system of state sovereignty toward a postliberal, plurinational sovereignty system that includes a separate nation-to-nation and consent-based shared sovereignty arrangement between states and indigenous peoples' (p. 83).

The *Declaration* checked state power by helping to frame public discourses of resistance. In Australia, the Rudd government (2007–10) reversed its predecessor's opposition to the *Declaration* as a mark of 'respect for Indigenous peoples' (Macklin, 2009), but without responding in any specific way to the reservations the previous government used to explain its opposition. In New Zealand, the Key and English governments (2008–present) have taken a similar position, indicative of a broadening perspective on indigenous rights, largely by virtue of the Maori party's presence in that country's coalition government. In New Zealand, the bounds of possibility have been extended, but perhaps without real governmental thought on just how far it is willing to see those new bounds of possibility tested. Indeed, the: 'Standards concerning indigenous rights are still fluid; the contours of international law are constantly stretched' (Xanthaki, 2008, p. 282), but the United Nations remains the only truly authoritative non-state body for the presentation and testing of indigenous claims in relative freedom from the populist and highly subjective prejudices that can contextualise domestic discussions. Indigenous peoples may view their rights as inherent, but pragmatically, they need to be justified to the international community. When indigeneity engages with normative liberal ideas about political arrangements it influences and shapes these to make them more responsive to indigenous claims, which is why its application to minority indigenous populations alone is to Fiji's great disadvantage.

The *Declaration* assumes political stability and principled arrangements for the distribution of public power and authority. Its potential to contribute to working out such arrangements, if it was drawn in to Fijian political discourse as the indigenous Chief Executive of the national Citizen's Constitutional Forum, Akuila Yabaki (2008), describes it:

> It [would] recognise our right to be different, and to act as an individual or as part of a community as we choose. It encourages participation in matters which affect us all such as education, social welfare, health, environment and governance without discrimination. From it we should learn that multiculturalism is what makes us all part of the common heritage of mankind. We are all entitled to exercise and practice our beliefs, cultures and religions, and should not interfere in the rights of other people to do the same.

The *Declaration* is also useful as an instrument of order and stability because it implies shared relational and relative national sovereignty. It provides a framework for thinking about indigeneity's limits as well as its possibilities.

> In the exercise of the rights enunciated in the present Declaration, human rights and fundamental freedoms of all shall be respected. The exercise of the rights set forth in this Declaration shall be subject only to such limitations as are determined by law, and in accordance with international human rights obligations. Any such limitations shall be non-discriminatory and strictly necessary solely for the purpose of securing recognition and respect for the rights and freedoms of others and for meeting the just and most compelling requirements of a democratic society. (United Nations, 2007a, 46(1))

Further:

> Indigenous peoples and individuals are free and equal to all other peoples and individuals and have the right to be free from any kind of discrimination, in the exercise of their rights, in particular that based on their indigenous origin or identity. (*United Nations Declaration on the Rights of Indigenous Peoples*, Article 2)

Conversely, indigeneity is limited if it is ill-equipped to admit the relationship between all groups' economic and political engagement with one another and any one group's capacity for self-determination. There are examples from other jurisdictions where the politics of indigeneity transcends, rather than encourages, the:

> mistaken premise that a choice must be made between an ethnic conflict model and an 'integration' model. The assumption has been that focusing on the ethnic division necessarily means stressing antagonistic polarity, and that the debate must be between such a model and an opposing one – which transcends the division by arguing that it is, in politics, mainly a function of elite or ruling-class strategies. (Norton, 2000, p. 89)

In Canada, for example, the 'inherent right of self-government of indigenous peoples':

> is based on the view that the Aboriginal peoples of Canada have the right to govern themselves in relation to matters that are internal to their communities, integral to their unique cultures, identities, traditions, languages and institutions, and with respect to their special relationship to their land and their resources. (Indian and Northern Affairs Canada, 1995)

The *Declaration* would, then, contribute to a theoretically cohesive and pragmatically instrumental account of indigeneity if its applicability to jurisdictions such as Fiji, was more certain, as it is clear that indigenous majority status in a multicultural population does not, in and of itself, remove postcolonial constraints on indigenous political authority.

The Declaration on the Rights of Indigenous Peoples and domestic politics

The importance of global developments in liberal democratic thought on the rights of indigenous peoples is all the more evident when set against examples of self-determination being more constrained by domestic factors than globalisation *per se*. In a recent example, the New Zealand parliament overrode claims to Maori customary title to the foreshore and seabed by vesting title solely in the Crown. The *Foreshore and Seabed Act 2004* was enacted after a tribal group,

Ngati Apa, was refused a commercial mussel farming licence over a customarily used area of foreshore and seabed. The point of legal contention was whether a tribe had a legal right to ask a Court to confirm customary title. The ensuing legal and political debates were protracted, complicated and controversial with an alarmist government, encouraged by populist opposition parties, promoting public suspicion that one tribe's customary title would necessarily deny all other citizens access to the entire coastline. Although this was never the Ngati Apa intention, public suspicion created a context for the Crown to contest the incremental re-casting of sovereignty by asserting its own absolute authority. The consequent Maori appeal to the United Nations to declare the *Foreshore and Seabed Act* incompatible with international norms of human rights and justice provided a contrasting illustration of the international moral constraints on domestic state sovereignty, especially as the United Nations' Committee on the Elimination of Racial Discrimination found that the legislation breached the *Convention on the Elimination of Racial Discrimination* (2005), and urged negotiations between the state and Maori to 'seek ways of mitigating its discriminatory effects' (United Nations Committee on the Elimination of All Forms of Racial Discrimination, 2005).

The Committee's findings and recommendations were affirmed by the United Nations' Special Rapporteur on the Fundamental Freedoms and Human Rights of Indigenous Peoples, and as part of their coalition government agreement in 2007, the National and Maori parties agreed to review the Act. The review ultimately recommended repeal of the legislation. Thus, even a settled political order that guarantees relatively high levels of indigenous political participation is not immune from allowing populist ideology to override a universally accepted human right. Significantly in this instance, domestic pressures, not globalisation, prevented Maori entry into a commercial market. The political disagreement between Maori and the Crown showed that Maori reclaim authority over their natural resources to support cultural, environmental and spiritual aspirations, but their claims also have an unapologetic economic purpose. Guardianship or stewardship, rather than 'ownership', of the foreshore and seabed is not, for example, as obviously 'opposed to monetary values...established by global capitalism' as Fenelon and Hall suggest (2008, p. 1884).

At the same time, however, the United Nations' restrictive understanding of indigeneity as belonging only to minority native populations left Fiji without recourse to an important instrument in international law to help it resolve domestic disagreement over the Qarase government's (2002–06) *Qoliqoli Bill 2006*, one of the two proposed Acts of Parliament precipitating that year's military coup. The two parliamentary Bills, one passed, and the other not, provide instructive contrast on indigenous rights to coastal resources. Lal (2009) explains that the Fijian legislation was intended:

> to transfer 'all proprietary rights to and interests in qoliqoli [foreshore] areas within Fiji fisheries waters [and] vest them in the qoliqoli owners.' By this process, the marine area from the foreshore to the high water mark would be declared 'native reserves', for the unfettered use and enjoyment of the resource owners. (p. 24)

A key difference with New Zealand was that Maori never sought 'unfettered use' of the resource. Pragmatic acceptance of the rights of others as well as economic considerations highlighted the practical limits that relative and relational political authority imposes on the claims that indigeneity can realistically make. In spite of military opposition being given civil credence by the reservations of the Fijian Law Society and national tourism industry, Qarase's Soqosoqo Duavata ni Lewenivanua (SDP) party still attracted 80 per cent of the indigenous vote at the 2006 election. After campaigning on the Bill, the Prime Minister claimed a mandate to enact it that, in turn, established the context for the removal of his government. The tourism industry objected on reasoned self-interested economic grounds. However, the Law Society observed that in transferring ownership, as distinct from *mana whenua* [guardianship], which Maori claimed in New Zealand, 'the state is in fact transferring to them the state's rights of sovereignty within these qoliqoli areas. The effect of this is that the qoliqoli could become autonomous areas whereby the owners of the qoliqoli could implement their own rules outside the regulation and control of the State' (Fijian Law Society, in Lal, 2009, p. 25). In other words, indigenous sovereign authority would be absolute; and unencumbered by the needs, rights, and interests of other citizens. However, the military reaction to the *Qoliqoli Bill* confirmed that Fijian sovereignty is a fractured and unstable construct increasingly distant from the people. The ensuing coup illustrated the importance of domestic, rather than international factors, in determining indigenous Fijian access to a share in domestic political authority.

The *Declaration* sets out principles to codify indigenous claims on the state and is equipped to set the terms of indigenous engagement in the state itself. While the context means that these general principles would need to be operationalised in different ways than in Australia or New

Zealand, for example, they remain relevant because it is indigeneity rather than population status alone that contextualises the rights, opportunities and constraints of postcolonial indigenous politics. The *Declaration*'s failure to consider indigenous politics in these terms is a significant weakness, especially in respect of Fiji where the principles it enunciates are exactly those that might fill the significant intellectual and political void in contemporary Fijian understandings of power and inter-ethnic relationships, especially as indigeneity's growing influence within the United Nations has otherwise heightened international scrutiny of colonial and assimilationist conceptions of citizenship. Developments in international law provide a principled framework for thinking about both the possibilities and limits to the rights of indigenous peoples in postcolonial societies.

Conclusion

Globalisation accounts for the colonisation of indigenous territories and its pursuit of capital expansion is sometimes allowed to override indigenous cultural imperatives. However, at the same time, in its contemporary phase, globalisation provides indigenous peoples with recourse to international law and economic opportunities to strengthen their positions vis-à-vis the state in the quest for specific and proportionate shares in national sovereignty. Indigenous/state political relationships are distinguished by state reliance on domestic laws and political influence to counter indigenous claims to shared sovereignty, which is becoming increasingly relative and relational, rather than the absolute indivisible and incontestable domain of the state. Instruments of international law such as the *Declaration* have become a site of tension between domestic authority and international norms of justice in New Zealand. At the same time, its inapplicability to Fiji deprives that country of a potential framework for mediating ideas about power, authority and their limits so that a relative and relational sovereignty can be developed. In short, far from being a neocolonial constraint on indigenous political aspirations, globalisation's opportunities make it an ambiguous political paradox and the following chapters show the ways in which indigenous engagement with national and international economies are preliminary to cultural self-determination as much as they are preliminary to material wellbeing. Indigenous economic engagement of these kinds is aided by the growing scrutiny of neocolonial constraints on indigenous citizenship provided by the developments at international law that this chapter has discussed. The universalisation of human rights has restrained the nation state's capacity to limit indigenous political rights and indigenous peoples in Australia and New Zealand have had recourse, through international legal instruments, to challenge the state's political authority.

SIX

Economic development as differentiated citizenship: Australia

Yindyamarra winhanga-nha [The wisdom of knowing how to live well in a world worth living in]

Introduction

Indigenous economic practice and aspirations emphasise economic activity's cultural context and purpose; practices and aspirations that routinely differ from Australian public policy's instinctive presumptions. In focusing on the politics of indigenous economic development, as differentiated citizenship and as an essential constituent of Australian reconciliation, this chapter notes the philosophical contrast between prevailing indigenous thought and policy measures such as the Commonwealth's *Indigenous Economic Development Strategy* and 'Closing the Gap in Indigenous Disadvantage'. The contrast reflects the view that a people's capacity to define itself is an important constituent of self-determination. It is especially important in preventing the development of negative and potentially prophetic stereotypes. In short: 'Aboriginal Australia must not be dominated by Mainstream Australia's perception of who we are' (Sarra, 2014, p. 79).

Indigenous actors' repeated emphasis on transgenerational wellbeing shows that economic development is understood as part of a complex policy domain closely intertwined with social stability, employment, health and educational opportunities. Indeed, there is a 'gap' to be 'closed' between indigenous experience and public policy, not just in relation to the labour market, but also in schooling where the idea of culturally cognisant pedagogy is sharply contested and provides an important contrast with New Zealand, which is explored in the following chapter, where Maori have assertively advanced the view that cultural equality in schooling is a mark of genuinely equal citizenship.

Access to functioning markets for education, housing, employment and access to the middle class are important determinants of prosperity. The relative size of the indigenous middle class is a measure of indigenous access to full and substantive citizenship and this chapter especially considers the proposition that 'culture counts' (Bishop and Glynn, 1999) in economic development and its determinants. Culture remains a possible determinant of material wellbeing even though it is true that at other times people may make deliberate choices about what they value that emphasise other priorities over the material. However, these choices exist at one extreme of a range of possibilities and the chapter shows, for example, that 'culture counts' in developing alternatives to passive welfare and in measures that realise not just the 'right' to self-determination, but its transformative capacity such that poverty need not remain colonialism's necessary legacy. The chapter shows that the education system's more effective support for the development of a larger indigenous middle class is an essential pre-condition for the power of self-determination. The following chapter shows that, in New Zealand, increases in the size of the Maori middle class has shown the interdependent relationship between cultural and material security.

Culture, economic development and the true 'gap' in indigenous public policy

Contemporary Australian discourse accepts relationships between economic development and self-determination, but is divided on the question of whether material security should be pursued through employment in the mainstream labour market alone or through 'hybrid' models of development (Altman, 2011). The contrast is between immediate utilitarian goals and development based on rights of indigeneity; between 'equality and sameness' or 'diversity and choice' (Altman and Rowse, 2005). Alternatively, differentiated citizenship removes the absolute distinction and allows the two to co-exist and contribute to self-determination in various but equally important ways, so that policy might transcend 'economic sameness' (Altman, 2011, p. 7), while still supporting engagement with the capitalist economy to support cultural as well as economic security.

While liberal citizenship can be a 'positive project of government' (Hindess, 2002, p. 134), it is also a 'positive project' of indigenous civil society. Public institutions and the rules by which they function are important but so, too, are indigenous institutions, especially as indigenous economic development is 'not just a technical problem that requires a technical solution' (Altman, 2011, p. 10). Culture is central to how one understands the purpose of economic activity. It underlies relationships between 'pride and identity' and opportunities for economic security (New South Wales Aboriginal Land Council,

2014, p. 8) to explain the New South Wales Aboriginal Land Council's aspiration for 'strong Aboriginal communities in which Aboriginal people actively influence and fully participate in social, economic and cultural life' (New South Wales Aboriginal Land Council, 2014, p. 8). There are also important relationships between 'customary rights' and 'social and economic wellbeing' and the Council continues to speak of land rights as 'empowerment' because 'economic development is necessary to give meaning to self-determination' (Deloitte Access Economics and New South Wales Aboriginal Land Council, 2013, p. 5). The same rationale explains the Cape York Institute's argument that: 'With economic development comes empowerment. Until the indigenous people of Cape York can largely generate their own incomes they will be dependent on income transfers, where someone else takes all of the rights and responsibilities to make decisions and take actions on behalf of a relatively powerless people' (Pearson, in Deloitte Access Economics and New South Wales Aboriginal Land Council, 2013, p. 7).

The New South Wales Land Council proposes simultaneous attention to commercial viability and 'distinctive Aboriginal values relating to such matters as work practices and relations, hierarchy and authority, the distribution of profits and…social viability' (Martin, 1995, p. 19). The Council positions economic aspirations as products of the values and experiences that give meaning to people's lives so that cultural 'match' between people and economic opportunities becomes an important determinant of development (Lindsay Barr and Reid, 2014) to explain why wealth maximising behaviour and rational self-interest are not the sole determinants of indigenous economic engagement; they separate cultural from economic aspirations (Jacobsen et al, 2005) and undermine circuitous relationships among social stability, employment, health, educational and economic opportunities.

Economic empowerment occurs in cultural context and indigenous peoples' renewed legal capacity, in some cases, to use traditionally owned resources for material purposes illustrates the cultural importance of connections between individual and collective wellbeing. In this context, material prosperity becomes just one of development's purposes, and scope must be retained to 'build on the rights, cultural assets and social networks of Indigenous people', so that policy does not 'ignore those or see them as a problem to be overcome' (Hunt, 2011, p. 9). In particular, communal resource ownership reflects indigenous peoples' trans-generational understanding of development and is preliminary to the maximisation of authority over their own affairs. From this perspective, one rationalises relationships between 'strengthening culture and protecting heritage…[and the] conservation of natural values' (North Australian Indigenous Land and Sea Management Alliance, 2013, p. 10). One also rationalises the aspiration of 'securing and managing our land…[and] protecting and promoting our culture, heritage and the environment' (New South Wales Aboriginal Land Council, 2014). Similarly: 'The stated vision is clear' for the Cape York Institute: 'long-term sustainable tourism development on Cape York and the Torres Strait that respects and celebrates the culture, traditions and lifestyle of the Indigenous and non-Indigenous people, enhances environmental integrity and creates economic and social growth' (Ruhanen and Whitford, 2014, p. 190).

For example, *Indigenous Business Australia* proposes indigenous entrepreneurship's potential to address 'disadvantage and [thus] make a sustained difference in the lives of indigenous peoples; 'Closing the "entrepreneurship Gap" is preliminary to the broader aims of closing the socio-economic, health and education gap between indigenous and non-indigenous Australians' (Morrison et al, 2014, p. 4). The capacity to use evidence to evaluate policy is also essential. This is how one knows that 'the gap [is or] is not closing' (Mundine, 2013).

Mundine's (2013) strategies for closing the entrepreneurial gap are based on four principles especially relevant to economic development: governance, land ownership, social stability and openness. Although indigenous people 'are the most highly governed' in Australia, there remain important characteristics of good governance missing from contemporary political arrangements. Good governance requires 'a stable, representative government, a functioning bureaucracy, no systemic corruption, the rule of law and transparency of dealings and fair, certain and transparent systems for dispute resolution', under conditions admitting that: 'We need governance to reflect the way indigenous people look at themselves, not the way others have chosen to look at them' (2013). In particular, 'the traditional neo-classical economic approach to private enterprise based solely on an individual entrepreneur maximising his or her profits is very wide of the mark for Indigenous enterprises' (Morrison et al, 2014, p. 13).

Indigenous businesses tend to exist for the benefit of the owners' broader family and community. They are 'often embedded in Indigenous community networks' to give *social capital* the same importance as *private capital* (Morrison et al, 2014, p. 15). As one participant in Morrison et al's (2014) study put it:

> [I]t's all about us blackfella's…my business. That's why I started it. To give the blackfella's a go…They can come into

the business, work here, maybe put them on a traineeship, you know, give them a real opportunity in a supportive environment.

So we try and give a lot of career development to our mob…They know whatever they choose to do, we can get them training to be able to accommodate…their position. (pp. 149–50)

Targeted policy attention to people's readiness for work is an important determinant of development (Australians for Native Title and Reconciliation, 2010) and, while most indigenous businesses prefer to employ indigenous workers, there remains a significant skills deficiency giving business, itself, an important function in the strengthening of human capacity. Similarly, Morrison et al (2014) were provided with many examples of businesses' cultural focus contributing to broader community wellbeing:

[T]he Gallery's main objective is to encourage…cultural maintenance through storytelling and the cultural production of artwork.

Everything is about our Aboriginal culture here, everything, from the way that I run my staff, from the type of food.

I think about my Grandmother really a lot…she was raised on a mission…She was a domestic, and recently we got some documents where she was fighting for her rights to be paid, or to see her family…she wasn't allowed to speak language…And even as an older lady, when she speaks about culture or language, she'd whisper it, because it was so ingrained. And those things are what really drives me, because I'm not only able to do it, but it's my responsibility to do it, so that my daughter will know our language and those stories. (p. 150)

Conversely, the absence of cultural pride is associated with underachievement (Sarra, 2007) and the theme's broader social significance is evident in the observation that:

The main basis for the business was to start Aboriginal kids wearing something that represents themselves, as opposed to wearing black American clothes…I felt uncomfortable about our kids aligning themselves with another culture…

when we…sell them the gear…we change the druggie
gangster culture to them wanting to be stockmen. So that
has a positive effect on the community, because they go
from wanting to be gangsters, with all the rubbish clothing,
to getting a job and working on the station and getting
involved in the rodeo and stock work. (Morrison et al,
2014, pp. 149–50)

In contrast, the Commonwealth's *Draft Indigenous Economic Development
Strategy*, released for consultation in 2011, focused principally on
labour market participation in isolation from the cultural context of
work. It lacked the 'strong rights-base' that underlies New Zealand
Maori economic opportunities and which North American research
has found to be a more effective basis for development (Hunt,
2011). The final *Strategy*, to 2018, 'provides a vision for government,
business and Indigenous and non-Indigenous Australians and outlines
actions for improving Indigenous economic development' (Australian
Government, 2011, p. 20).

The *Strategy* proposed 'targeted reforms to help close the gap in
essential infrastructure, and develop a strategic policy framework
for infrastructure provision in remote communities' (p. 69). It set
out policy priorities and 'reporting arrangements' intended to allow
greater evaluative depth than has traditionally distinguished indigenous
policy. It claimed a concern for 'the major actions the Government
is taking to achieve its goal of improved economic development for
Indigenous Australians' (p. 69). However, it did not admit that the
goal requires a more dramatic shift from the underlying philosophical
position that Scambary (2013) found in mining agreements, between
2003 and 2007, where government policy 'sought to de-emphasise the
cultural behaviour or imperatives of Indigenous people in undertaking
economic action in favour of a mainstream approach to economic
development' (p. viii). The point is also evident when comparing
the *Strategy*'s egalitarian objectives, with those of *Closing the Gap in
Indigenous Disadvantage*, neither of which gave adequate regard to
cultural imperatives and 'Closing the Gap' sought serious indigenous
engagement only *after* the policy's initial implementation. Indeed, in
its submission on the draft *Strategy*, Australians for Native Title and
Reconciliation (2010) thought it sufficiently remarkable to make
special note of the commitment to 'work collaboratively' by 'genuinely
engaging with Indigenous Australians in formulating policy, [and]
acknowledging that policy reforms are more likely to be successful
when they are informed by those affected' (p. 7).

There remains a particular 'gap' to be closed between indigenous identified possibilities and policy recognition to suggest that in some respects 'governmental policy settings have been frozen in the apologetic 1970s' view of the Aboriginal world' (Langton, 2012). Altman (2011) is also correct to observe that: 'It is impossible to establish an economic development strategy for the present and future if there is no engagement or understanding of the past; and an acknowledgement of deep economic development policy failure' (p. 6). Altman's is one of the reasons why on their own, statistical measures of wellbeing, oversimplify indigenous 'need'. In its submission on the draft *Strategy* the North Australian Indigenous Land and Sea Management Alliance (2013) made a number of proposals not accepted into the final document. These showed the complexities of indigenous economic development that because of restrictions on indigenous deliberative capacity are not always admitted into public policy. For example, the Alliance especially noted the importance of:

- hypothecation of a substantial proportion of resource revenues to Indigenous economic development, addressing both employment and enterprise creation;
- review of government environmental offsets and social benefits packages associated with major development projects, with redesign to favour creation and industry-supported incubation of Indigenous businesses to deliver on commitments;
- serious, integrated planning processes that:
  - instead of setting up competing development and conservation plans, treat both together;
  - deploy economic development as a solution to improve and sustain environmental quality and address social problems;
  - support local and finer scale (property-level) planning to inform regional plans;
- changes in law governing access to resources associated with land ownership: to facilitate rather than inhibit economic use by Indigenous people, including native title interests;
- financial assistance to carbon farming enterprises to support them in the period between start-up and first sales of credits;

- processes for overcoming bureaucratic disjunctions and incompatibilities that inhibit coherent programmes drawing on multiple sources; and
- greater flexibility to match government programmes of all sorts to deeper understanding of local context and aspirations. (p. 4)

The Alliance also stressed:

- developments requiring substantial modification of the landscape or extraction of renewable natural resources always confront trade-offs, even in relatively undeveloped regions: something is lost for every gain;
- cumulatively significant areas of soils suitable for irrigated or rain-fed agriculture are present but scattered in mosaics rather than large, uniformly favourable tracts of country: most of the region lacks suitable combinations of soils and water for broad-scale agriculture;
- options exist for productive livelihoods in delivery of ecosystem services and tourism that do not depend on major modification of landscapes or ecosystem processes;
- Indigenous views of values that demand protection are too little considered in decisions about acceptable trade-offs;
- in many parts of north Australia, existing Indigenous livelihoods do not depend entirely on monetary exchange and those aspects of livelihoods should not be compromised. (p. 8)

The efficacy of the *Strategy*'s intention to close the gap in 'essential infrastructure' depends on the efficacy of accompanying policies to close the gap in the provision of health and education services of the same quality available to non-indigenous citizens. Self-determination requires economic empowerment through the housing and labour markets, equitable employment opportunities for women, and a particular focus on younger people's education and training needs. 'Schools should…be appealing and effective for indigenous children' (Mundine, 2013) and focused on the provision of 'high quality, equitable student outcomes' (p. 3), especially as 58 per cent of the indigenous population is under the age of 25, and economic development cannot be sustained without the education system's full and effective contribution.

The relationship between poor education and low employment levels has long been admitted in public policy rhetoric, yet policy solutions remain elusive, and poor education, poor health and social dysfunction are often structural barriers to indigenous peoples acquiring the full benefits of labour market participation. Culture is elsewhere accepted as integral to effective schooling (Bishop and Glynn, 1999) and its capacity to make differentiated citizenship work in practice makes the school a site of sharply contested perspectives; especially as societies contemplate the affirmation of the United Nations' *Declaration* that: 'Indigenous peoples have the right to establish and control their educational systems and institutions providing education in their own languages, in a manner appropriate to their cultural methods of teaching and learning' (United Nations, 2007a, Article 14, 1).

Equal access to culturally cognisant schooling is a mark of equal citizenship. Equitable access to political, economic and social liberties is also an outcome of the just distribution of educational opportunities, which also equips people with the political capacity to demand cultural respect and group recognition from public institutions. However, the former Education Minister Julia Gillard's restrictions on bilingual schooling illustrated indigeneity's marginal public policy status. In contrast, in 2015 the New South Wales government retained at least a notional commitment to the teaching of indigenous languages in the public education system such that: 'This is the first generation (of children) who have actually been given permission to speak their language' (McNaboe, 2015). Gillard's view held currency through a politics of exclusion to show why indigenous participation at every level of the education system, as student, teacher, administrator and policy maker is important. Indeed, Sarra (2007) found that indigenous parents' high expectations of systemic performance lacked influence because 'they had no idea about how to pursue it' (Sarra, 2007, p. 76). In other words, they had no meaningful or understandable deliberative capacity.

Ladwig and Sarra's (2009) *Structured Review of the Northern Territory Department of Education and Training* responded to entrenched underperformance in Northern Territory schools (Ladwig and Sarra, 2009). While the Northern Territory education system has the infrastructural capacity to raise the quality of its work (Ladwig and Sarra, 2009), the fact remains that failure to do so is the outcome of an entrenched political culture unable to consider, in substantive ways, the meaning of citizenship. That there is a need, in the Northern Territory, 'to establish regular review of school and systemic performance' (Ladwig and Sarra, 2009, p. 8) further illustrates the failure of the policy process to respond to a relationship between evidence and practice.

This systemic failure occurs even as much is known about the benefits of robust policy evaluation and about the pedagogies, practices and institutional arrangements more likely to work for indigenous people. The objective of 'delivering the goods' to all students 'no matter who they are or where they live' (p. 8) is not easily realisable, but decisions about how seriously to pursue such an objective is deeply entrenched in political values.

Sarra (2007) stresses the practical relationship between self-determination and effective schooling with a foundational purpose of schooling being 'getting the children to believe they could be as smart as any other child from any other school, and develop into strong, young, black, powerful people' (p. 79). The report argued that the Department of Education and Training had only just reached the point where the public could 'justifiably raise its expectation' that good quality education could be provided (p. 11) as 'it is well known... that the Northern Territory has too long lived under the cloud of low expectations' (p. 11). It is evident that systemic, as well as teacher expectations, are important to the 'pedagogy for emancipation' that Sarra seeks (2014, p. 78).

The New South Wales Ombudsman has an evaluative role over a number of indigenous policy measures. Its statutory independence and separation from policy delivery makes its perspectives unique; they stand apart from the political constraints of resourcing and electoral acceptability in much the same fashion as New Zealand's Education Review Office is able to review schools and schooling independently of the wider education bureaucracy. In its review of indigenous economic policy, in 2016, the Ombudsman endorsed the New South Wales Land Council's view that: 'The role of government must shift from delivering systems predicated on disadvantage, to facilitating the aspirations, priorities and self-determination of Aboriginal peoples. Governments must be prepared to move into an innovative space to encourage Aboriginal self-determination, and long-term partnerships with industry' (Ombudsman, New South Wales, 2016).

The Ombudsman, however, found that these aspirations are constrained by inadequate economic investment, poor policy integration, accountability and delivery, low rates of ownership and employment, compounded by the negative relationship between the rate of imprisonment and economic outcomes. The Ombudsman's recommendations for addressing these instances of policy failure were directed, mainly, to the state's Department of Education and Training. That focus indicates *both* the importance of education to self-determination and the extent of policy incoherence in that domain. The Ombudsman recommended:

> That the Department of Education (Aboriginal Affairs) takes account of the observations made in this report, and includes the following features in the Aboriginal Economic Prosperity Framework:

> a. A clear vision of what it aims to achieve over the short, medium and longer term.
> b. A tiered approach to ensure focus on individuals, enterprises and communities.
> c. Consideration of available evidence about promising or proven initiatives in NSW and elsewhere.
> d. Means by which to address existing barriers contributing to economic marginalisation of Aboriginal people/enterprises, including through:
>   i. improving educational outcomes and transitioning to post-school options
>   ii. reducing the ongoing impact of incarceration on economic outcomes
>   iii. eliminating pockets of financial exclusion and building financial literacy
>   iv. fostering employment opportunities in the public and private sectors
>   v. creating pathways to home ownership – helping individuals to raise capital.
> e. Means by which the significant Government investment in growing the NSW economy and other existing opportunities can be harnessed, including by:
>   i. leveraging mainstream economic development initiatives
>   ii. embedding the framework within broader regional and state-wide economic development efforts and facilitating place-based approaches to building local economies
>   iii. recognising the assets and comparative advantages of Aboriginal communities
>   iv. facilitating collaboration and partnerships
>   v. supporting the entrepreneurial capacity of Aboriginal people and organisations

vi. using government procurement processes to incentivise the government/private sector to engage Aboriginal enterprises.

f. Flexibility – so that adjustments can be made where problems are identified along the way and/or new information comes to light about better approaches.

g. Sufficient reach and authority to ensure that legal and policy developments in other portfolios consider the potential impact on Aboriginal economic outcomes, similar to regulatory or environmental impact statements.

h. Clear responsibilities ascribed to relevant agencies and positions which are in turn linked to individual performance contracts.

i. Robust governance arrangements which:
    i. coordinate existing and future efforts to strengthen Aboriginal economic prosperity by the government, private and non-government sectors
    ii. empower individuals with sufficient authority to lead the necessary reforms, and
    iii. are supported by regular and open reporting on progress, informed by a genuine dialogue with Aboriginal leadership on what meaningful indicators of performance should look like. (Ombudsman, New South Wales, 2015, p. 32)

The need for policy based on evidence of what works is especially important in education where expectations are strongly influenced by fashion and ideology. Education's transformative potential is well understood, but compromised, by political and professional factors that combine, in effect, to leave disproportionate numbers of indigenous people excluded from the 'real economy', especially the primary labour market. In the absence of measures to close these gaps: 'It is difficult to see how the federal policy on indigenous economic development is of any help at all in overcoming welfare dependency' (Langton, 2012), particularly as welfare is a relatively 'easy' solution to the absence of functioning labour markets or to addressing systemic barriers to indigenous access to those markets through racism and poor education, for example.

Access to markets, mining and the middle class

In urban areas, where most indigenous people reside, it is not the absence of commerce that impedes indigenous economic participation, but the absence of markets that function effectively for indigenous citizens. The education market's ineffectiveness, restricted access to markets for health services and racism in the housing and labour markets contribute to indigenous economic marginalisation. For example, for Langton (2012), there remain too 'few incentives for [economic] participation and many disincentives'. Although it is essential, it is not sufficient to argue, in response, for increased educational investment. Similarly, measures to help welfare recipients manage their incomes may enhance social stability and improve familial care but can, at the same time, undermine the self-responsibility that cultural integrity once promoted and that is a precondition for living a life that one has reason to value. However, Forrest (2014) correctly, and importantly, notes the significance of accountability measures to ensure that public money provided to government service providers is efficaciously spent.

There are economic and social arguments for denying welfare assistance to young people who choose not to engage in education or work. However, the practicality and justice of such a requirement is that there must be both functioning labour and educational markets. Often, neither is the case and where they are present, the alternative markets of Altman's 'hybrid economy', discussed later in this chapter, ought not be dismissed, even though Forrest (2014) is correct to emphasise that: 'there is no employment gap, or disparity, for the first Australians who are educated at the same level as other Australians, the full force of our community leaders and governments must pack behind the achievement of parity in educational outcomes as a national priority' (p. ii).

The Australian Indigenous Chamber of Commerce (2013) emphasises 'real' jobs and private ownership as the basis for full participation in 'Australia's free market commercial system' to contrast with the former Community Development and Employment Programme (CDEP) which encouraged welfare dependency. For Langton (2012), CDEP and the Intervention are 'exceptionalist initiatives' that 'have isolated the Aboriginal world from Australian economic and social life', with the 'Intervention' an example of 'a failure of state relationships rather than an appropriate and sustainable response to the challenge of Indigenous vulnerability'. It, too, placed unrealistic confidence in mainstream labour markets, as they are presently constructed, to provide certain paths to stability. Functioning markets' elusiveness shows, among other considerations, the importance of extra-state relationships to sustainable self-determination. The development of these relationships requires focus beyond the incidental benefits of commercial activity concerned principally with 'creating wealth for state and corporate appropriation' (Howitt, 2012). State and corporate investment in indigenous communities does not, on its own, provide sufficient wealth-creating opportunities to constitute 'development' (Howitt, 2012). However, focusing disproportionately on labour market participation, as the path to prosperity, can disconnect people from culture and diminish the inherently cultural character of work itself. Yet, on the other hand understating indigenous employment growth, especially in the primary labour market, is a path to poverty.

Although 'unimaginable' 50 years ago (Langton, 2012), increasing the size of the indigenous middle class is economically significant and challenges an expectation of an inherent conflict between indigenous lifestyles and material affluence. The presumption of conflict simplifies indigenous cultural priorities and overlooks poverty and social dysfunction's profound impact on cultural integrity to presume the inevitability and, even propriety, of indigenous citizens never joining the national political community as materially equal. It is a view that presents a trade-off between political and, thus, economic equality and the maintenance of culture. Poverty, then, becomes a cultural necessity and differentiated citizenship is illegitimised. Indeed, this book's considered reference to diverse indigenous perspectives shows that perpetual poverty need not remain colonialism's legacy and the choice between cultural integrity and economic security can be an externally constructed false dichotomy. The transition to an at least proportionate indigenous middle class would indicate the substantive occurrence of indigenous access to the national political community as full citizens, and by way of further illustration, the following chapter explores the growth in the New Zealand Maori middle class as a variable contributing simultaneously to cultural revitalisation and material security. The example illustrates differentiated citizenship's practical utility and adds to the case for economic engagement, sensitive to the *particular* as well as the *general* needs of indigenous peoples and, ideally, expanding 'the capabilities or freedom of individuals to improve their well-being and to realise what they value' (Sengupta, p. 868 in Jacobsen et al, 2005). Such an approach can account for cultural imperatives in ways that, for example, Scambary (2013) proposes where mining agreements ought to admit indigenous concepts of 'productivity and value', so that indigenous peoples are not defined 'as underdeveloped' (p. 15), but as people of agency, with capacity to seek commercial relationships consistent with their own cultural and economic aspirations. For example, Langton (2012) observes that the *Mabo* judgment's recognition of extant indigenous land rights offers qualified opportunities for self-determination through the commercial development of land. The newly recognised 'right to negotiate' means that mining offers substantial potential benefits to indigenous land owners. The conditional right to negotiate followed the High Court's *Mabo* (1992) decision. It removed the presumption that indigenous people had no legitimate interest in others' commercial exploitation of their lands, and Langton (2012) proposes 'changing the [mining] paradigm' to ensure that indigenous peoples actively exercise the right to negotiate mining agreements. However, this potential is balanced by the industry's capacity to undermine cultural imperatives and disturb alternative economic possibilities. As Altman and Rowse (2005) note, 'to change peoples' forms of economic activity is to transform them culturally' (p. 176), so that 'when confronted by large-scale mineral development, indigenous peoples may struggle within development discourse to express the centrality of everyday custom and belief to their future priorities, and of the style and nature of their engagement' (Scambary, 2013, p. 198). Yet, mining has also provided opportunities beyond 'balancing pressures to survive in the modern economy with the needs and desire to retain culture' (Taylor and Scambary, 2005, p. 27). Legal and institutional arrangements are, then, required to remove, rather than confirm the 'narrative of failure' that Altman (2011, p. 1) finds in contemporary policy discourse.

Langton and Longbottom's (2012) argument for greater legal certainty to define relationships between mining companies and indigenous landowners is significant to 'economic empowerment and development' (p. 3). There is a particular need for policy that engages, rather than simply compensates, indigenous peoples for mining on their lands because the construction of 'compensation' as welfare may simply shift indigenous dependence from the state to the mining company (Scambary, 2013). There is no indigenous right of veto over mining licences, as the *Declaration on the Rights of Indigenous Peoples* and other international legal instruments insist, so it is 'ingenuity and leadership' that counts in concluding favourable land access agreements (Langton, 2012).

Howlett's (2008) case study of the Century Zinc mining proposal in the Gulf of Carpentaria between 1987 and 1997 found that 'the arms of the state involved...in the negotiations acted to ensure the development of the mine went ahead against the wishes of the majority of Indigenous people in the region' (p. 221). Only very rarely does economic expansion see the state intervene to override the objections of individual property title holders, and the fact that it continues to occur in relation to communally owned indigenous land does suggest a lesser property right, which inevitably confers a lesser citizenship status on indigenous property owners.

Economic expansion can impinge on indigenous property ownership and cultural integrity, but that is an argument for the regulation of development to protect human rights and freedoms and for respect for indigenous property rights. It is not an argument that globalisation is *always* and *necessarily* injurious to indigenous wellbeing. Nevertheless, the right to negotiate has, even with its constraints, shown the connection between collective self-determination through 'symbolic' rights and personal self-determination through the 'substantive' right to employment in the 'real' labour market. However, the distinction between policies of symbolism and substance is rhetorically overstated. The relationship between each set of priorities is deeply intertwined; both practically and philosophically.

Mining has brought functioning labour markets to many remote communities and outside staff recruitment difficulties can make corporate engagement with local indigenous communities a matter of pragmatic necessity (Langton, 2012). Mining is the single most significant contributor to indigenous entrepreneurial development. For example, the agreement between Fortescue Metals and the Western Australian Njamal people provides for co-ownership and operation of a magnetite mine on traditional lands. Forrest (2014) explained the relationship:

> Recognising that an economic hand-up is always better than a hand-out, in December 2011, Fortescue Metals Group developed a programme to award $1 billion worth of contracts to First Australian businesses within two years, to create sustainable economic futures for first Australians through employment and the active stimulation of first Australian businesses...
>
> It has now awarded 156 contracts and subcontracts totalling $1.5 billion to more than 50 small and large first Australian businesses and joint ventures...
>
> Fortescue's approach drives outcomes by including a requirement for tenderers to provide first Australian engagement strategies that identify measurable indigenous employment and supplier targets in their tender documents. The successful contractor's performance is monitored

regularly as part of Fortescue's active contract management processes. All contractors are well aware of Fortescue's commitment to indigenous engagement, and failure to meet their contractual obligations affects their prospects of doing business with Fortescue in the future. (p. 183)

All major mining enterprises employ indigenous workers. They also provide entrepreneurial opportunities to indigenous businesses. Yet, there must still be scope, through differentiated citizenship, for 'hybrid economies' of the kind Altman (2011) proposes. Just as excluding people from empowerment through the mainstream labour market compromises capacity to live lives that they have 'reason to value' (Sen, 1999), so does the exclusion of hybrid models from the 'real economy' that might allow people to develop, for themselves, conceptions of the good life. Sustainable economic development requires that mining is not permitted to acquire singular significance to become the only path to prosperity (Langton, 2012). The intention to broaden the indigenous economy explains Forrest's (2014) recommendation that indigenous business development ought to be supported through tax incentives to indigenous businesses able to 'create real jobs' (pp. 162–3); a proposal that stands in marked contrast with prevailing liberal democratic emphasis on individual equality, just as the related proposal to support indigenous business development through preferential government procurement practices is inconsistent with the principle that governments ought to protect an economic level playing field (p. 168). One needs then, to consider what arguments might exist in reparative justice to support these proposals. Pragmatically, one ought also consider how these measures would be distinct from the deeply harmful affirmative action practices employed in Fiji during much of the 1980s and 1990s. The risk for Australia, as it has been in New Zealand, is that affirmative action policies become the subject of middle-class capture. The National Australia Bank's largely successful indigenous employment policies mitigate against such risks by relying on targets, rather than quotas; they do not, for example, guarantee employment without the requisite skills and are responsive to the Bank's business case for improving services to indigenous people.

Economic participation as 'recognition'

Political acceptability requires proponents to justify policy measures that transcend normative liberal conceptions of justice; conceptions which generally accept unequal economic outcomes on the assumption that they are, at least, the product of egalitarian opportunities and thus the result of personal choices rather than injustice in the distribution of substantive opportunities to make decisions commensurate with economic wellbeing.

Forrest's understanding of what it means to be 'recognised' is grounded in the meaningful capacity for economic engagement, not as an alternative to living a life that is culturally purposeful, but as a necessary and just constituent of human equality. Indeed, misrecognition prevents people from functioning 'as self-realizing agents' (Kompridis, 2007, p. 278). However, Forrest's remedial measures would not be required in the presence of functioning educational and labour markets. The case for remedialism is that it is necessary to bring people to participatory parity. However, if parity of esteem genuinely distinguished indigenous peoples' lives there would be no need for remedial policies, there would, instead, be the 'capabilities' that indigenous peoples routinely seek. For example, the Cape York Institute (2005) argues that both state policies and local institutional arrangements must be stable, cohesive and able to enhance peoples' capabilities. In particular, they must be able to support essential 'pre-requisites for economic development'. These are:

- incentives for people to benefit from work;
- incentives for people to be educated and healthy;
- good governance;
- access to financial capital to build assets;
- good infrastructure;
- social capital/order (respect, trust, accountability, enforcement of law);
- protection of property (legal protection of individual ownership).

Indigenous aspirations may also extend beyond overcoming welfare dependence to trans-generational wealth building. For example, the North Australian Indigenous Land and Sea Management Alliance (2013) proposes that economic opportunities be evaluated from the perspective of community need before corporate need, with a particular focus on long-term benefits because: 'Communities of remote and regional northern Australia are presently challenged to act as more than troubled observers of plans made and decisions taken principally by external parties…[where] public expenditure on development opportunities tends to be focused on corporate rather than community needs' (p. 13).

Just as governments use sovereign authority to limit the domestic significance of international law, it is often governments, not globalisation, that compromise the connection between economic development and self-determination. Indigenous economic development is principally encumbered by their less than proportionate share of national sovereignty that, in turn, limits access to the rights of citizenship. In its overly zealous attempt at environmental protection, Queensland's *Wild Rivers Act 2005* was an example of a policy measure that set aside successful indigenous environmental management practices established over thousands of years, as well as a range of native title rights essential to the preservation of traditional lifestyles and daily sustenance. The Act was repealed in 2014 largely because, as the chairperson of the Cape York Land Council put it: 'This legislation…jeopardise[s] future development and enterprise for Aboriginal people of the Cape hoping to become self sufficient with the return of their traditional country through business enterprises such as cattle, development and other activities. It also restricts the traditional use of some water systems in Cape York' (Ross, 2009).

The Act was allegedly passed without consultation with the Cape York indigenous communities and was discriminatory in its explicit failure to recognise the continuation of native title (Gusmerini, 2006).

It is for these reasons that Altman's (2011) hybrid economy becomes an expression of differentiated citizenship. Altman proposes defining relationships and opportunities in ways that remove the narrative of failure from policy discourse by recognising indigenous peoples' 'aspirations and agency to pursue alternate forms of livelihood from those imagined for them by the Australian government' (p. 9). The proposition is for a broader policy focus, concerned with possibilities and aspirations beyond 'socio–economic sameness'. For example, 'hybrid' economic opportunities might be pursued where environmental and cultural variables create opportunities outside the mainstream labour market, especially where such markets are underdeveloped (Howitt, 2012; Altman, 2011). The argument is to provide people with choices about the kinds of economic activities that they wish to privilege, and to respond to the proposition that indigenous economic development is most compromised when indigenous peoples are prevented from conceptualising development for themselves. As, for example, Altman (2011) puts it: 'A theoretical, abstract, and somewhat reductionist strategy for development is being proposed because those charged with the policy formulation process do not have the means to engage with the empirical reality of communities and regions; or with the inevitable wide range of aspirations that Indigenous people will hold' (Altman, 2011).

For the Cape York Institute, Sen (1999) and Nussbaum's (1987) capabilities approach to development describes the conditions *for* development and the outcomes *of* development. The Institute's 'Capabilities Indicators' propose alternatives to passive welfare so that one might focus not so much on a 'right' to self-determination, but on the 'power' of self-determination. Conversely, when policy avoids culture or privileges deficit over possibility, it makes 'invisible', 'the forms of productivity associated with the customary sector' (Scambary, 2013) such as those that Altman's (2011) hybrid economy presumes in proposing the development of an indigenous conservation workforce 'on country' to challenge Closing the Gaps' narrower conception of development. Altman shows that there are possibilities for economic activity even where markets are underdeveloped. By way of further example, Altman (2005) suggests that the indigenous art industry in the Maningrida region alone was worth $1.5 million annually. The region provided further economic opportunities in wildlife harvesting and natural resource management. For Altman (2005), economic development is based on a 'fundamental honesty about the structural limitations to Indigenous economic development, given the quality of the land base, the resources available to invest in development, and the weak property rights and commercially viable resources' (p. 6). There are, in fact, precedents for policy arrangements of the sort that Altman imagines. For example, an obvious congruence between the cultural and the economic informs the Commonwealth's Working on Country programme, introduced in Australia in 2007. The programme 'represents a symbolic and practical breakthrough in recognizing, respecting, and recurrently resourcing innovative community-based resource management effort on the indigenous-owned estate' (Altman and Kerins, 2008). Far from being an unproductive 'work for the dole' scheme, Working on Country, involves work of significant national environmental benefit that can reasonably attract state funding as a public good. The economic development opportunities available to indigenous people on their own lands have often been overlooked as sources of 'real jobs,' especially in the remotest parts of Australia where access to mainstream labor markets is limited, but where environmental management opportunities arise from the 'biodiverse and ecologically' intact nature of the land' (Altman et al, 2007, p. 36).

Sustainable and economically viable projects in the Northern Territory have included 'carbon abatement projects, weed and feral animal management, quarantine services, water resource management, coastal surveillance, and wildlife and fire management' (Altman et al, 2007, 35). Altman et al (2007) see this as part of a 'livelihoods' approach to economic development, which introduces a 'customary' sector to the state and private sectors as sources of income in remote and very remote parts of Australia, where the market alone seems unlikely to lead the kind of development required to alleviate poverty, which is estimated as being as high as 40 per cent in these areas.

The Australian bush foods industry is estimated to be worth $16 million annually and has potential for further development (Cleary et al, 2005). In other words, the customary sector needs to be well integrated into the 'real' economy (Altman et al, 2007). These initiatives ought to sit alongside educational, training and recruitment imperatives to increase private sector employment opportunities, especially among urban dwelling indigenous people. However, Australia does, in a broader sense, struggle to work out how the international tests of 'objectiveness, reasonableness, necessity, and proportionality' (Xanthaki, 2008, p. 282) ought to apply to the distribution of public authority. State resistance to indigenous claims are more assertive in Australia where indigenous demographic characteristics inhibit coordinated assertions of extant political rights. Opportunities to participate in the mainstream global economy and to benefit more fully from evolutions in international law are also challenged by the stronger: 'Possessive logic of patriarchal white sovereignty [that] works ideologically to naturalise the nation as a white possession by informing and circulating a coherent set of meanings about white possession as part of common sense knowledge and socially produced conventions' (Moreton-Robinson, 2004, p. 1).

Resistance to guaranteed indigenous representation in parliaments, the parliamentary neutralisation of the more far-reaching land rights found in the *Mabo* (1992) and *Wik* (1996) decisions of the High Court of Australia, and the marginalisation of local communities from discussions about *Queensland's Wild Rivers Act 2005* and the Northern Territory Emergency Response (Intervention) in 2007 are all illustrative, as is the more recent exclusion of indigenous peoples from initial policy discussions on Closing the Gap in Indigenous Disadvantage.

Conclusion

The different perspectives that exist on the purpose and proper character of indigenous economic development reflect the policy domain's inherent complexities, but also the philosophical inconsistencies and policy incoherence that continues to distinguish indigenous affairs.

For Altman (2011), this requires 'the multi-partisan attention of the most transparent institution [the Parliament] available in Australia in a fraught policy environment where the boundaries between politicians, the bureaucracy and business are becoming increasingly blurred'. Transparent policy debate may facilitate greater indigenous deliberative inclusion and avoid the reductionist conceptualisation of indigenous policy to statistically measurable points of distinction with other citizens, where self-determination as 'exercising the right to take responsibility' (New South Wales Aboriginal Land Council, 2014) is compromised. Greater policy bipartisanship, too, would facilitate certainty and indigenous civil society's capacity to support economic development (Australians for Native Title and Reconciliation, 2010).

While public policy is cautious in the recognition it gives to the cultural location of economic development; it is clear that for indigenous peoples economic activity serves a diminished purpose when it is removed from that context. Culture is also preliminary to effective schooling which is, in turn, a determinant of indigenous access to labour markets, utilisation of land rights for material purposes and access to the middle class which can be an important constituent of equal citizenship and participatory parity. The following chapter shows that these arguments are also relevant to New Zealand where a stronger politics of indigeneity asserts relationships between culture and economic agency. The chapter extends the argument that modern economic globalisation does not necessarily set indigenous claims aside; rather it provides new contexts for their expression, new constraints on their realisation, and new avenues for their pursuit, meaning that the contemporary Maori economy is distinguished by experiences of 'a complex mix of policy, history, culture, luck and timing' (New Zealand Institute of Economic Research, 2003). It is also distinguished by significant opportunity.

SEVEN

Economic development as differentiated citizenship: New Zealand

Maaku ano e hanga tooku nei whare [I will build my own house] (King Tawhiao)

Introduction

Citizenship is a determinant of indigenous economic opportunities; it defines the ways in which people 'belong' to the national political community and influences access to the 'sovereign and economic independence' that Maori seek (O'Sullivan and Dana, 2008). Personal engagement in the national economy through the housing and labour markets is economically important, but also a mark of the extent to which substantive differentiated citizenship actually occurs. Collective interests are pursued with the benefit of a trans-generational timeframe, and with the support of compensation for Crown breaches of the Treaty of Waitangi. At the same time, the notion of distinctive 'Maori' economic development recognises a politics of difference in contexts where being Maori is important and where 'Maori business is New Zealand business' (Westpac New Zealand, 2014). Just as it is in Australia, it is cultural values that determine the purpose and parameters of economic activity. It influences the ways in which economic agency is understood and, generally, leads Maori to pursue the opportunities that international capitalism provides, rather than succumb to the victimhood of its constraints.

Economic development policy is decreasingly viewed from deficit perspectives but, instead, as a matter of agency. Similar values explain increasing Maori insistence on the education system's more effective support of economic aspirations, especially as the potential 'demographic dividend' that the Maori population structure creates depends on the education system increasing its responsiveness to Maori needs and aspirations. This is most likely to occur through modes of differentiation, as reconciliation, that counter systemic racism and low systemic expectations of Maori achievement. The chapter presents the Maori developed and highly effective teacher professional training programmes, extended from Bishop et al's (2010) *Scaling up Education Reform: Addressing the Politics of Disparity* as examples of policy development through explicit Maori engagement, and which show that the citizen is, indeed, 'one who deliberates' (Aristotle, 1988).

Economic development

Economic development, as differentiated citizenship, responds to the 'characteristics inherent in how Māori view the world…[which are] important in assessing and proposing Māori economic development policy' (New Zealand Institute of Economic Research, 2003).

> [E]conomic development is a component of a broader, integrated system of strategic thought, activity and kaupapa, undertaken by the tribe in order for it to enhance and distribute mana and matauranga. It provides for social meaning and cohesion, identity, understanding of relationships…amongst ourselves, but also between all people…It provides for an understanding of benefits and burdens as part of a collective way of life…it builds sustainable hapu communities and addresses the gaps and underlying unity structures, so that present and future generations enjoy oranga whanui, access to power influence and choice of their way of life. (Gage, in Smith et al, 2015, p. 77)

Although contemporary differentiated citizenship is a significant intellectual evolution from prevailing thought in 1974 it does continue to reflect the Prime Minister, Norman Kirk's, view that: 'We are one nation in which all have equal rights, but…in no circumstances should we by any law or Act demand that any part of the New Zealand community should have to give up any part of its inheritance, its culture, or its identity to play its part in this nation' (Kirk, 1974). In 2017, culture remains Maori economic development's distinguishing point. 'If Māori do not feel secure about their culture, commercialisation will be seen as a threat, and will be resisted. In this sense, grievances and insecurity spill over into a self-imposed limit on economic development' (New Zealand Institute of Economic Research, 2003, p. 18). In particular, 'A system of property rights in relation to Maori owned or controlled assets needs to reconcile the Maori view of asset ownership and the factors which enable the economic returns on these assets to be maximised' (New Zealand Institute of Economic Research, 2003, p. 50).

As well as contextualising economic development, cultural values set its parameters. For example, Smith et al (2015) found the prevalent view, among four New Zealand iwi, that 'financial gains and individual benefits should not outweigh those of the collective. Factors for success need to be inclusive of the social, cultural, environmental, and political aspirations of the collective, and tensions between them should be mitigated' (p. 47). For these reasons, Coleman et al's (2005) description of the Maori economy as a 'transformation of Maori from members of a tribal-based, communal culture at the beginning of the nineteenth century to members of an individualistic capitalistic culture at the end of the twentieth century' (p. 17) misrepresents its contemporary character and diminishes Maori economic agency. Similarly, Rata (2003) undermines Maori economic agency in proposing that 'tribal capitalism' demonstrates ways in which 'a local movement can become reorganised into the global system' to create 'doubly oppressive social and economic structures: the oppressive political and social relations of traditional societies in conjunction with the exploitative economic relations inherent to capitalism' (p. 44). Alternatively, where safeguards against elite capture are in place, tribal capitalism may innovatively protect group identity, especially through language and culture, and use collective resources in new and evolving contexts. Successful strategies for self-determination depend on how indigeneity engages with other people and how indigenous claims are recognised in relation to the rights of others. Differentiated liberal citizenship potentially provides an ordered framework for such engagement.

Personal wellbeing is principally derived from integration into the national economy, largely through employment and home ownership. Communal interests are also important, and the increased cultural security that has distinguished Maori society over the last 30 years is partly attributable to increased capacity to benefit from land ownership and from the long-term focus that tribal entities' are able to take, unconstrained by the need to provide an immediate return to shareholders. The trans-generational time horizon allows one Maori incorporation, for example, to adopt a '100 year strategic plan that builds on the [more than 100-year-old] founding principles: to retain ownership, tread lightly upon the land, engage with the local community and ensure our mokopuna's mokopuna [grandchildren's grandchildren] live a healthier, wealthier life' (Westpac New Zealand, 2014). It is through collective wealth's contribution to the creation of educational and employment opportunities that a stronger relationship between collective and household wellbeing may emerge and it is for these reasons that:

> In a post-settlement context, Maori owners of capital have the means and moral obligation to engage in the broader goal of realising the potential of all Maori, not just elites. For iwi this means having a robust and transparent distributional model of governance that genuinely represents the interests of the collective. Most iwi will be keen to avoid privatised dependency and to foster greater participation and connectedness. Drawing those on the periphery firmly into the centre of iwi wealth will be a difficult but necessary task. (Kukutai, 2015)

In short, culture matters.

The tribe's long-term focus positions it to exploit capitalist modes of economic arrangement. The tribe need not focus solely on the maximum return to shareholders in the shortest possible time. Its permanency, trans-generational investment horizon, and constant geopolitical attachment to its people gives it incomparable stability. Rather than constituting resistance to globalisation (Fenelon and Hall, 2008, p. 1869), the collective management of tribal resources is as old as the tribe itself and provides ways of conducting economic relationships to ensure the prevalence of cultural preferences in property ownership. While neoliberalism's minimalising of the claims of the poor and marginalised has a disproportionate impact on indigenous peoples, it remains the case that it was neoliberal public sector reforms, from the 1980s onwards, that created space for substantive Maori involvement in the public policy process (O'Sullivan, 2007). In environments that otherwise privilege the individual over the group, tribal authorities play significant roles in public policy development and delivery (O'Sullivan, 2007). The introduction of 'choice' to service delivery created opportunities for Maori organisations to engage in primary health care and social services according to their own cultural preferences. Similarly, there was an expansion in the number of schools teaching in the Maori language and to some extent according to preferred Maori pedagogies. The prevailing Maori philosophy was that 'Maori should formulate policies for Maori and the role of the Crown should be to ensure that those policies were integrated into a workable state framework' (Durie, 2003, p. 304). Maori were equally determined in their view that 'Maori progress, whether in commerce, education or science, could not be accomplished without taking cognisance of Maori values and the realities of modern Maori experience' (Durie, 2003, p. 304). An absolute congruence between cultural and economic imperatives emerged on the grounds that cultural security is available only as a function of economic security. At the same time, the Maori population's increasing economic significance enhances its authority vis-à-vis the state, while national sovereignty's evolving character diminishes the state's capacity to dominate. However, marginalisation does continue where intellectual and political discourses position indigenous peoples as inevitable victims, always and necessarily unable to benefit, in their own terms, from engagement in the global economy. Instead, Maori might reasonably expect to participate in economic development on their own terms and to avoid confinement 'to victimhood' (MacDonald and Muldoon, 2006, p. 212). One of the ways in which this occurs is through the partial restoration of the Maori asset base through settlements of claims against the Crown for breaches of the Treaty of Waitangi.

Treaty settlements

Ngai Tahu is a tribe of approximately 39,000 members with an asset base in excess of $500 million. It is governed by a broadly representative Runanga (council) selected through the direct participation of tribal members. Ngai Tahu's wealth is largely derived from the development and utilisation of traditional resources through extensive property holdings, tourism and fisheries. Commercial profits are used to support cultural and educational aspirations as well as to meet social imperatives (Te Runanga o Ngai Tahu, *Annual Report*, 2008). So it is that: 'Binary understandings of indigenous peoples as either ecological natives or colonised subjects are simplistic and inadequate' (Bargh, 2012, p. 281). Indeed, as van Meijl (2015) puts it, in relation to contemporary water claims, 'it is necessary to avoid a sharp contrast between custom and commodity, between a spiritual conception of water and the commercial exploitation of water, or between pre-industrial or "indigenous" conceptualisations of the commons and the seemingly irreversible global trend towards privatisation of the public domain' (p. 220).

Privileging the spiritual alone is not part of the Maori tradition, even though it is true that the personification of the natural environment precludes thinking about the physical world as a set of tradable commodities and 'Maori claims of ownership are primarily generated by shifts in state policy' (van Meijl, 2015, p. 220). For example, Treaty settlements, especially those that have responded to the privatisation of public resources have created new contexts for thinking about the interdependent relationship between cultural and economic aspirations.

The Lange (1984–89) government's privatisation policy brought the question of property rights into sharp public policy focus and showed the importance of economic opportunities through differentiated citizenship. It introduced the idea that water, fisheries and even the radio frequency spectrum were not part of the public domain but tradable property rights owned and potentially sold by the Crown. While Maori resisted the imposition of state notions of 'ownership' over kaitiakitanga, a new conception of 'ownership' was brought into Maori Crown discourse, to re-shape the socio-cultural factors that determine the purpose of property rights.

The creation of tradable fishing quota was a resource management measure introduced in 1986. It raised the question of who actually owned the fisheries in the first instance; whose are they to sell or allocate to private commercial interests? The 'commodification of the common heritage' (Frame, 2001, p. 23) prompted Maori to assert ownership as both Treaty right and commercial opportunity and, as Hooper (2000) summarises it:

> [T]he introduction of a property rights system for fisheries not only gave rise to the largest indigenous rights claim in the country's history, it also provided the means for indigenous rights to be recognised, ensuring the sustainable utilization of fisheries, while providing for indigenous rights holders to realise their own…social and economic aspirations. (p. 18)

In effect, the proposed Quota Management System (QMS) formalised Maori exclusion from the fishing industry and, thus, access to a traditional resource because they lacked the financial capacity to purchase quota (de Alessi, 2012). The Muriwhenua iwi consortium claimed, before the Waitangi Tribunal, that the QMS was 'a transfer by the Crown of fishing rights that the Muriwhenua people have not relinquished' (de Alessi, 2012, p. 401). The claim was upheld and in order for the QMS to proceed the government purchased and allocated 10 per cent of the inshore fishery to an especially established Maori Fisheries Commission. However, a further claim was that earlier Crown interference with traditional fishing rights had prevented their expansion and warranted further redress. By way of settlement, further quota and a share in a multimillion dollar fishing company was purchased and allocated to the Commission (de Alessi, 2012). In 2015, the Commission held net assets to the value of $227 million, while the iwi-owned Aotearoa Fisheries Ltd recorded a $22 million profit for the year ended September 2014 (Aotearoa Fisheries Ltd, 2015).

A further example of the close relationship between the cultural and commercial is the Waitangi Tribunal's (2014) decision setting out the ways in which Rotorua's geothermal resources have traditionally been used for economic as well as social and cultural purposes (p. 1469). In this context, Bargh (2012) argues that natural resources, such as geothermal energy, provide development models capable of contributing 'to a more sustainable global political economy' (p. 272) made possible by the *Maori (Te Ture Whenua Maori) Land Act 1993* shifting the Maori Land Court's initial focus on land alienation to one of retention and development, including *inter alia*, geothermal development (Bargh, 2012). Bargh (2012) proposes mana [authority], utu [balance], kaitiakitanga [guardianship] and whakapapa [genealogical connections] as 'ethical coordinates' that might distinguish the economic use of Maori natural resources (p. 277).

Mana is an especially important concept in asset management. It is a personally held attribute that can be diminished or enhanced by 'behaviours that respect both people and the natural environment'. Mana contextualises the purpose of economic activity. At the same time, kaitiakitanga has particular implications for the distribution of economic surpluses (Bargh, 2012, p. 277). For example, the Crown's proposed partial privatisation of electricity generating companies along the Waikato river raised the question of resource ownership. The Waikato iwi's principal concern was to secure ancestral authority over the river. The commercial context where it became necessary to assert this extant right re-emphasised the relationship between culture and commerce.

Indigeneity, the Maori economy and the demographic dividend

The relationship between culture and corporate economic development, as differentiated citizenship, is theoretically clear and Bargh (2012), for example, proceeds from Gibson-Graham and Roelvink's (2010) proposition of 'an economy as a space of negotiated interdependence rather than a functional (or dysfunctional) growth machine' (p. 335). However, what remains unclear are the ways in which collective wealth will be employed to raise household wealth as the basis of whanau [family] and personal self-determination. For example, realising Maori potential may require iwi to take a more assertive role in developing educational priorities as, for example, the Waikato-Tainui Strategy imagines in stressing the significance of relationships among culture, education, economic wellbeing and self-determination. These are relationships that extend King Tawhiao's vision *Maaku ano e hanga tooku nei whare* [I will build my own house] (Waikato-Tainui, 2015b) and underlie its intention to pursue:

1. a pride and commitment to uphold their tribal identity and integrity;
2. a diligence to succeed in education and beyond; and
3. a self-determination for socio–economic independence. (Waikato-Tainui, 2015b, p. 1)

From these perspectives, Maori must logically reject the assertion that Treaty settlements have allowed capitalism to create an 'ambiguous assimilation of Maori tribes into the changing New Zealand political economy' (Webster, 2002, p. 342), even as others, such as Bargh (2012), do find a need to guard, culturally, against capitalism's unconstrained possibilities, with debates over New Zealand's acquiescence to the Trans-Pacific Partnership Treaty polarising Maori opinion just as they polarise broader public conceptions of New Zealand's engagement with global capitalism.

Policies grounded in rights of indigeneity, coupled with supporting institutional arrangements create substantive opportunities for self-determination; and cultural revitalisation is among those factors contributing to economic development. The appointment, in 2014, of the Maori party's co-leader as both Minister of Maori Affairs and associate Minister of Economic Development emphasised the relationship between the cultural and economic spheres. Policy 'focus on institutions is particularly useful for Maori economic development as it allows the discussion to incorporate issues such as belief systems, and the structure of property rights…it provides a useful framework to examine the key differences between Maori and non-Maori pursuit of economic success' (New Zealand Institute of Economic Research, 2003, p. 49).

Rights broaden and contextualise economic aspirations. They challenge dependent 'bicultural partnership' with the state (O'Sullivan, 2007), show that biculturalism's '"two people" paradigm on the edge of the global economy' (Kukutai, 2015) inadequately describes the opportunities that differentiated citizenship provides, and explains why 'interest in Maori economic development is not just about social responsibility or Treaty [of Waitangi] risk management. Instead, it is a policy area with significant potential to enhance New Zealand's overall economic performance' (New Zealand Institute of Economic Research, 2003), especially as New Zealand's partial recognition of certain 'rights' of indigeneity occurs alongside the national economic 'need' for proportionate Maori contributions, especially as the Maori population has increased from 7 per cent in 1951 to 14.6 per cent in 2015 (Statistics New Zealand, 2016), and is projected to reach 18 per cent of the national population by 2025 (Te Puni Kōkiri, 2010). This national economic imperative allows cultural considerations and self-determination, with its trans-generational focus, to influence economic thought and practice.

It is in this context that, in 2014, the Iwi Chairs' Forum has sought a $1 billion public contribution to the development of 'underperforming' Maori land. The request appealed to restitutive justice, but was also pragmatically responsive to the Ministry of Primary Industries' projection of an $8 billion benefit, over ten years, from the full utilisation of Maori land. The Ministry has projected a further benefit as the creation of 3,600 new jobs (Iwi Chairs' Forum, 2014). The Ministry of Maori Development's (Te Puni Kōkiri, 2014) analysis of the Waikato Maori economy (a tribal region in the upper North Island) shows similar scope for improved performance, even though incremental 'absolute and relative socio-economic gains' have occurred consistently since the 1970s (Chapple, 2000, p. 2), and from 2001 to 2010 the Maori economic asset base increased from $9.4 billion to $36.9 billion (Westpac New Zealand, 2014). Since 1986, the Maori Labour Force Participation Rate has increased, while non-Maori participation has decreased (Ministry of Business Innovation and Employment, 2015).

Public policy aspirations to reduce the size of government continue to create opportunities for the development of an iwi 'shadow state'. For example, the Key and English governments' (2008–) intention to privatise public housing creates new opportunities for Maori to support home ownership as a determinant of economic security, but also creates employment and training opportunities to position it to benefit from increasing national demand for housing. The use of Maori land to address inadequate land supply, for new housing, further explains the Iwi Chairs' Forum's interest in housing as a policy domain with significance beyond the immediate needs of Maori public housing tenants. The Forum might also strengthen differentiated citizenship by engaging with the generally wealthier and better educated 'global Maori diaspora' which is 'not simply a practical matter of leveraging skills and capital. It also involves grappling with tricky questions about collective identity obligations, community boundaries, and belonging' (Kukutai, 2015). Ultimately, differentiated citizenship allows indigenous peoples to position themselves so that they are seen by others as contributors rather than burdens on national economic aspirations.

In 2014, Maori contributed 8 per cent to the GDP of the Waikato regional economy. While sufficient to show that: 'Today, the vision of the disappearing native has been firmly dispelled' (Kukutai, 2015, p. 3), the contribution was not commensurate with the 21.9 per cent Maori share of the regional population (Te Puni Kōkiri, 2014). In 2015, just 33 per cent of the Waikato working age population lacks a formal qualification and just 10 per cent hold a university degree (Waikato-Tainui, 2015a), and while the overall number of Maori leaving school without a university entrance qualification has decreased, the differential with the national population remains significant and economically harmful.

The *Ngapuhi Strategic Direction for 2014 to 2019* proceeds from a tribal 17.4 per cent unemployment rate and median annual income of $21,700; some $7,000 less than the national median. It proceeds also from a home ownership rate of just 26.6 per cent (Te Runanga-A-Iwi-O-Ngapuhi, 2013). Meanwhile, the Waikato Maori median income differential of 25 per cent is explained by disproportionate Maori employment in low skilled, low paid industries. The number of Maori not in employment education and training (NEET) has fallen by 1.8 percentage points, to 20.9 per cent, in the three years to June 2015.

The number of Maori in skilled occupations is gradually increasing as is the number of job opportunities in these occupations (Ministry of Business Innovation and Employment, 2015). However, the 'average' image that these data present need to be disaggregated to establish that disadvantage is not evenly distributed among the Maori population and that there is scope for selective policy focus to secure significant self-determining 'demographic dividends' (Jackson, 2011, p. 66). In this context, increasing Maori capacity for employment in the primary labour market is an urgent policy imperative.

Inter-group variations in wellbeing commonly arise from unjust distributions of the rights, privileges and burdens of citizenship but so, too, can intra-group variations. The failure to give due consideration to differences in the distribution of power, authority and privilege *within* groups can lead to an incomplete understanding of the determinants of relative advantage and disadvantage and, thus, the *particular* policy measures that might extend wellbeing. The failure to analyse measures of wellbeing in these terms leads to the conclusion that there are no instances of Maori prosperity and that 'Maori ethnicity is socio-economic destiny' (Chapple, 2000, p. 10). It is, then, useful to analyse the sociological variables contributing to Chapple's (2000) observation that: 'The Maori ethnic group is not a group whose boundaries are well defined by socio-economic failure' (p. 11). Kukutai (2015) consequently finds 'a segmented opportunity structure that is open to those with certain kinds of ties to Maori ethnicity, but relatively closed to others' (p. 3). The costs and benefits shift with changing political context (Kukutai, 2015). For example, the Maori language has shifted from an object of ridicule in the education system to an important employment attribute. The social isolation that might once have been Maori language speakers' experience has been displaced with professional employment opportunities that create access to the middle class.

For Maori women, sex is of sufficient importance to suggest particular policy focus on their needs as distinct from the needs of Maori *per se*. Age and education are more significant than ethnicity as predictors of income (Chapple, 2000). However, as Maori are disproportionately young and poorly educated, there is an obvious case for particular policy attention on the educational needs of young Maori people. Maori employment is also concentrated in 'low productivity' industries (Te Puni Kōkiri, 2014). A further example is that low incomes and poor education are disproportionately concentrated in rural areas to make rurality a significant constraint on wellbeing (Chapple, 2000). In response, targeted policy attention to the particular needs of low income Maori, as a group that is a distinct subset of all low income earners is warranted.

Raising educational performance is preliminary to the broader economic imperative of raising the size of the Maori middle class. While relationships between class and identity need to be examined in the 'context of Maori cultural and political revitalization' (Kukutai, 2015, p. 2), it remains that raising household wellbeing requires increasing the size of the Maori middle class which, while growing, is still proportionately smaller and less wealthy, than the non-Maori middle-class, as 'inequality has been re-indigenised in ways that have enabled a minority of Maori to advance, but cemented the disadvantaged position of those already marginalised' (Kukutai, 2015, p. 43). For example, urban migration, beginning in the 1950s, was a response to growing low skilled employment opportunities in manufacturing. This followed considered public policy choices that limited educational opportunities for Maori for whom working-class concentration, itself, became a determinant of further opportunities. The relationship between education and class explains why increasing the relative size of its middle class is an objective that features so strongly in Waikato's Tribal Education Strategy *Ko te Mana Matauranga* (Waikato-Tainui, 2015a).

The Strategy emphasises measures to promote savings, home ownership and financial planning. 'What is critical is that each tribal member is free to determine their own destiny, empowered to reach their goals and all the while strong in their tikanga [culture] and secure in their reo [language]' (Waikato-Tainui, 2015a, p. 3). The Strategy must, however, be able to engage the state, which controls schooling, and which remains unsuccessful in securing the Waikato aspiration of having all its members in possession of a post-secondary school qualification. Although the goal is a long-term one that the tribe does not expect to achieve before 2050, it will remain elusive without the considered support of the state, with the politics of education reform particularly influencing that aspiration. Educational underachievement coupled with extensive evidence of labour market discrimination means that Chapple (2000) cannot conclude that 'age, education and literacy's' power in explaining the income differential means that 'the pattern of employment disparity does not support the hypothesis that racial discrimination is particularly important in explaining the large variation in employment chances over time' (p. 19). For example, restricting Maori economic capacity was the explicit intention of Maori land and education policies at least until the mid-twentieth century. As Clarence Beeby, Director-General of Education during the 1930s explained, the purpose of Native Schools was 'to lead the lad to be a good farmer and the girl to be a good farmer's wife'. They would then copy 'the nuclear family of the pakeha social order' (Beeby, in Hill, 2004, p. 182). Similar assimilationist values also compromised the capacity of Maori Trust Boards to support material prosperity in the ways that they could use Maori land.

Notwithstanding racism, ethnic differences in age structure does create unique opportunities for Maori, and explain why improving the education system's effectiveness is an urgent policy priority among Maori civil society. For example, the differential in educational attainment may reduce 'simply because' of the Maori population being disproportionately of the age where qualifications are most commonly attained. The Maori population's median age is 23.4 years, compared with a national median of 38 years and 15–24 year olds comprise 31 per cent of the Maori working-age population (Statistics New Zealand, 2013). These demographic characteristics mean that Maori income earning potential will rise at a faster rate than it has in recent years (Jackson, 2011).

This 'demographic dividend', however, does not automatically lead to an 'economic dividend' (Jackson, 2011). That requires particular policy interventions developed with reference to broader cultural and economic variables. The opportunities that the 'demographic dividend' creates will be quickly set aside if the younger subset of the Maori population does not contribute proportionately. On the other hand, the potential 'economic dividend' remains until this group retires from the workforce (Jackson, 2011). 'The importance of recognising and proactively investing in the dividend years for Maori in order to transform them to economic windfalls cannot be overemphasised' (Jackson, 2011, p. 70).

The greatest opportunity to extract a demographic dividend occurs while the proportion of the population that has yet to reach the age of entry into the workforce remains above 30 per cent. That proportion reached a peak of 50 per cent in 1971, at which time, education policies remained determinedly focused on preparing Maori for employment in low skilled manual labour and paid little official regard to the proposition that 'culture counts' in education (Bishop and Glynn, 1999). The education system's contribution to Maori economic underachievement is significant, but with the pre-working age population projected not to fall below 30 per cent, until 2026, there remains an opportunity for the dividend to be pursued (Jackson, 2011). This requires greater insistence on educational quality and focus. The Iwi Chairs' Forum (2014) argues that the education system might better support the development of Maori assets and many iwi authorities seek focused relationships with schools and universities. Iwi relationships with tertiary education institutions are extending the idea of culturally responsive education and training. For example, Ngai Tahu's *Te Tapuae o Rehua* partnership with two polytechnics and three universities is illustrative (Savage et al, 2014) and, among other considerations, draws on opportunities that the Christchurch post-earthquake 'rebuild' has created for the development of Maori trade training.

Te Kotahitanga: the Maori citizen deliberates

Racism in schools was a recurrent theme to which the Te Kotahitanga teacher professional development project responded from the mid-2000s. Te Kotahitanga is grounded in Maori students' 'voice' and provided Maori with deliberative input on the question of what works for themselves in secondary schooling. It provided an opportunity for Maori people to set out the pedagogic conditions from which a theory of best teaching practice was developed (Bishop et al, 2010).

'Emancipatory approaches tackle disparity from the premise that those who experience discrepancies know best what the problems are and are therefore more likely to have the solutions' (Savage et al, 2014, p. 90). Cook-Sather et al (2015) have also found examples of student achievement increasing when deliberative opportunities have been structured into the policy process. 'These actions can also contribute to the conceptualisation of teaching, learning and the ways we study as being more collaborative processes' (Bishop et al, 2010, p. 3). Indeed, the Te Kotahitanga 'Effective Teaching Profile' illustrates more than any other instrument in indigenous education policy the nexus between structured deliberation and 'street level' policy practice (Bishop et al, 2010). The Profile was developed from the clear Maori description of relationships between culture and educational achievement. It emphasised:

1. *Manaakitanga* – teachers care for their students as culturally located human beings above all else.
2. *Mana motuhake* – teachers care for the performance of their students.
3. *Nga whakapiringatanga* – teachers are able to create a secure, well-managed learning environment.
4. *Wananga* – teachers are able to engage in effective teaching interactions with Māori students as Māori.
5. *Ako* – teachers can use strategies that promote effective teaching interactions and relationships with their learners.
6. *Kotahitanga* – teachers promote, monitor and reflect on outcomes that in turn lead to improvements in educational achievement for Māori students. (Bishop et al., 2010)

Te Kotahitanga provided both a theoretical and practical policy rationale for the argument that 'rather than continuing to look to the majority culture for solutions…perhaps the answers to Maori educational achievement and disparities actually lie elsewhere, in the sense-making and knowledge-generating processes of the culture the system marginalises' (Bishop et al, 2010, p. 2).

Student deliberation allowed the following representative Maori perspectives to be raised and hold influence. Instances of racism were explicitly identified and the relationship between racism and achievement exposed.

> I'm a Maori, they should ask me about Maori things…I've got the goods on this but they never ask me. I'm a dumb Maori I suppose. Yeah, they asked the Asian girl about

her culture. They never ask us about ours. (Bishop et al, 2003, p. 48)

Mrs S…can't even say my name…and I always argue with her. She makes me feel like I've got a dumb name and I'm dumb…She goes, well, that is what I have got down here, and I go, "No, it isn't my name", and then I just let her go off. I know what she's going to say. I've heard it all before. (Bishop et al., 2003, p. 50)

I was in her office and like you couldn't see it but she just said "What's that around your neck?" and I go "It's my greenstone." And she just got the scissors and chopped it off…My Koro has blessed it I don't know how many times…Probably because we have all been saying we don't want to take it off, they are beginning to understand…That it's something precious to you. Yeah, just like their wedding rings are precious to them. (Bishop et al, 2003, p. 55)

We're average, we behave and so we aren't Maori…All we hear about are Maori on the field smoking, and the kapa haka group. (Bishop et al, 2003, p. 48)

The contrast with the perspectives of teachers and principals who traditionally enjoy greater policy influence shows the significance of wider deliberation. Teachers observed that:

Well I believe that it is the home background to a large extent, I believe that it is parental expectation. They don't turn up to school on a regular basis. They are more interested in things outside the classroom rather than achieving academically…their determination to get some academic success is lacking and it is that which I find very frustrating. I feel it comes from the home and I am not criticising the home, I am just saying that it's throughout Maoridom to a large extent. (Bishop et al, 2003, pp. 82–3)

Most of the students in the…room have close contacts with tikanga. They are used to karakia… there is an inbuilt expectation of how people behave in terms of tikanga. The…group I expect to behave and their tuakana make sure they do. (Bishop et al, 2003, p. 87)

Thinking about Maori students' underachievement in deficit terms undermines teacher agency and self-efficacy (Bishop et al, 2010), which can have prophetic influence for both teacher and student. Hattie (2003) found consistent achievement differentials whatever the socio-economic status of the school, suggesting that 'the evidence is pointing more to the relationships between teacher and Maori students as the major issue – it is a matter of cultural relationships not socio-economic resources as these differences occur at ALL levels of socio-economic status' (p. 7).

> We are dealing, it would seem, not so much with culturally deprived children as with culturally deprived schools. And the task to be accomplished is not to revise, and amend, and repair deficient children, but to alter and transform the atmosphere and operations of the schools to which we commit these children. Only by changing the nature of the educational experience can we change the product. To continue to define the difficulty as inherent in the raw material, the children – is plainly to blame the victim and to acquiesce in the continuation of educational inequality. (Ryan, 1976, pp. 61–2)

Te Kotahitanga's student narratives provided a comprehensive theoretical challenge to schooling's assimilationist tendencies, while Te Kotahitanga itself shows Maori asserting education's transformational capacity through considered deliberation. Maori expectations of cultural responsiveness and broader quality are clear and show that while schools may be 'in essence colonial institutions' (Hohepa, 2013, p. 621), it does not follow that they must remain assimilationist in their effect. The body of scholarship proceeding from the Te Kotahitanga project is extensive and provides just one substantive description of the conditions under which schools might recognise indigenous conceptions of the 'good life' to allow the system to realise its transformative capacity.

Substantive public deliberation through participation in education and policy practice would ideally mean that there are 'no inherent limits to what is possible' (Penetito, 2011, p. 4) and for Penetito (2011) 'a sense of radical hopefulness' distinguishes contemporary education policy (p. 1) because: 'The work by Bishop, Berryman et al (2006; 2010) is beginning to shape as the best thing that has happened in mainstream secondary education, in the interests of Maori learners ever, in my view' (Penetito, 2011, p. 10).

While families exert the greatest influence on decisions to remain at school, their influences are followed by those of the wider community (Sherriff, 2010) where a culture of achievement, grounded in confidence in the school itself is an important variable suggesting the further significance of Maori deliberative influence over the ways in which schools are culturally responsive and admit the Maori desire 'to achieve as Maori'. Deliberating through leadership in the education system is an important constituent of indigenous peoples' assertion of self-determination. Indeed, leadership 'has been identified as a key factor in raising achievement' (Hohepa, 2013, p. 628).

Conclusion

The relationship between economic agency and differentiated citizenship is close and deeply intertwined. It proceeds from wider relationships between culture and what people expect from economic activity. It proceeds also from the central role that differentiated citizenship plays in admitting culture into public policy. The relationships among economic opportunities, Treaty settlements and educational effectiveness are also important marks of substantive differentiated citizenship. These are constituents of a politics of indigeneity that sees Maori economic activity as an essential expression of agency. Indigeneity is a theoretical position that does not see Maori ethnicity as synonymous with victimhood, but is a position concerned with self-determination as cultural independence, economic interdependence and that deliberates in public affairs to assert its expectations of the state. The chapter has shown that the politics of indigeneity is able to assert its claims to self-determination, even as Maori remain a minority population, because self-determination is accepted as a relative and relational concept. The following chapter shows that, in contrast, the potential political strength that might otherwise flow from majority population status is compromised because the foundational point that self-determination is not absolute and not found in isolation from broader sites of political power is misunderstood. The chapter argues that differentiated liberal citizenship provides a promising alternative framework for understanding and responding to relationships between political power and economic agency.

EIGHT

Economic development as differentiated citizenship: Fiji

Introduction

Indigenous Fijians' relative lack of economic self-determination occurs at the intersection of political instability, incoherent understandings of the nature of political relationships and the underutilisation of natural resources. Of this book's three nations of interest it is Fiji that most lacks a coherent philosophy of indigenous self-determination, which is the point that most significantly sets that country's indigenous politics apart from those of Australia and New Zealand. Although the indigenous Australian pursuit of self-determination occurs in a contradictory and philosophically inconsistent policy environment and the aspiration is by no means assured in New Zealand, it is clear that the indigenous peoples of both those jurisdictions have well developed understandings of what self-determination means and its relationship to broader political philosophies, opportunities and constraints. Self-determination in Australia and New Zealand is also responsive to the prevailing economic environment.

The absence of meaningful indigenous Fijian self-determination occurs as economic growth over the 30 years to 2011 averaged 2.1 per cent of GDP (Chand, 2015). Just as it is in Australia and New Zealand, Fijian indigenous economic development is complex and contested; complicated because: 'The present in terms of the level of economic development in Fiji can be explained by the past, and particularly the distribution of political power' (Chand, 2015).

Indigenous Fijians own 84 per cent of the country's land, form the greater part of the population, and have, under earlier Constitutions, enjoyed guaranteed parliamentary majorities. Fiji's political culture remains unable to consider the comprehensive land reform that is required to raise the returns to indigenous land holders and, in contrast, New Zealand Maori have relatively higher levels of wealth and political influence because they are able to exercise more proportionate and particular shares in national sovereignty, in stable and secure economic and political environments. Economic weakness is among the outcomes of the pressure that is placed on an aggressively nationalist politics of indigeneity to secure Fijian 'paramountcy' through political and economic privilege. Yet the material wellbeing of indigenous Fijians remains heavily dependent on foreign investment which, in contrast, requires political stability. Foreign investment has rarely met government targets of 25 per cent of GDP (Asian Development Bank, 2014). In 2010, private sector investment was just 3 per cent of GDP and its annual average over the years 2006–13 was 8.7 per cent (Asian Development Bank, 2014). This chapter argues that economic development is more likely to occur through policies and practices of differentiated citizenship that are recognisant of political authority's true character and relative and relational nature. There are also lessons to be drawn from jurisdictions like Australia and New Zealand on the ways in which non–absolutist, relative and relational understandings of political power need not leave indigenous peoples bereft of political voice. The greatest constraint on any developments in Fijian political thought and practice is that constitutionally, sovereignty does not belong to the people and contemporary political values and institutional arrangements are:

> very largely the creation of one individual, and when Bainimarama goes, one way or another, we may well witness a resurgence of indigenous nationalism and at least some of the privileges of chiefly status and authority in Fiji's national politics. In the final analysis, however, much will depend on who controls the military. (Lawson and Hagan Lawson, 2015, p. 15)

While election campaign manifestoes for the 2014 election emphasised democracy of a very limited kind, the connection between democracy and public sovereignty remains elusive. Certainly, some kind of philosophical settlement of this tension would contribute to both political and economic stability. The question is also one of whether liberalism can satisfy an indigenous demand for 'ethnic democracy' (Lawson, 2012, p. 293).

The politics of indigeneity versus the economics of chaos

Fiji's unattractiveness to foreign investors diminishes opportunities for the development of export industries, which are especially important given that remittances are second to tourism as Fiji's principal source of foreign exchange (Asian Development Bank, 2014) and given the irony in Bainimarama's observation, before the 2006 coup, that 'if we don't act [against the Qarase government], this country is going to go to the dogs and no investor will want to come here' (in Ratuva, 2007, p. 36). Fiji's highly regulated marketing arrangements and export licensing regime further inhibit opportunities for export-led growth. Its fishing industry, which is integral to indigenous affirmative action policies, operates well below maximum sustainable levels (World Trade Organization, 2009).

The Bainimarama government's (2006–) concern for increased private sector investment is compromised, principally, by the uncertain political environment that the government itself has reinforced. Nor is its stated interest in improved national governance consistent with an ideological resistance to taking account of the *particular* needs and rights of indigenous peoples; the possibility elsewhere admitted by differentiated citizenship. Yet, the government has expressed confidence that its newly created 'political stability' will have a positive impact on the tourism industry (Republic of Fiji, 2013a).

Indigenous Fijians do not enjoy access to public institutions able to promote political stability. For example, the 'independent and impartial judiciary', Public Accountability and Transparency Commission, Code of Conduct for Parliamentarians and Civil Servants and Freedom of Information laws (Republic of Fiji, 2013b) operate within the prevailing authoritarian political culture and the liberal values that one would ideally find in these kinds of institutions may not, in fact, develop. There also remains irony in the government's description of its 2015 Budget as 'Turning Promises into Deeds' (Republic of Fiji, 2015) and the country's basic infrastructural and educational opportunities also inhibit development, even as there are emergent signs of improvement. For example, in 2013 and 2014, growth was 4.6 per cent and 3.8 per cent respectively, and the Reserve Bank's deputy governor hopefully remarked that: 'We now have four years of continuous growth, not normally seen in our history' (Naiyaga, 2014, p. 1).

Sugar production and tourism also increased and there has been stable inflation and employment growth. In 2014, public health and education expenditure increased by 18 per cent (Chand, 2015) and Fiji is introducing free schooling to Year 12, which has, along with the state funding of transport to school, removed a significant obstacle for many families. In contrast, fishing and mining are projected to decline (Republic of Fiji, 2013a) and, if it is to occur, economic development must circumvent a prevailing intellectual climate of fear and tension where ultimate sovereignty belongs to the military and where claims to indigenous paramountcy makes ethnicity the principal context for expressing political rights and assessing economic opportunities (Ratuva, 2014).

Paramountcy obstructs self-determination. It sits alongside protectionism's residual legacy, where 'The social Darwinian policy of the colonial state suggested that, to be "protected" from the evil vagaries of foreign cultures, the indigenous population had to be cocooned into traditional cultural institutions and subsistence communal life separate from other ethnic groups' (Ratuva, 2014, p. 137). Protectionism confined indigenous economic activity to unskilled labour and restricted opportunities to utilise natural resources. Military sovereignty further constrains policy debate as well as the free academic research that elsewhere contributes to policy formation.

Immediately prior to the coups in 1986, the Fijian Labour party proposed the distinct separation of indigenous political authority from the state's so that 'chiefly authority could remain in ritual spheres, but individual equality prevail in political practice' (Lal, 1992, p. 263). This distinct separation of the indigenous realm from the state is inconsistent with differentiated citizenship's concern for overlapping sites of indigenous authority, shared authority within the nation state and distinct indigenous authority over their own affairs. However, institutionalised chiefly influence has a 'rather bleak' future to suggest both need and scope for a revised and inclusive politics of indigeneity guided, in the interests of liberal acceptability and theoretical coherence, by the United Nations' *Declaration on the Rights of Indigenous Peoples*.

The separation of authority may have contributed to what Horscroft (2002) describes as an indigenous 'consciousness that their culture is antithetical to economic success' (p. 66) which may, in turn, help to explain the view that prosperity depended on affirmative action policies that made indigenous 'belonging' to the state conditional on Indian exclusion. Indeed, the absence of substantive economic security both requires and contributes to cultural resilience; its limited presence is a key determinant of indigenous Fijian discontent, contributing to perceived Indian dominance of the state (Horscroft, 2002). Indeed, the coup culture's logic is partly drawn from the discourse of 'backward Fijian and advanced Fiji Indians' (White, 2001, p. 317), as part of a prophetic politics of deficit where 'the most benign group attributes... [have] become entrenched in processes of self identification' (White, 2001, p. 317). While it is true that some people will choose lifestyles that make material prosperity less likely, it may not be reasonable for Duncan et al (2014) to position Fijian culture *per se* as a constraint on economic development, as if deep material poverty was an accepted constituent of the good life. For the Fijian, they suggest, 'the *vanua*

[land], the *lotu* [religion], and the *matanitu* [government] were the three broad parts of society that his life revolved around. In each of these entities, the Fijian saw things from the traditional perspective – that is, the Fijian versions of land, religion and government' (Duncan et al, 2014, p. 48). The argument presumes singular and static conceptions of land, religion and government and accepts that these are always and necessarily inconsistent with material wellbeing. It may be that people value and privilege certain other things over the material, but inadequate accounts of political authority's relative and relational character also help to explain constraints on indigenous Fijian self-determination.

Differentiated citizenship admits that indigenous rights are determinants of economic agency, though not useful as a singular path to prosperity, to suggest a policy focus where liberal egalitarianism's limits are recognised but not, uncritically, set aside. Neither paramountcy nor affirmative action has enhanced indigenous self-determination in substantive and sustainable ways (Ratuva, 2014), and it is both Indian and indigenous Fijians who reasonably claim economic vulnerability, even though indigenous Fijians have potentially greater political capacity to counter that vulnerability than almost any indigenous group in the world.

Affirmative action policies were developed to further the interests of majority population groups and necessarily include aspirations beyond fair economic opportunities. In Fiji, affirmative action helped 'spawn communal strife' (Ratuva, 2014, p. 139). Its rationale was to entrench privilege and economic advantage. It was used 'as leverage for ethnic appeasement, mobilisation of electoral support and self-enrichment', in similar fashion to its application in jurisdictions such as Malaysia and South Africa, from where the Fijian policy was adapted. As in Fiji, it was employed in these jurisdictions, not so much to correct structural injustice, but to serve the interests of the already politically dominant (Ratuva, 2014, p. 139). On the other hand, political stability requires substantive recognition of the ways in which demographic dominance does not, as a matter of course, translate into political equality. Extant rights of indigeneity remain important concerns because behind the 'support for extreme forms of nationalism' that created public support for the coups and putsch lies a 'sense of marginalisation from the political and economic mainstream of Fiji society' (Fiji Community Development Program, 2011). Addressing political and economic alienation is preliminary to the stability that improved indigenous wellbeing requires, and is an essential principle of the Fiji Community Development Program (2011). However, 'dialogue and understanding of the conflicting dimensions of development, to ensure that development is equitable and inclusive across all of Fiji's regions, and among all of its communities' is required (Prasad et al, 2001, p. 12). The obstacle is that the conditions that genuine dialogue presumes are not present and the Fijian community sector is also unable 'to formulate programs independently of changing cycles of donor policies' (Fiji Community Development Program, 2011). The indigenous Fijian economy exists, then, in a state of dependence to leave the claim to 'paramountcy' as one of empty rhetoric. It was, ironically, political instability that prevented the implementation of affirmative action policies during the 1980s and 1990s. Their rejection was one of the reasons for Bainimarama's coup (Ratuva, 2015b).

Ongoing political instability, and the Bainimarama government's insistence on non-racial public policy, makes reliance on state policies of ethnic privilege an unlikely path to sustainable development. It is also not consistent with the indigenous acquisition of a just and meaningful share in national political sovereignty. Ratuva (2015b) proposes that such vision needs:

> to ensure the availability of resources for growth in the private sector; reform of the system of direct and indirect taxation, to minimise market distortions and improve incentives for risk taking and effort; a wages policy that recognises the paramount importance of maintaining international competitiveness; and the mobilization of all sectors of the community in support of economic expansion, in particular, increased indigenous Fijian participation in commerce and industry. (p. 17)

'Reducing inter-ethnic socio-economic inequality in Fiji must instead rely on politically more demanding redistribution, requiring political negotiation' (Ratuva, 2001, p. 24). It is, in turn, a matter of increasing urgency for a Fijian politics of indigeneity to develop principles from which to negotiate and to incorporate ways of recognising others' rights as preliminary to the meaningful advancement of indigenous opportunities. For example, the Asian Development Bank (2009) presumed connections between democracy and socio-economic development in recommending:

> stabilised macroeconomic factors; increased economic contribution of the tourism sector; diversified and expanded manufacturing and commercial sectors, an improved

> business regulatory environment; improved community livelihoods through micro, small, and medium-sized businesses; provision of secure long-term incomes for resource owners…[and] restructuring of the sugar industry; widened coverage of financial services and deepened financial markets; and access to cost-efficient infrastructure services. (p. 4)

Just as the restoration of Maori commercial fishing has provided significant opportunities in New Zealand, there is important scope within the Fijian economy for that industry's development, even as Fiji presently 'lacks an overarching vision for its economic development that addresses overfishing in both its inshore and offshore fisheries' (de Mers and Kahui, 2012, p. 188). Overfishing occurs, partly, as a function of economic underdevelopment providing few alternative employment options, especially in rural communities (de Mers and Kahui, 2012). Similarly, tourism is an important foreign exchange earner for Fiji, but does not contribute sufficiently to poverty reduction. Policy might, instead, proceed from the approach known as 'pro-poor tourism'. From that perspective, policy would promote stronger supply chain relationships with agricultural and fishing industry producers which would support smaller domestically owned businesses traditionally unable to compete with large foreign-owned operators (Scheyvens and Russell, 2010).

The connection between culture and economy is most apparent through natural resource management and does, as Chand (2015) argues, provide good prospects for stability and prosperity as long as political divisions can be set aside. It is especially important to reverse the colonial policies that made ethnicity a point of stratification in the national workforce (Prasad et al, 2001). 'Fiji has yet to build a nation congruent with its state and still lacks a sovereign, collective, unified people whose will the state expresses and enacts' (Kelly and Kaplan, 2009, p. 184). Fiji lacks the institutional means to establish political consensus, which is preliminary to development and to raising the standard of living of the 34 per cent of Fijians living below the poverty line.

In 2010, the military government amended land leasing arrangements by requiring the distribution of rental income to individual landholders. The practice was to circumvent the retention of income by some chiefs for themselves rather than using it, as tradition required, to attend to the needs of the whole community. While the policy may have appealed to egalitarian values, its primary intent was to undermine chiefly authority. Certainly, it has been the sustained failure of chiefly leadership that 'produced a tradition/modernity binary' (Lawson and Hagan Lawson, 2015, p. 12) that Bainimarama used effectively to court the votes of Fijian commoners to whose material interests Fiji First consciously appealed. Indeed, during the 2014 election campaign Bainimarama noted that:

> Our ownership of 91 per cent of the country's land is guaranteed in our Constitution; our freedom to be Christians and follow Jesus Christ is also guaranteed; there are many more of us than any other race and our birth rate is higher; our children have never lived longer because of better health services; my Government's free primary and secondary schooling means that, for the first time, every i'Taukei child can get an education; those young people have never had a better chance to go to university or a technical college because of our scholarships and tertiary loans; the i'Taukei language is now a compulsory subject in our primary schools so it is also secure; our culture and traditions are thriving. So I ask you: How are we threatened? The answer is that WE ARE NOT. It is a big lie to try to spread fear when there is no reason for the i'Taukei to fear anything. We are strong. We are proud. And to say that we need protection is an insult. It demeans us as a people. (Bainimarama, 2014)

> My Government gave you the money you receive from the land you lease to decide for yourselves how it is spent. We empowered you, the ordinary people, by giving you the power to decide. That is democracy. But these people want to take that money back from you and give it to the chiefs to decide for you. They don't want you to have your say. They think they know better. Well, that is not democracy. That is a hereditary elite telling you what is best for you. (Bainimarama, 2014)

> Don't turn the clock back. Insist on keeping what is yours. The chiefs have their place and we all respect the chiefly system. But we want them to lead by example in their public and personal lives. And we want them to serve us, as well as lead us, not take our money and tell us what to do.

> Or try to manipulate us with false warnings about threats
> to our way of life when none exist. (Bainimarama, 2014)

As a claimed measure of its commitment to indigenous peoples'
material prosperity Bainimarama further campaigned, in 2014, on
the promise that:

> We will set aside $10 million to help the i'Taukei use
> their land for subdivision and development. For too long,
> landowners have leased out land for others to develop
> and make huge profits. We will encourage landowners to
> become landlords while reaping direct commercial benefits
> from their land. The funding will be made available as a
> grant to assist landowners to meet development costs, such
> as the provision of electricity water and roads. This will not
> only empower the i'Taukei but also contribute to national
> economic development. (Bainimarama, 2014)

The government underwrites up to 50 per cent of the value of public
loans to indigenous businesses in the event that these 'go bad' (Naiyaga,
2014, p. 1). It does so with the Reserve Bank deputy Governor's
caution that while assistance for business development is important:
'we must also be careful not to give too much [sic] handouts as it has
the potential to create this "handout mentality with no responsibility
and accountability as it is given free". We must change this handout
mentality' (Naiyaga, 2014, p. 1).

The Bank's politicisation means that one must expect its long-term
location in the national political economy to remain subservient
to military oversight and it is untrue for the deputy Governor to
propose that 'the concerted effort by Government towards an inclusive
parliamentary democracy in 2014 has also been a major contributor to
regained confidence among investors and consumers alike' (Naiyaga,
2014, p. 1). Fiji's parliamentary democracy is not inclusive; nor is
it free and independent and there is a constitutionally protected
possibility of parliamentary democracy being, once again, set aside
for reasons determined by the military alone. The Prime Minister's
personal volatility is significant and an important contributor to Fiji's
unpredictable political future. The Prime Minister is a destabilising
influence on contemporary political culture. By way of example, in
2013, the Catholic priest, Kevin Barr, became the subject of a removal
order from the country.

Although the removal order was subsequently rescinded after representations to Bainimarama, it provides an example of the Prime Minister's personal character. In 2012, Barr had written a facetious letter to the editor of the *Fiji Sun* in which he commented on the country's increasingly close relationship with China, by proposing that the Union Jack be replaced with the Chinese flag on the national ensign. Bainimarama's response exposed the folly of too close a political association between the Church and the regime. In a leaked letter to the Australian High Commission in Suva, Barr alleged receiving a phone call from Bainimarama in which he demanded an apology for the letter. The demand allegedly included the comment that Barr was anti-government and a 'fucked up priest' (Field, 2013). Barr's later response to a Prime Ministerial text message of the same vein was allegedly to say that he was simply not in agreement with some government decisions. The response, according to Barr's communication with the High Commission, was a text message reading 'Fuck U arsehole. Stay well away from me' (Field, 2013). Yet, it is only in climates of political stability that indigenous claims can be made and responded to with a coherent balance between principle and pragmatism.

Economic policy, stability and differentiated citizenship

The political tension arising from inequality was apparent during the 2014 election campaign. The electoral competition between Fiji First and the Social Democratic Liberal Party (SODELPA) was one where Fiji First 'pushed for fundamental reform and transformation' while SODELPA was 'protective of neo-traditional values' and the presumption was that the two perspectives were incompatible (Ratuva, 2015a), and not reconcilable through a form of differentiated citizenship that the United Nations' *Declaration on the Rights of Indigenous Peoples* (2007a) might help to develop. Indeed, in 2009, the argument of the Fiji Native Tribal Congress (Fiji Native Tribal Congress, 2012) for the resurrection of democracy was made with reference to the *Declaration*'s imperative 'to protect, maintain and advance the rights of Fiji's native population…in a manner that balances those rights equitably with the rights of other individuals and groups in Fiji'. McCreery (2012), similarly argued that the *Declaration*'s focus on development over welfarism 'represents best practice for Indigenous peoples, states and private enterprises wanting to revitalise Indigenous led economic development' (p. 1).

Yet there still remain moral and pragmatic justifications for viewing economic development policy through indigeneity's lens. These justifications make indigenous Fijian exclusion from the *Declaration* a particular constraint on the development of a coherent, just and pragmatic politics of indigeneity. Its inapplicability deprives Fiji of a politically and jurisprudentially developed framework for examining reasonable constraints on political power, just as much as it provides ways of contemplating that: 'Indigenous peoples have more than just the right to be beneficiaries of externally controlled economic systems' (McCreery, 2012).

Economic development presumes liberal democratic stability which, in real terms, is not achieved by dismissing the 'ethnic democratic' practice of communal representation in parliament, while also diminishing the essential liberal tenets of free speech, freedom of association and a free and independent press. There is an important distinction between wanting to 'control' the state, as Lawson (2012) understands 'ethnic democracy', and wanting to hold a *particular* share in its sovereign authority. Economic security, and the foundational contribution it makes to self-determination, is an essential indicator of that authority's meaningful presence. It is a measure of differentiated citizenship, showing why 'it would not do to dichotomise' liberal and ethnic democracy (Lawson, 2012, p. 294). Further: 'It is only a matter of time before a government sponsored by the Fiji Military Forces loses office in a national election: will Fiji prove its resilience to yet another coup' (Chand, 2015)? The answer may lie in the extent to which indigenous people perceive that their economic security is sufficient to allow the true exercise of the right to self-determination, even as the role of economic wellbeing in maintaining relative political authority is not well understood. A further contributing factor is that the government's *Agricultural Investment Guide* makes no mention of the particular or unique contributions that indigenous peoples and their natural resources might make to national development (Republic of Fiji, 2013a).

The absence of differentiated citizenship's pragmatic opportunities leaves paramountcy, as an incoherent and underdeveloped account of political power, an unsatisfactory philosophical basis from which political rights and economic opportunities are determined. It is paramountcy, more than any other variable that explains the entrenchment of indigenous economic disadvantage. The important contrast, with Australia and New Zealand, is that in those jurisdictions rights grounded in first occupancy are pursued, not as ends in themselves, but as foundations for engaging with prevailing political and economic systems. This underlying pragmatism allows indigenous policy to challenge the liberal tendency to place 'more weight on economic freedom than on personal freedom or civil liberties' (Quiggin, 2005, p. 32), and to show that political authority is preliminary to economic opportunities. In particular, differentiated citizenship provides context for assessing and pursuing new objectives in land policy where Dodd (2012) 'identifies broad competing principles of inalienability and sustenance as the fundamental objectives of landholding customs' (p. 8). From some indigenous points of view, land rights are a mark of who is, and who is not, a Fijian (Dodd, 2012). Yet, they have not provided economic security to either indigenous or Indo-Fijians. Land reform that minimises land tenure's underlying contribution to ethnic division, is essential to both political stability and improved economic wellbeing: 88 per cent of Fijian land is held under communal title and its use is a significant point of Fijian national conflict. In an important contrast with Australia and New Zealand, Fijian land ownership is not causally related to collective development opportunities.

Arguments over land expose, more than any other variable, the relationship between coherent and broadly accepted theories of power and self-determination. In other jurisdictions, customary understanding of relationships between natural resource use and material wellbeing has evolved, to create opportunities that remain elusive to indigenous Fijians, whose inability to accept that political power is relative and relational to others' expectations, restricts opportunities to benefit materially from resource ownership.

The privileging of land leasing over communal use by landowners themselves has compromised the development of an indigenous economy. The income that leases provide is often not sufficient to ameliorate owners' material poverty and land management practices that do not foster the development of mature markets, for land produce. Inadequate 'access to finance, inadequate returns to private investment, and appropriability of returns on investment remain among economic development's "binding constraints"' (Duncan et al, 2014, p. 40). These constraints show the limits of an isolable approach to self-determination and obstacles to transferring leases diminish their economic value and is an example of Fiji not providing strong incentives for entrepreneurial activity (Duncan et al, 2014, p. 40). There is no reason for confidence in the Minister for Primary Industry's hopeful suggestion that the government 'fully recognise[s] the importance of private investment in realising these opportunities and we will continue to create an environment that will allow private investment to take place' (Republic of Fiji, 2013a, p. 7). The ways in which people think about land ownership and how decisions should be made over its use are deeply intertwined with people's conceptions of the good life. It is also important that just one third of indigenous land is 'accessible' and 'cultivable' (Fonmanu et al, 2003).

Land policy reflects an underlying clash between 'traditional and introduced economic systems' (Duncan et al, 2014, p. 186) and it is a reflection of inadequate indigenous understandings of the nature of political power that leads to the observation that 'the primary difficulty in achieving sustained, effective economic reform has been the lack of motivation to undertake collective action that will weaken the village level power of the chiefs, which translates into power at the national level (Duncan et al, 2014, p. 186). The purposes for which long-term leases may be granted need to be broadened, provided that all efforts are also made to ensure that indigenous peoples, themselves, make better use of their land holdings. For example, agricultural leases remove an important economic opportunity from indigenous peoples; 99 year leases to tourist operators have, in contrast, allowed international companies to invest in the local tourism market. However, it is important that these do not 'crowd out' local indigenous ventures in this potentially most lucrative industry.

The Bainimarama government claims that its agricultural policy is underpinned by three objectives: 'Empowering Fijians, Modernising our Nation, and Strengthening our Economy' (Republic of Fiji, 2013a). However, it is an enormous rhetorical overstatement for the Prime Minister also to propose that Fiji is 'world renowned as a leading agricultural producing country' (Republic of Fiji, 2013a, p. 6), even as agriculture contributes 82 per cent of Fijian GDP, accounts for 41 per cent of export earnings and employs 28 per cent of the population (Republic of Fiji, 2013a). It is also true that it is Bainimarama's authoritarian and incoherent approach to government that most constrains the investment that he proposes, even though it is true that the government has extended agricultural tax concessions to foreign investment (Republic of Fiji, 2013a).

Elsewhere, differentiated citizenship creates opportunities for indigenous peoples to challenge the 'state as an antagonist of indigenous rights' (Howitt, 2012), even as resource rights may be conditioned and constrained by acceptance that one's own capacity for self-determination is balanced by non-indigenous peoples' assertion of that same right. Rights come, then, to be 'defined in relation to real or perceived threats or challenges posed by "other" groups, and are often fluid – changing in response to economic and political circumstances' (Prasad et al, 2001, p. 3). The return of substantive sovereignty from the military to the people is also preliminary to the ideal that:

The Fijian government, assisted by the international community, must build consensus through inclusive policy development involving Parliament, civil society, and multilateral and bilateral development institutions, in the formulation, implementation and review of policies and programmes. It should promote dialogue and understanding on the conflict dimensions of development, to ensure that development is equitable and inclusive across all of Fiji's regions, and among all of its communities. (Prasad et al, 2001, p. 12)

A similar conception of power is evident in the Fiji Community Development Program's (2001) argument that the community sector might: 'Contribute to poverty alleviation through empowerment and the provision of services and acting as policy advocates; and supporting processes of democratisation and demand for good governance through strengthening multi-stakeholder partnerships and planning, improving accountability and transparency and increasing the participation of marginalised groups' (p. 14).

Australasian experiences demonstrate a well-developed civil society's importance to economic development. Strengthening indigenous civil society distinguishes the politics of indigeneity in both Australia and New Zealand and helps to explain increases in relative indigenous political influence in both jurisdictions. The Fijian community sector, including religious organisations, brings stability to an environment otherwise compromised by the absence of certain and shared public sovereignty. The Community Development Program's democratic objectives do, however, presume sovereignty's return to the people, where civil society's 'dual role' includes 'contributing to poverty alleviation through empowerment and the provision of services and acting as policy advocates; and supporting processes of democratisation and demand for good governance' (Fiji Community Development Program, 2011, p. 14) where, among other considerations, limited physical infrastructure: roads, water, electricity and poor education and health might also be addressed. However, the 'protective labour policy' legacy (Prasad et al, 2001, p. 3) and more recent affirmative action policies mitigated against the need for effective education policy and Fijian community sector organisations identify the importance of the development of financial management, evaluation and policy development skills, for example. The state offers considerable assistance with the costs of education but, pedagogically, the system's effectiveness is not consistent with increasing people's opportunities for greater self-determination. School ineffectiveness is also compounded by a significant distinction between urban and rural schools, with resources and teaching quality noticeably poorer in rural areas where an estimated 60 per cent of indigenous Fijians have completed at least part of their schooling (White, 2001). Indeed, White (2001) attributes the coup, in 2000, 'to growing dual burdens of low educational attainment and stigmatising discourses compounded by the…election of…a government headed by a Fiji Indian prime minister' (p. 305).

The 2015 Budget established education as a priority, with the sector attracting 16.8 per cent of the year's expenditure in recognition of a need for 'better learning standards and improved student outcomes' (Republic of Fiji, 2015, p. 60). On the other hand, however, the number of new school graduates each year well exceeds job growth and it is only high levels of emigration that prevent exponential increases in unemployment (Duncan et al, 2014) to show that Fijian economic development requires better developed labour markets.

Conclusion

Protectionism meant that indigenous people were excluded from mainstream economic opportunities and it was the ensuing material poverty that encouraged support for an exclusive and isolationist paramountcy. Isolationism retains influence to distinguish Fiji from New Zealand where indigenous engagement with the national and global economies is well-developed and from Australia where it is, at least, pursued. In those jurisdictions differentiation contextualises engagement whereas in Fiji it contextualises exclusion. The important point for the politics of indigeneity is that not only might it concern itself with the terms of belonging to the state but also with the terms of belonging to an economic order. Land reform is especially important in this sense, as is the dismantling of affirmative action policies and the de-politicisation of the banking industry. Ultimately as the 2014 election campaign showed, economic inequality and political instability occurred in a circuitous relationship.

Conclusion

The book's opening chapter described reconciliation as a theoretical framework from which contemporary indigenous politics is played out across Australia, Fiji and New Zealand; jurisdictions with marked contextual differences, but sharing a need for ordered and relationally just terms of association among indigenous peoples, the state and wider societies as they respond to British colonial legacies. While grounded in Christian public theology, reconciliation transcends the notion of a sacramental relationship between God and penitent involving sorrow, forgiveness and correcting broken relationships, to provide a metaphor for just intra-national relationships. Religious discourses of reconciliation have influenced secular indigenous politics in each jurisdiction. They help to rationalise the politics of indigeneity's juxtaposition with liberal democracy to position differentiated citizenship as a legitimate constituent of the liberal political arrangements that prevail in Australia and New Zealand and that the international community seeks to impose on Fiji.

It is from secular reconciliation that the book's concern for a theoretically defensible differentiated citizenship proceeds. This is because Australian secular politics finds recourse to policies of relational justice not just in the common law but also in reconciliation's moral presumptions. In New Zealand, these same presumptions are brought into policy practice with reference to the Treaty of Waitangi under which successive governments have offered apologies and recompense for land alienation and other breaches of extant rights of prior occupancy. However, in both jurisdictions reconciliation is variously understood and deep philosophical divisions remain over the ways in which indigenous peoples should be free to express their liberal democratic citizenship. Reconciliation's principal concern is to resolve those differences. It does so by turning to practical politics to work out the limits and possibilities for 'living together differently' – a process that is complicated and compromised in Fiji where Christian churches have, instead, contributed significantly to reconciliation's cooption into an aggressive and assertive indigenous nationalism. Indeed, Fiji provides an important case study in the constraints of religious idealism, as reconciliation's moral legitimacy and political efficacy are tested in ways that do not occur in jurisdictions where other groups' relative power prevents the assertions of absolute indigenous paramountcy. The contrast with Australia and New Zealand shows the importance of stable political institutions to self-determination. Stability allows a coherent politics of indigeneity to form as both a theory of justice and a political strategy asserting the terms on which indigenous peoples wish to belong to the nation state.

The politics of indigeneity is grounded in claims to extant political rights that are distinct from the general rights of ethnic minorities preceded by multicultural theories of liberal citizenship. The politics of indigeneity is concerned with culture's place in public policy; it understands individual liberty as conditional on culturally framed group rights. It challenges the bounds of liberal possibility by juxtaposing indigenous notions of political authority with western liberal theory to make it a politics of both resistance and transformation. It has particular implications for the ways in which democratic arrangements are made, especially for the ways in which health and social services are delivered. It sets educational and economic aspirations that do not confine people to victimhood, and privileges culturally framed collective as well as personal agency.

The politics of indigeneity asserts the development of language and culture as legitimate, not just in the private sphere, but also in the public where languages might be deliberately developed and maintained in schools and used in judicial and parliamentary proceedings. Indigeneity translates reconciliation into practical politics through culture's normative recognition and through substantive indigenous policy engagement. It seeks to draw indigenous rights into a theoretical account of liberal citizenship that is inclusive and that holds substantive meaning for indigenous peoples. In these ways it reframes debates about public sovereignty's character and location and can legitimise sovereignty only if it is shared and distributed among sites of traditional indigenous authority, as well as providing substantive indigenous deliberative opportunities within the state itself.

When the state recognises traditional indigenous authority it recognises the indigenous claim to *particular* rather than simply *proportionate* shares in national sovereignty. This is morally required because indigenous peoples have never voluntarily ceded sovereignty and have no reason to accept the state as their sole point of political identity. Thus, group rights matter. They are expressed through a 'politics of presence' that is institutionalised yet perpetually contested in New Zealand, asserted but without sustained substantive impact in Australia, and explicitly rejected in Fiji where the politics of indigeneity is volatile and underdeveloped.

Although indigenous peoples are, as a whole, materially poor their *particular* colonial context means that egalitarian justice's concern for the welfare of poor people is insufficient to challenge political authority's inequitable distribution. Attending to the material needs of poor people is just, but does not reshape the ways in which public sovereignty is understood so that its inclusive potential might be reached. Nor does it respect the agency that indigenous people seek to make sure that they, themselves, 'count' in *particular* ways in public policy formation.

Indigenous politics are complex and multifaceted and a theoretical understanding of indigeneity *per se* is preliminary to thinking about the nature of the political authority that indigenous peoples might reasonably enjoy as an alternative to the assimilationist presumption that still carries some weight in Australia and New Zealand. It is also preliminary to modifying the claim to exclusive paramountcy that is sought on the one hand in Fiji and the strictly non-racial military supervised polity that is sought on the other. Indeed, it is contemporary Fiji's inability to consider these political complexities in an ordered and coherent fashion that most suggests the need for principled theoretically consistent and clear accounts of the rights of indigenous peoples in the contemporary state. Such an account of indigenous peoples' place within the state is preliminary to self-determination and must be developed with reference to citizenship; an ideological concept that sets the nature and terms of indigenous belonging.

Citizenship has equal capacity to constrain or empower indigenous peoples. However, its history has been one of constraint through the narrow interpretation of its possibilities. It has been used to construct culturally homogenous national identities proceeding from the assumption that all people may join the national political community as equals, but only by thinking and behaving in singular cultural terms. Citizenship's exclusive framing by the state has masked its alternative emancipatory capacity and potential for integration into a substantive self-determination. In this way, it has been structured towards indigenous people not seeing the state as theirs; as something to which they might belong in substantively equal terms. Alternatively, indigenous self-determination can be supported when liberal democratic citizenship is differentiated to provide for public recognition and substantive deliberation in public affairs, where citizenship's focus on the rights, privileges and responsibilities of the individual is extended to consider those of the group. It is through group recognition that citizenship can admit the social and cultural contexts in which indigenous peoples find personal liberty.

Liberal citizenship's emancipatory potential is that liberalism is a theory of political relationships that arose to allow diverse perspectives to be considered in public decision-making. In its own terms, it ought not fear difference but provide the institutional means for considering peoples' different expectations of citizenship and interpretations of the good life. Liberalism is, then, equipped to create a more just political order than was possible under pre-democratic colonial arrangements where people were subjects of the Crown, not equal citizens of a nation state, with the guaranteed capacity to deliberate. From this perspective, indigeneity's purpose becomes one of influencing the political order to accept particular forms of indigenous deliberation, such as guaranteed representation in parliaments.

Differentiated citizenship is a politics of inclusion based on recognising that individual identity is the product of cultural context and that it is from culture that political identities may arise to contest colonialism's legacy as a set of ideas competing for popular ascendancy with indigeneity's moral arguments for self-determination.

In Fiji, differentiated citizenship's potential to give expression to indigenous political aspirations in the liberal language of international acceptability may provide a theoretically coherent alternative to the haphazard, aggressive, inwardly obsessive focus of contemporary indigenous nationalism, which precludes the political stability that meaningful and sustainable self-determination requires. Culturally contextualised participatory parity creates varying degrees of deliberative opportunity for minority indigenous populations in jurisdictions such as Australia and New Zealand, but is also particularly relevant to contemporary Fijian politics as providing an ordered and cohesive framework for thinking about how that country's political institutions and values might respond to its colonial past.

Contemporary indigenous politics in Australia and New Zealand demonstrate both democratic inclusion and exclusion. However, examples from both these jurisdictions demonstrate scope for the concept to contribute stability and coherence to Fiji by helping to work out the terms of different peoples' 'belonging together differently'. Citizenship's contribution is that it helps to codify the terms on which people belong to the state and the rules for political engagement.

The values that a community holds about what it means to be a citizen frames debates about the form that public institutions should take. It also contextualises debates about the ways in which people participate in those institutions. Public attitudes towards citizenship determine its willingness to allow decision-making on the basis of 'participatory parity' or on the assumption that political participation must be according to a culturally homogenous ideal. In short, citizenship's construction determines whether culture does or does not count in public affairs.

Citizenship's inclusive and emancipatory potential is, then, realised with the juxtaposition of the politics of indigeneity with liberal political theory to create two-tiered differentiation, where indigenous peoples enjoy 'participatory parity' with other citizens in their contributions to public decision-making and enjoy independent authority over their own affairs. Differentiated citizenship of this kind provides a foundation for relationally just terms of association between indigenous and other members of the political community; as contributors to a nation state which while a product of colonial aggression, is potentially transformed with time and evolving conceptions of justice, to create opportunities for pragmatic self-determination in circumstances where the full and exclusive restoration of indigenous authority cannot, practically, occur. It is through citizenship that ideas about public authority are developed. Self-determination's relative and relational character requires indigenous political voice within the structures and institutions where citizenship is expressed. It is only through that voice that indigenous peoples are able to contribute to the constant contestation of political priorities and re-shaping of political values that determine how each might interpret the 'good life' in the modern state. However, political authority is not located within the state alone. It is also found in indigenous peoples' relationships with global economic, political and jurisprudential developments.

Self-determination's relative and relational character means that its substantive expression occurs within a global economy and a global market of ideas about the proper rights of indigenous peoples vis-à-vis the nation state. While colonisation itself is the product of oppressive economic expansion justified by principles of convenience developed at international law, the collective security that indigenous peoples aim to restore rests, in modern times, on economic agency and engagement with the international economy.

Globalisation was the principal cause of the usurpation of indigenous political rights and economic opportunities. However, its contemporary form provides important opportunities for indigenous peoples to challenge dependent relationships with the nation state through economic development and through the formation of alliances of common aspiration with indigenous peoples in other parts of the world. Indeed, the United Nations' *Declaration on the Rights of Indigenous Peoples* (2007a) is the outcome of international political cooperation among indigenous peoples including those of Australia and New Zealand who have, in turn, found recourse to its legal precepts in successful challenges to state political authority.

The universalisation of human rights has made an important contribution to indigenous peoples' reclamation of political agency. Indeed, contemporary obstacles to indigenous self-determination are much more the product of domestic constraints than globalisation itself. Economically, it is globalisation's contemporary regulation rather than the concept *per se* that has the potential to constrain indigenous peoples' opportunities to pursue self-defined paths to greater material wellbeing. The cooption of indigenous peoples' experiences into others' resistance to globalisation can, indeed, be a form of neocolonialism, paying no regard to an indigenous desire for material security and for important relationships between material and cultural security. The ways in which indigenous peoples actively pursue economic agency indicates that they find no cultural virtue in poverty; just as they find no certainty in relying on the modern state to admit each and every expression of self-determination that indigenous perspectives might rationalise. In Fiji, in particular, indigenous peoples' relative political power is a consequence of domestic constraints. In contrast, their limited economic opportunities are the product of global tourism, fishing and cultural exports along with military participation in United Nations' peacekeeping missions. Strengthened global influences through the extension of the limits and possibilities of the *Declaration on the Rights of Indigenous Peoples* to Fijians as a majority indigenous population would constrain military sovereignty, and introduce and develop the idea of self-determination as relative and relational to ordered political and economic engagement with others. Indeed, indigenous economic agency is the most significant determinant and pre-condition for substantive self-determination.

Indigenous economic activity's cultural context and purpose often distinguishes it from state policy imperatives and is, thus, most likely to occur with substantive purpose in the context of differentiated citizenship. Economic agency is preliminary to reconciliation and personal capacity to make decisions about what one values and to construct a meaningful conception of the 'good life'. These considerations distinguish indigenous peoples' economic agency from Australian policies such as the *Indigenous Economic Development Strategy* and 'Closing the Gap in Indigenous Disadvantage' which focused principally on an economically utilitarian view of self-determination as available only through individual participation in the mainstream labour market. Instead, indigenous views tend to be broader and assume a trans-generational culturally grounded focus that adds significant complexity to public policies aimed at improving the quality of indigenous people's lives. It may be important, in egalitarian justice, to close statistical gaps in education, income and health. But it is a matter of overriding importance to close gaps in relational justice that inhibit indigenous agency in the education and labour markets and in the health system where racism and inattentiveness to the claims of culture create gaps between indigenous experience and policy outcomes.

Education, in particular, is a site of contestation over the proper place of indigenous cultures in public life. Whereas the New Zealand education system accepts a role in the maintenance and development of the Maori language as both recognition of the right to language *per se* and as a matter of restitutive justice, there is not as comprehensive an understanding of language and education in these terms in Australia. While there is incremental policy change towards the recognition of language and some attention to the pedagogic implications of culture there is, in Australia, no equivalent to the New Zealand Te Kotahitanga project's influence on schooling as a measure that consciously sought Maori deliberation in its development.

Effective education is important to self-determination because education is a determinant of access to the middle class. The relative size of the indigenous middle class is a measure of differentiated citizenship's substantive presence. It is an expression not just of the 'right' to self-determination, but the 'power' of self-determination: the ways in which citizenship has been able to challenge poverty as colonialism's necessary legacy.

Economic development's cultural context has widespread implications for the politics of indigeneity, which presumes an extant right to resource utilisation for economic gain, and for indigenous economic engagement for their own purposes, often based on alliances of common aspiration beyond the state. Indeed, for indigenous peoples, extra-state relationships provide opportunities to set aside the dependence and vulnerability that colonial policies impose. It is important to self-determination that indigenous people's access to lives that they have reason to value (Sen, 1999) are not unbreakably connected to the preferences and prejudices of the state. Indigenous Australian civil society is acutely aware of that possibility and its own policy preferences are sharply focused beyond the state, just as they are in New Zealand where through differentiated citizenship Maori assert a particular economic agency which, in turn, affirms the terms on which they choose to 'belong' to the modern state.

Settlements for Crown breaches of the Treaty of Waitangi provide particular context to contemporary Maori economic development, with cultural distinctiveness an important characteristic of collective economic pursuits. While cultural values set economic activity's purpose and engagement, Maori economic development receives public policy support in a more focused fashion than applies to indigenous Australia. The greater relative Maori population size and greater relative value of the Maori economy means that national wellbeing depends on Maori wellbeing in ways that are not comparable in Australia. However, as in Australia, the education system does not meet indigenous expectations and has not been able to achieve the 'demographic dividend' that the Maori population structure makes possible. Addressing this instance of profound policy failure is, incrementally, receiving greater policy attention and the Te Kotahitanga secondary school teacher development programme was an important example of conscious, culturally framed, Maori deliberative engagement in the policy process. Te Kotahitanga's effectiveness was its contribution to increased Maori attainment of national qualifications. It illustrated differentiated citizenship both in the approach it took to Maori deliberation and in the substantive presumptions it made about how Maori are best taught at school. It showed how differentiated citizenship is preliminary to a culture's acceptance into public policy.

Differentiated citizenship gives practical expression to the politics of indigeneity, and shows that this is not a defensive politics that sees relative Maori disadvantage as inevitable or immutable. Instead, it is an assertive politics of agency and presence that consistently and publicly places on the public record its expectations of the state in matters such as education, while simultaneously presuming the right and capacity for independence over Maori peoples' own affairs. In contrast with the Fijian politics of indigeneity which does not admit self-determination's relativity to others, nor its status as the product of interdependent relationships, the New Zealand politics of indigeneity's more nuanced understanding of political authority and relationships means that it has enjoyed some influence over the exercise of public sovereignty while also being intellectually well placed to maintain strategies of resistance to the state's claim to absolute authority.

The New Zealand politics of indigeneity responds to a political environment in which self-determination is neither absolute nor isolated from broader expressions of political authority. This is its point of distinction from Fiji where relative population size might ordinarily be expected to provide indigenous Fijians with greater political influence than is presently enjoyed. Relative population size ordinarily offers significant political advantage but, in Fiji's case, political instability coupled with an insufficiently well-developed and executed indigenous account of political possibilities compromises that advantage. However, the indigenous Fijian politics does not diminish the politics of indigeneity's relevance. The country's shifting population structure is an outcome of its colonial history and a common experience shared with indigenous peoples in other parts of the world, which brings similarity to the underlying political questions that need to be answered about self-determination and indigeneity as a politics of possibility. In particular, Fijian economic opportunities are dependent on a coherent and consistent account of political authority concerned more with self-determination's capacity than with its perceived exclusive rights.

The restoration of public sovereignty is the first and essential condition for substantive indigenous Fijian self-determination. Public sovereignty is not, ideally, expressed through indigenous 'paramountcy' because a politics of isolation cannot provide the political and economic relationships that self-determination requires. Instead, differentiated citizenship with reference to the principles, limits and possibilities embodied in the *Declaration on the Rights of Indigenous Peoples* (United Nations, 2007a) could establish a coherent, pragmatic yet assertive politics of indigeneity able to reconfigure Fijian politics in ways that would ensure *particular* indigenous belonging to the state. Belonging through an assured and *particular* share in public sovereignty is an aspiration that can only be pursued in circuitous relationship with measures to address entrenched economic underdevelopment in a jurisdiction where indigenous lives are distinguished by poverty, ill-health, unemployment and limited education. This is the outcome of political exclusion beginning with the protectionism of British colonial rule, followed by the inability to make use of the extensive natural resources that remain under indigenous control, exclusive accounts of indigenous political authority, and finally the formal vesting of sovereignty in the military. As this book's cross jurisdictional comparison has shown, negative power relationships and their responses, as a politics of possibility, are the products of the structure of citizenship, not simply relative numeric status. In Australasia indigenous political disadvantage, and its responses, are a function of prevailing ideas about justice and political organisation, while in Fiji the politics of indigeneity's transformative capacity requires a fuller conception of power than racial restrictions on who can or cannot hold the office of Prime Minister or President.

As a politics of transformation indigeneity's concern is an on-going one. Self-determination is its ultimate purpose which means that it is neither static nor absolute. Political contexts evolve and self-determination cannot effectively occur as an isolationist approach to political power. There will always remain scope for the principles which this book sets out to inform the analysis of indigenous politics and policy. For example, Australian public policy broadly, but vaguely, accepts that indigenous people are entitled to a particular kind of belonging to the nation state. However, the question of just how substantive that recognition should be and by whom and how the question should be settled is one that will become especially important as Australia considers a government proposal to amend the Commonwealth Constitution to recognise indigenous prior occupancy. The debate that is preceding a national referendum on the proposal is providing indigenous peoples with an opportunity to set out what it is, exactly, that they seek from Constitutional recognition, and from self-determination. Both reason and prejudice distinguish wider public responses and whichever it is that assumes ascendant influence there will, at least, bring further clarity to the question of how indigenous peoples reasonably belong to the modern political community.

Similar questions pre-occupy New Zealand public policy, including the policy space that Maori might enjoy to strengthen traditional tribal authorities as sites of differentiated citizenship. The question of what it means, exactly, to be a citizen of an iwi is as important as the question of what it means to be a Maori citizen of the nation state. Treaty of Waitangi settlements shape and influence the meanings of both kinds of citizenship. Yet the context in which they do so is one where Maori expectations of schooling are still to be realised, where the public health system is not as effective for Maori as it is for other citizens and where Maori continue to find racism in public life. For example, there appear discrepancies in the judicial sentencing of Maori and non-Maori offenders convicted of similar crimes. Maori experience of discrimination in the labour market continues. Yet indigeneity, as a politics of potential means that Maori are well placed to respond to these instances of prejudice and to pursue aspirations based on what they, themselves, hold important. The contrast with Fiji could not be starker. In that country, indigeneity's potential is restrained, especially as the country's most significant contemporary political concern is the government's proposed village by-laws which contemplate the regulation of almost every facet of people's lives in the country's 1172 indigenous villages.

The proposal includes the regulation of clothing, compelling people to own a home before they marry, and strictly prescribing the roles that people must play in village administration. The by-law is intended to uphold traditional cultural values and provide a more certain foundation for material security. It was circulated for consultation in November 2016. However, given Fiji's conditional and authoritarian democracy it is unlikely that the consultation will be genuine or that robust and considered responses to the draft will emerge. Neither the *Fiji Sun* nor the *Fiji Times* have taken independent positions and there is not a free civil society able to contribute to debates on the level of regulation that is proposed. The absence of a coherent and pragmatic indigenous conception of political power also compromises the capacity for indigenous deliberation on a policy proposal that will constrain people's opportunity to make considered decisions for themselves on which aspirations they wish to privilege and pursue. Conversely, the book's consideration of indigeneity as a politics of potential provides broad principles and values against which political arrangements might be assessed. It sets out ways in which peoples might belong together differently within a single nation state where cultural values and aspirations legitimately contextualise public as well as private life for peoples who did not consent to the displacement of their political authority. Their contemporary and abiding presence as distinct peoples depends on particular recognition and just normative relationships with others as both members of their own communities and as substantively equal members of an inclusive nation state.

References

Alfred, T. 2009. *First Nation Perspectives on Political Identity*. Ottawa: Assembly of First Nations.

Alley, R. 2010. Fiji under Bainimarama. *The Journal of Pacific History*, 45, 145–53.

Altman, J. C. 2005. Economic futures on Aboriginal land in remote and very remote Australia: Hybrid economies and joint ventures. *Culture, Economy and Governance in Aboriginal Australia*. Sydney: University of Sydney Press, 121–134.

Altman, J. C. 2011. *The Draft Indigenous Economic Development Strategy: A Critical Response*. Canberra: Centre for Aboriginal Economic Policy Research, Australian National University.

Altman, J. and Kerins, S. 2008. *Submission to the Senate Standing Committee on Environment, Communications and the Arts inquiry into the operation of the Environment Protection and Biodiversity Conservation Act 1999*. Canberra: Centre for Aboriginal Economic Policy Research, Australian National University.

Altman, J. and Rowse, T. 2005. Indigenous Affairs. In P. Saunders and J. Walter (eds) *Ideas and Influence: Social Science and Public Policy in Australia*. Sydney: UNSW Press.

Altman, J., Buchanan, G. and Larsen, L. 2007. *The Environmental Significance of the Indigenous Estate: natural resource management as economic development in remote Australia*. Canberra: Centre for Aboriginal Economic Policy Research, Australian National University.

Anaya, S. 2008. *The Human Rights of Indigenous Peoples, in Light of the New Declaration, and the Challenge of Making Them Operative: Report of the Special Rapporteur on the Situation of Human Rights and Fundamental Freedoms of Indigenous People*. New York: United Nations.

Anderson, A. 2012. *Address to the Northern Territory Legislative Assembly, 1 November 2012*, www.alicespringsnews.com.au/2012/11/03/indigenous-adults-must-grow-up-so-that-indigenous-children-can-depend-on-them-says-alison-anderson/

Anderson, P. 2014. *Launching 2030: A Vision for Aboriginal and Torres Strait Islander Health*, www.lowitja.org.au/sites/default/files/docs/Futures-6-March-2014-Pat-Anderson.pdf

Anglican and Catholic Bishops. 2004. *Statement on the Foreshore and Seabed Legislation*, www.catholic.org.nz/nzcbc/fx-view-article.cfm?ctype=BSART&loadref=83&id=64

Aotearoa Fisheries Limited. 2015. *Annual Report*. Auckland: Aotearoa Fisheries Limited.

Aristotle. 1988. *The Politics*. Cambridge: Cambridge University Press.

Asian Development Bank. 2009. Fiji: Country Strategy and Program Update, www.adb.org/documents/fiji-country-strategy-and-program-update-april-2009

Asian Development Bank. 2014. Country Partnership Strategy, Fiji, 2014–2018, www.adb.org/documents/fiji-country-partnership-strategy-2014-2018

Australian Government. 1998. Native Title Amendment Bill 1997, *Federal Register of Legislation*, www.legislation.gov.au/Details/C2004B00162

Australian Government. 2011. *Indigenous Economic Development Strategy 2011–2018*. Canberra: Australian Government.

Australian Indigenous Chamber of Commerce. 2013. *Seven Point Reform Agenda*, www.indigenouschamber.org.au/about/our-agenda/

Australian Indigenous Doctors' Association. 2008. *Submission to the Northern Territory Emergency Response Review Board*. www.aida.org.au/pdf/submissions/Submission_8.pdf

Australian Institute of Health and Welfare (AIHW). 2015. *Australia's Welfare 2015*, Australia's welfare series 12. Cat. no. AUS 189. Canberra: AIHW, www.aihw.gov.au/WorkArea/DownloadAsset.aspx?id=60129552019

Australians for Native Title and Reconciliation. 2010. *Submission to the Indigenous Economic Development Strategy: Draft for Consultation and Action Plan 2010–2012*, http://irca.net.au/sites/default/files/public/documents/PDF/Government_Docs/ieds_2011_2018.pdf

Bainimarama, F. 2005. *Draft Submission to Parliament on The Promotion of Reconciliation, Tolerance and Unity Bill 2005*, Suva: Republic of Fiji.

Bainimarama, F. 2006. *Fiji Sun*, 1 November.

Bainimarama, F. 2014. *Speech at the Opening of the Savusavu Market*. www.fiji.gov.fj/Media-Center/Speeches/PM-BAINIMARAMA---SPEECH-AT-OPENING-OF-ADDITION-(1).aspx

Banks, R. 2007. *United Nations General Assembly Declaration on the Rights of Indigenous Peoples Explanation of Vote by New Zealand Permanent Representative H E Ms Rosemary Banks*. New York: New Zealand Permanent Mission to the United Nations, www.nzembassy.com/info.cfm?c=51&l=124&CFID=7984901&CFTOKEN=19347722&s=to&p=63315

Bargh, M. 2012. Rethinking and re-shaping indigenous economies: Māori geothermal energy enterprises. *Journal of Enterprising Communities: People and Places in the Global Economy*. 6, 3, 271–83.

Barry, N.P. 1990. The philosophy of the welfare state. *Critical Review*, 4, 545–68.

Benhabib, S. 1996. Introduction. In S. Benhabib (ed.) *Democracy and Difference: Contesting the Boundaries of the Political*. Princeton, NJ: Princeton University Press.

Benhabib, S. 2002. *The Claims of Culture: Equality and Diversity in the Global Era*. Princeton, NJ: Princeton University.

Bennett, M. 2005. Indigeneity as self-determination. *Indigenous Law Journal*, 4, 71–115.

Bishop, R. and Glynn, T. 1999. *Culture Counts: Changing Power Relations in Education*. Palmerston North: Dunmore Press.

Bishop, R., Berryman, M., Tiakiwai, S. and Richardson, C. 2003. *Te Kōtahitanga: The Experiences of Year 9 and 10 Māori Students in Mainstream Classrooms*. Wellington: Ministry of Education.

Bishop, R., O'Sullivan, D. and Berryman, M. 2010. *Scaling up Education Reform: Addressing the Politics of Disparity*. Wellington: NZCER Press.

Blunden, A. 2004. *Nancy Fraser on Recognition and Redistribution*, http://home.mira.net/~andy/works/fraser-review.htm

Bohman, J. 1995. Public reason and cultural pluralism: Political liberalism and the problem of moral conflict. *Political Theory*, 23, 253–79.

Boston, J., Martin, J., Pallot, J. and Walsh, P. 1996. *Public management: the New Zealand model*. Auckland: Oxford University Press.

Brands, J. 2014. *The Shape of Things to Come: Visions for the future of Aboriginal and Torres Strait Islander health research*. Melbourne: The Lowitja Institute.

Brash, D. 2004. *Nationhood*. An Address to the Orewa Rotary Club, www.national.org.nz/speech_article.aspx?ArticleID=1614

Brett, J. 2005. Relaxed and comfortable: The Liberal Party's Australia. *The Australian Quarterly Essay*. Melbourne: Schwartz Publishing Pty.

Byrd, J.A. and Heyer, K.C. 2008. Introduction: International Discourses of Indigenous Rights and Responsibilities. *Alternatives*, 33, 1–5.

Cairns, A. C. 2000. *Citizens Plus: Aboriginal Peoples and the Canadian State*. Vancouver: UBC Press.

Cairns, A. 2003. Afterword: International dimensions of the citizen issue for indigenous peoples/nations. *Citizenship Studies*, 7, 497–503.

Calma, T. 2005. *Aboriginal and Torres Strait Islander Social Justice Commissioner Social Justice Report 2005*. Sydney: Human Rights and Equal Opportunity Commission.

Calma, T. 2008. *Building a Sustainable National Indigenous Representative Body*. Sydney: Aboriginal and Torres Strait Islander Social Justice Commissioner.

Cape York Institute. 2005. *Viewpoint*. http://capeyorkpartnership. org.au/wp-content/uploads/2013/08/6-20Freedom-20capabiltiies-20and-20Cape-20York-20reform-20agenda.pdf

Carens, J. H. 1992. Democracy and respect for difference: The case of Fiji. *University of Michigan Journal of Law Reform*, 25, 547.

Catholic News. 2007. Fiji Archbishop attacks Australia over 'Colonial' Coup Critique, *Catholic News*, 25 January, http://cathnews.acu.edu. au/701/141.php

Cavagnoli, D. 2014. *Investigating Variations in Labour Force Participation Rates of Māori and Non-Māori in New Zealand*. Wellington: Victoria University of Wellington.

Chand, S. 2015. The political economy of Fiji: Past, present, and prospects. *The Round Table*, 104, 199–208.

Chapple, S. 2000. *Maori Socio-Economic Disparty*. Wellington: Ministry of Social Policy.

Clarke, J. 2006. Desegregating the Indigenous Rights Agenda. *Australian Journal of Legal Philosophy*, 31, 119–26.

Cleary, J., McGregor, M., Bryecson, K. and James, C. 2005. *Development of a Value-Driven Bush Foods Industry Chain that Rewards Aboriginal People*. Port Augusta, SA: Desert Knowledge Cooperative Research Centre.

Coleman, A., Dixon, S. and Mare, D. 2005. Wellington: New Zealand Business Roundtable.

Commonwealth of Australia. 2013. *National Aboriginal and Torres Strait Islander Health Plan 2013–2023*. Canberra: Commonwealth of Australia, www.health.gov.au/internet/publications/publishing.nsf/ Content/oatsih-healthplan-toc

Congregation for Catholic Education. 1997. *The Catholic School on the Threshold of the Third Millennium*, www.ewtn.com/library/curia/ ccemille.htm

Cook, I. 2004. *Government and Democracy in Australia*. Melbourne: Oxford University Press.

Cook-Sather, A., Clarke, B., Condon, D., Cushman, K., Demetriou, H. and Easton, L. 2015. *Learning from the Student's Perspective: A Sourcebook for Effective Teaching*. Abingdon: Routledge.

Council for Aboriginal Reconciliation. 2003. *Chairperson's Introduction*, www.austlii.edu.au/au/orgs/car/council/spl98_20/intro.htm

Council of Australian Governments. 2009. *COAG Meeting Communiqué*, 2 July 2009, www.coag.gov.au/meeting-outcomes/ coag-meeting-communiqu%C3%A9-2-july-2009

Council of Australian Governments. 2010. *National Indigenous Reform Agreement (Closing the Gap)*, www.coag.gov.au/intergov_agreements/ federal_financial_relations/docs/IGA_FFR_ScheduleF_National_ Indigenous_Reform_Agreement.pdf

Cunneen, C. 1992. Judicial Racism. *Aboriginal Law Bulletin*. 44, 2, 1–9.

Daes, E.-I. A. 2008. An overview of the history of indigenous peoples: self-determination and the United Nations. *Cambridge Review of International Affairs*, 21, 7–26.

Dahl, A. 2016. Nullifying Settler Democracy: William Apess and the Paradox of Settler Sovereignty. *Polity*. 48, 2, 279–304.

Dakuvula, J. 2004. *Citizenship Education Case Study: Politics of Ethnicity, Citizenship, and the Rule of Law in Fiji*. Asian South Pacific Bureau of Adult Education.

Dance, K. 1998. 'We are sorry' words which aren't enough, but a vital beginning. *Media Release*. Broome, WA: Roman Catholic Diocese of Broome.

De Alessi, M. 2012. The political economy of fishing rights and claims: The Maori experience in New Zealand. *Journal of Agrarian Change*, 12, 390–412.

De Mers, A. and Kahui, V. 2012. An overview of Fiji's fisheries development. *Marine Policy*, 36, 174–9.

Delanty, G. 2000. *Citizenship in a Global Age*. Philadelphia, PA: Open University Press.

Deloitte Access Economics and New South Wales Aboriginal Land Council. 2013. *Economic Development Strategy Research Summary Report*. Sydney: Deloitte Access Economics.

De Torre, J. M. 2000. *Human Rights, Natural Law and Thomas Aquinas*, http://catholicsocialscientists.org/cssr/Archival/2001/ Torre_187-206.pdf

Delanty, G. 2000. *Citizenship in a Global Age*, Philadelphia, PA: Open University Press.

Dodd, M. 2012. *Reform of Leasing Regimes for Customary Land in Fiji*. BL (Hons) dissertation, Otago: University of Otago.

Dodson, M. 1994. The human rights situation of indigenous peoples of Australia, Paper Presented to the Intergovernmental Work Group for Indigenous Affairs, Copenhagen. *Indigenous affairs*, 30–45.

Dodson, M. and Wilson, R. 1997. *Bringing them Home: Report of the National Inquiry into the Separation of Aboriginal and Torres Strait Islander Children from their Families*. Sydney: Human Rights and Equal Opportunity Commission.

Duncan, R., Codippily, H., Duituturaga, E. and Bulatale, R. 2014. *Identifying Binding Constraints in Pacific Island Economies*, Honolulu: East-West Center.

Durie, M. 2003. *Nga Kahui Pou: Launching Maori Futures*. Wellington: Huia.

Durie, M. 2005. *Nga Tai Matatu: Tides of Maori Endurance*. Melbourne: Oxford University Press.

Fenelon, J. and Hall, T. 2008. Revitalization and indigenous resistance to globalization and neoliberalism. *American Behavioral Scientist*, 51, 1867–901.

Field, M. 2013. Military ruler lets old priest stay, *Stuff*, www.stuff.co.nz/world/ south-pacific/8227392/Military-ruler-lets-old-priest-stay

Fiji Community Development Program. 2011. Program Design Document, http://dfat.gov.au/about-us/publications/Pages/fiji-community-development-program-fcdp-design-document.aspx

Fiji Native Tribal Congress. 2012. *Supplementary Report to the Committee on the Elimination of Racial Discrimination for the Republic of Fiji*. Suva: Fiji Native Tribal Congress.

Fiji Post. 2001. *Fiji Post*. 24 August.

Fiji Post. 2007. *Fiji Post*. 21 April.

Fiji Times. 2001. *Fiji Times*, 7 April.

Finlayson, C. 2009. *Speech to Te Kokiri Ngatahi: Hui to Progress Treaty Settlements*. www.beehive.govt.nz/speech/speech-te-kokiri-ngatahi-hui-progress-treaty-settlements

Finlayson, C. 2014a. *Address to Tuhoe-Crown Settlement Day in Taneatua*, www.beehive.govt.nz/speech/address-tuhoe-crown-settlement-day-taneatua

Finlayson, C. 2014b. Finlayson dismisses findings of Waitangi Tribunal report. *Maori Television*, 17 November, www.maoritelevision.com/news/regional/finlayson-dismisses-findings-waitangi-tribunal-report

Firth, S. and Fraenkel, J. 2007. Preface: Fiji's perpetual legitimacy crisis. In S. Firth, and J. Fraenkel (eds) *From Election to Coup in Fiji: The 2006 Campaign and its Aftermath*. Canberra: ANU E-Press.

Fleras, A. 1999. Politicising indigeneity: Ethno-politics in White Settler Dominions. In P. Havemann (ed) *Indigenous Peoples' Rights in Australia, Canada, and New Zealand*. Auckland: Oxford University Press.

Fleras, A. 2000. The politics of jurisdiction: Pathway or predicament. In D. Long and O.P. Dickason (eds) *Visions of the Heart: Canadian Aboriginal Issues* (2nd edn). Toronto: Harcourt Canada.

Fonmanu, K.R., Ting, L. and Williamson, I.P. 2003. Dispute resolution for customary lands: Some lessons from Fiji. *Survey Review*, 37, 177–89.

Forrest, A. 2014. *The Forrest Review: Creating Parity*, Canberra, Commonwealth of Australia.

Fraenkel, J. 2015. The remorseless power of incumbency in Fiji's September 2014 Election. *The Round Table*, 104, 151–64.

Fraenkel, J. and Firth, S. 2006. The enigmas of Fiji's good governance coup. In J. Fraenkel, S. Firth (Author) and B. V. Lal (eds) *The 2006 Military Takeover in Fiji: A Coup to End All Coups?*. Canberra: ANU E-Press.

Frame, A. and Te Mātāhauariki Institute. 2001. *Property and the Treaty of Waitangi: a tragedy of the commodities?* Hamilton: Te Matahauariki Institute, University of Waikato.

Fraser, N. 2003. *Redistribution or Recognition?: A Political–Philosophical Exchange*. New York: Verso Books.

Friedman, J. 1999. Indigenous struggles and the discreet charm of the Bourgeoisie. *The Australian Journal of Anthropology*, 10, 1–14.

Fry, G. 2000. Political legitimacy and the post-colonial state in the Pacific: Reflections on some common threads in the Fiji and Solomon Island coups. *Pacifica Review*, 12, 3, 295–304.

Galston, W.A. and Galston, W.W.A. 1991. *Liberal Purposes: Goods, Virtues, and Diversity in the Liberal State*. Cambridge: Cambridge University Press.

Garrett, G. 1993. A place of one's own: Reflections on a theology of space. *St Mark's Review*. 4, 3–7.

Gibson-Graham, J.K. and Roelvink, G. 2010. An economic ethics for the Anthropocene. *Antipode*. 41, 1, 320–46.

Gusmerini, P. 2006. *The Wild Rivers Act 2005 (QLD)*. Sydney: Australasian Legal Information Institute, www.austlii.edu.au/

Habermas, J. 1994. Citizenship and National Identity. In V. Steenbergen (ed.) *The Condition of Citizenship.* London: Sage Publications.

Hally, C. 1998. Reconstructing the moral order of society by forgiveness and reconciliation. *Aboriginal Issues Newsletter*, 2, 2.

Hattie, J. 1999. Influences on student learning. *Professorial Inaugural Lecture*, Auckland: University of Auckland.

Hattie, J. 2003. New Zealand education snapsot. Paper presented at the *Knowledge Wave 2003*. Auckland: The Leadership Forum.

Heater, D. 2004. *Citizenship: The Civic Ideal in World History, Politics and Education*. Manchester: Manchester University Press.

Held, D. 1989. Citizenship and Autonomy. In D. Held and J. Thompson (eds) *Social Theory of Modern Societies*. Cambridge: Cambridge University Press.

Held, D. 1995. *Democracy and the Global Order: From the Modern State to Cosmopolitan Governance*. Cambridge: Polity Press.

High Court of New Zealand. 1987. *New Zealand Maori Council v. Attorney-General, [1987] 1 NZLR, 641.* Wellington: High Court Wellington.

Hill, R. S. 2004. *State Authority, Indigenous Autonomy: Crown Maori Relations in New Zealand/Aotearoa 1900–1950.* Wellington: Victoria University Press.

Hill, R. 2007. *Declaration on the Rights of Indigenous Peoples: Explanation of Vote by the Hon. Robert Hill Ambassador and Permanent Representative of Australia to the United Nations.* New York: Australian Permanent Mission to the United Missions, www.fns.bc.ca/info/UNDeclaration/ Stmnts%20Made%20by%20States%20Before%20and%20After%20 the%20Vote/Australia.pdf

Hill, R. and Bönisch-Brednich, B. 2007. Politicizing the past: Indigenous scholarship and Crown–Maori reparations processes in New Zealand. *Social and Legal Studies*, 16, 163–81.

Hindess, B. 2000. Limits to citizenship. In W. Hudson and J. Kane (eds) *Rethinking Australian Citizenship.* Cambridge: Cambridge University Press.

Hindess, B. 2002. Neo-liberal citizenship. *Citizenship Studies*, 6, 127–43.

Hobbes, T. 1998. *Leviathan.* Oxford: Oxford University Press.

Hocking, B. and Hocking, B. 1999. Australian Aboriginal property rights as issues of indigenous sovereignty and citizenship. *Ratio Juris*, 12, 196–225.

Hohepa, M. K. 2013. Educational leadership and indigeneity: Doing things the same, differently. *American Journal of Education*, 119, 617–31.

Hooper, M. 2000. Maori power. In K. G. Kumar (ed.) *Sizing Up: Property Rights and Fisheries Management. A Collection of Articles from SAMUDRA Report*, pp. 18–22. Chennai: International Collective in Support of Fishworkers.

Horscroft, V. 2002. *The Politics of Ethnicity in the Fiji Islands: Competing Ideologies of Indigenous Paramountcy and Individual Equality in Political Dialogue.* MPhil dissertation, Oxford: University of Oxford.

Howard, J. 2000. Practical reconciliation. In M. Grattan (ed.) *Essays on Australian Reconciliation.* Melbourne: Bookman Press Pty Ltd.

Howitt, R. 2012. Sustainable indigenous futures in remote indigenous areas: relationships, processes and failed state approaches. *GeoJournal*, 77, 817–28.

Howlett, C. 2008. *Indigenous Peoples and Mining Negotiations: The Role of the State. A Case Study of Century Zinc Mine in the Gulf of Carpentaria.* PhD dissertation, Nathan, QLD: Griffith University.

Hunt, J. 2011. *Learning from Success: A Response to the Draft Indigenous Economic Development Strategy*. Canberra: Centre for Aboriginal Economic Policy Research, Australian National University.

Independent Iwi Working Group on Constitutional Transformation Matike Mai Aotearoa. 2016. *He Whakaaro Here Whakaumu Mo Aotearoa: The Report of Matike Mai Aotearoa*. www.converge.org.nz/pma/MatikeMaiAotearoaReport.pdf

Indian and Northern Affairs Canada. 1995. *The Government of Canada's Approach to Implementation of the Inherent Right and the Negotiation of Aboriginal Self-Government*, www.ainc-inac.gc.ca/al/ldc/ccl/pubs/sg/sg-eng.asp

Ingram, D. 2003. Between political liberalism and postnational cosmopolitanism: Toward an alternative theory of human rights. *Political Theory*, 31, 359–91.

Ivanitz, M. 2002. Democracy and indigenous self-determination. In A. Carter and G. Stokes (eds) *Democratic Theory Today*, pp. 121–48. Cambridge: Polity Press.

Ivison, D. 2002. *Postcolonial Liberalism*. Cambridge: Cambridge University Press.

Ivison, D., Patton, P. and Sanders, W. 2000. Introduction. In D. Ivison, P. Patton and W. Sanders (eds) *Political Theory and the Rights of Indigenous Peoples*. Cambridge: Cambridge University Press.

Iwi Chairs' Forum. 2014. Iwi Collective proposals: Briefing for the deputy Prime Minister, Minister of Housing and Minister for the Environment, www.ranginui.co.nz/vdb/document/202

Jacobsen, B., Jones, C. R. and Wybrow, R. 2005. Indigenous economic development policy: A discussion of theoretical foundations. *Social Change in the 21st Century*. Brisbane, QLD: Queensland University of Technology.

Jackson, N. 2011. Maori and the [potential] Demographic Dividend. *New Zealand Population Review*, 37, 65.

Jackson, R. 1999. Sovereignty in world politics: A glance at the conceptual and historical landscape. In R. Jackson (ed.) *Sovereignty at the Millenium*. Oxford: Blackwell Publishers.

James, R. 1997. Rousseau's Knot: The entanglement of liberal democracy and racism. In G. Cowlishaw and B. Morris (eds) *Race Matters: Indigenous Australians and 'Our' Society*. Canberra: Aboriginal Studies Press.

John Paul II. 1983. *The Code of Canon Law*. London: Collins Liturgical Publications.

John Paul II. 1986. Meeting with New Zealand Bishops. *Peace: The Message of the Gospel. Complete Texts of Addresses Given by Pope John Paul II During his Pastoral Visit to New Zealand 22–24 November 1986.* Wellington: Catholic Communications for the New Zealand Catholic Bishops' Conference.

John Paul II. 1996. Address to Aboriginal and Torres Strait Islanders. In S. Cornish (ed). *Always the Same Spirit.* Homebush, NSW: St. Paul's Publications.

John Paul II. 2001. *Ecclesia in Oceania.* Vatican City, www.vatican.va/holy_father/john_paul_ii/apost_exhortations/documents/hf_jp-ii_exh_20011122_ecclesia-in-oceania_en.html

Johnson, J. T. 2008. Indigeneity's challenges to the white settler-state: Creating a third space for dynamic citizenship. *Alternatives*, 33, 29–52.

Johnston, E. 1991. *Royal Commission into Aboriginal Deaths in Custody: National Report.* Canberra: Australian Government Publishing Service.

Kant, I. 1970. *Kant's Political Writings.* Cambridge: Cambridge University Press.

Kelly, J. and Kaplan, M. 2009. Legal fictions after Empire. In D. Howland and L. White (eds) *The State of Sovereignty: Territories, Laws, Populations.* Bloomington, IN: Indiana University Press.

Kelsey, J. 2005a. Maori, te Tiriti, and globalisation: The invisible hand of the colonial state. In M. Belgrave, M. Kawharu and D. Williams (eds) *Waitangi revisited: Perspectives on the Treaty of Waitangi.* Auckland: Oxford University Press.

Kelsey, J. 2005b. World trade and small nations in the South Pacific Region. *Kansas Journal of Law and Public Policy*, 14, 247–306.

Kenrick, J. 2006. The concept of indigeneity: Discussion of Alan Barnard's 'Kalahari revisionism, Vienna and the 'indigenous peoples' debate. *Social Anthropology*, 14, 19–21.

Kirk, N. 1974. *New Zealand Parliamentary Debates* 391, p. 2691. Wellington: New Zealand Government.

Kompridis, N. 2007. Struggling over the Meaning of Recognition A Matter of Identity, Justice, or Freedom? *European Journal of Political Theory*, 6, 3, 277–89.

Kukathas, C. 1992. Are there any cultural rights? *Political Theory*, 20, 105–39.

Kukutai, T. 2015. Imaging a post-settlement future: In this together?, *PostTreaty Settlements.org.nz*, http://posttreatysettlements.org.nz/imagining-a-post-settlement-future-in-this-together/

Kymlicka, W. 1989. *Liberalism, Community and Culture.* Oxford: Clarendon Press.

Kymlicka, W. 1996. *Multicultural Citizenship*. Oxford: Oxford University Press.

Kymlicka, W. 1999. Theorizing indigenous rights. *University of Toronto Law Journal*, 49, 281–611.

Kymlicka, W. 2000. American multiculturalism and the 'nations within'. In D. Ivison, P. Patton and W. Sanders (eds) *Political Theory and the Rights of Indigenous Peoples*. Cambridge: Cambridge University Press.

Kymlicka, W. and Norman, W. 1994. Return of the citizen: A survey of recent work on citizenship theory. *Ethics*, 104, 352–81.

Ladwig, J. and Sarra, C. 2009. *2009 Structural Review of the Northern Territory Department of Education and Training: Delivering the Goods*. Darwin: Northern Territory Government.

Lal, B. V. 1992. *Broken Waves: A History of the Fiji Islands in the Twentieth Century*. Honolulu, HI: University of Hawaii Press.

Lal, B. V. 2002. Making history, becoming history: Reflections on the Fijian coups and constitutions. *The Contemporary Pacific*, 14, 148–67.

Lal, B. V. 2006. *Islands of Turmoil: Elections and Politics in Fiji*. Canberra: ANU e-Press and Asia Pacific Press.

Lal, B. 2009. 'Anxiety, uncertainty and fear in our land': Fiji's road to military coup, 2006. In J. Fraenkel, S. Firth and B. Lal (eds) *The 2006 Military Takeover in FIJI: a Coup to End All Coups?* Canberra: ANU E Press.

Lal, B. 2012. *Intersections: History, Memory, Disciplines*. Canberra: ANYE Press.

Lal, B. V. 2015. Editorial: Fiji: The road to 2014 and beyond. *The Round Table*, 104, 85–92.

Langton, M. 2012. Changing the paradigm: Mining companies, native title and Aboriginal Australians. *ABC Radio Boyer Lecture*, www.abc.net.au/radionational/programs/boyerlectures/boyers-ep1/4305610

Langton, M. and Longbottom, J. 2012. Introduction. In M. Langton and J. Longbottom (eds) *Community Futures, Legal Architecture: Foundations for Indigenous Peoples in the Global Mining Boom*. London: Routledge.

Larson, E. and Aminzade, R. 2007. Nation-states confront the global: Discourses of indigenous rights in Fiji and Tanzania. *The Sociological Quarterly*, 48, 801–31.

Latham, M. 2000. *Modernization as Ideology: American Social Science and 'Nation-Building' in the Kennedy Era*. Chapel Hill, NC: University of North Carolina Press.

Lauderdale, P. 2008. Indigenous peoples in the face of globalization. *American Behavioral Scientist*, 51, 1836–43.

Lawrence, R. and Gibson, C. 2007. Obliging indigenous citizens? Shared responsibility agreements in Australian Aboriginal communities. *Cultural Studies*, 21, 650–71.

Lawson, S. 2004. Nationalism versus constitutionalism in Fiji. *Nations and Nationalism*, 10, 519–38.

Lawson, S. 2012. Indigenous nationalism, 'Ethnic Democracy,' and the prospects for a liberal constitutional order in Fiji. *Nationalism and Ethnic Politics*, 18, 293–315.

Lawson, S. 2015. Fiji's foreign relations: retrospect and prospect. *The Round Table*, 104, 209–20.

Lawson, S. and Hagan Lawson, E. 2015. *Chiefly Leadership in Fiji: Past, Present, and Future.* State, Society and Governance in Melanesia Program. Discussion Paper. Canberra: Australian National University.

Lenzerini, F. 2005. Sovereignty revisited: International law and parallel sovereignty of indigenous peoples. *An International Symposium. A Modern Concept of Sovereignty: Perspectives from the US and Europe,* University of Siena.

Lightfoot, S. 2008. Indigenous rights in international politics: The cases of overcompliant liberal states. *Alternatives: Global, Local, Political,* 33, 83–104.

Lindsay Barr, T. and Reid, J. 2014. Centralized decentralization for tribal business development. *Journal of Enterprising Communities: People and Places in the Global Economy,* 8, 217–32.

Locke, J. 1887. *Locke on Civil Government.* London: George Routledge and Sons.

Loughlin, M. 2003. Ten tenets of sovereignty. In N. Walker (ed.) *Sovereignty in Transition: Essays in European Law.* Oxford: Hart Publishing.

Maaka, R. and Fleras, A. 2005. *The Politics of Indigeneity: Challenging the State in Canada and Aotearoa/New Zealand.* Dunedin: University of Otago Press.

Maaka, R. and Fleras, A. 2009a. *Indigenizing Policymaking by Mainstreaming Indigeneity: Towards an Indigenous Grounded Analysis (IGA) Policy Framework as Participatory Governance.* Wellington: Victoria University of Wellington.

Maaka, R. and Fleras, A. 2009b. *Mainstreaming Indigeneity by Indigenizing Policymaking: Towards an Indigenous Grounded Analysis Framework as Policy Paradigm.* http://articles.indigenouspolicy.org/index.php/ipj/article/download/67/37

Macdonald, L.T.A.O.T. and Muldoon, P. 2006. Globalisation, neoliberalism and the struggle for Indigenous citizenship. *Australian Journal of Political Science,* 41, 2, 209–23.

Macedo, S. 1997. In defense of liberal public reason: Are slavery and abortion hard cases. *American Journal of Jurisprudence*, 42, 1, 1–29.

Macklin, J. 2009. *Statement on the United Nations Declaration on the Rights of Indigenous Peoples*. Canberra, www.un.org/esa/socdev/unpfii/documents/Australia_official_statement_endorsement_UNDRIP.pdf

Mansbridge, J. 1996. Using power/fighting power: The polity. In S. Benhabib (ed.) *Democracy and Difference: Contesting the Boundaries of the Political*. Princeton, NJ: Princeton University Press.

Marks, K. 2014. Fiji Military Leader Admits Beatings, Torture. *The Age*. 20 June. www.theage.com.au/world/fiji-military-leader-admits-beatings-torture-20140620-zsg90.html

Marshall, T. H. 1963. *Class, Citizenship, and Social Class*. New York: Anchor Books.

Martin, D. 1995. *Money, business and culture: issues for Aboriginal economic policy*, CAEPR Discussion Paper No. 101, CAEPR, ANU, Canberra.

Martin, D. F. 2001. *Is welfare dependency 'welfare poison'? An assessment of Noel Pearson's proposals for Aboriginal welfare reform*. Canberra: Centre for Aboriginal Economic Policy Research, Australian National University.

McCarthy, S. 2011. Soldiers, chiefs and church: Unstable democracy in Fiji. *International Political Science Review*, 32, 563–78.

McCorquodale, R. 2006. Beyond state sovereignty: The international legal system and non-state participants. *International Law: Revista Colombiana de Derecho Internacional*, 103–60.

McCreery, R. 2012. Promoting indigenous-led economic development: Why parties should consult the UNDRIP. *Indigenous Law Bulletin*, 8, 16.

McHugh, P.G. 2005. Living with rights aboriginally: Constitutionalism and Maori in the 1990s. In M. Belgrave, M. Kawharu and D. Williams (eds) *Waitangi Revisited: Perspectives on the Treaty of Waitangi*. Melbourne: Oxford University Press.

McNaboe, D. 2015. *Sydney Morning Herald*, 1 March.

Ministry of Business Innovation and Employment. 2015. *The Māori Economy*, www.mbie.govt.nz/info-services/infrastructure-growth/maori-economic-development/the-maori-economy

Mitzsal, B. 2005. Memory and democracy. *American Behavioral Scientist*, 48, 1320–38

Moore, D., Scotte, G., Drew, R., Smith, J. and Whelen, C. 2014. *Decentralising Welfare – Te Mana o Tuhoe*, www.srgexpert.com/wp-content/uploads/2015/11/Decentralising-welfare-te-mana-motuhake-o-tuhoe.pdf

Moreton-Robinson, A. 2000. *Talkin' up the White Woman: Indigenous Women and Feminism*. St Lucia, QLD: University of Queensland Press.

Moreton-Robinson, A. 2004. The possessive logic of patriarchal white sovereignty: The High Court and the Yorta Yorta Decision. In D. Riggs (ed.) *Taking up the Challenge: Critical Race and Whiteness Studies in a Postcolonising Nation*. Belair, SA: Crawford House Publishing.

Moreton-Robinson, A. 2005. Patriarchal whiteness, self-determination and indigenous women: The invisibility of structural privilege and the visibility of oppression. In B. Hocking (ed.) *Unfinished Constitutional Business?: Rethinking Indigenous Self-determination*. Canberra: Aboriginal Studies Press.

Mörkenstam, U. 2015. Recognition as if sovereigns? A procedural understanding of indigenous self-determination. *Citizenship Studies*. 19, 6-7, 634–48.

Morrison, M., Collins, J., Basu, P. and Krivokapic-Skoko, B. 2014. *Determining the Factors Influencing the Success of Private and Community-Owned Indigenous Businesses Across Remote, Regional and Urban Australia*, Final Report Prepared for the Australian Research Council and Indigenous Business Australia. Bathurst: Charles Sturt University.

Mouffe, C. 2006. Democracy, power and the 'political'. In S. Benhabib (ed.) *Democracy and Difference: Contesting the Boundaries of the Political*. Princeton, NJ: Princeton University Press.

Muehlebach, A. 2001. Making place at the United Nations: An anthropological inquiry into the United Nations Working Group on Indigenous Populations. *Cultural Anthropology*, 16, 415–35.

Muldoon, P. 2003. Reconciliation and political legitimacy: The Old Australia and the New South Africa. *The Australian Journal of Politics and History*, 49, 182–97.

Mundine, W. 2013. Shooting an elephant: Four giant steps. Address to the Garma Festival Corporate Dinner. *Australian Indigenous Chamber of Commerce*, www.indigenouschamber.org.au/wp-content/uploads/2013/08/Speech-to-Garma-Festival.pdf

Naidu, V. 2009. Draft report: Fiji Islands country profile on excluded groups. *Unpublished Report for UNESCAP*. Suva: UNESCAP.

Naiyaga, I. 2014. Address to the Fiji Indigenous Business Council Symposium 'Indigenous Business – creating our future'. Suva: Reserve Bank of Fiji.

Nana, G., Stokes, F. and Molano, W. 2011. *The Asset Base, Income, Expenditure and GDP of the 2010 Maori Economy*. Wellington: BERL Economics and Te Puni Kokiri.

Nettheim, G. 1998. The international law context. In N. Peterson and W. Sanders (eds) *Citizenship and Indigenous Australians: Changing Conceptions and Possibilities.* Cambridge: Cambridge University Press.

New South Wales Aboriginal Land Council. 2014. *Economic Development Policy.* Sydney: New South Wales Aboriginal Land Council.

New Zealand Government. 1985. *Treaty of Waitangi Amendment Act 1985*, www.nzlii.org/nz/legis/hist_act/towaa19851985n148306/

New Zealand Government. 1995. *Waikato Raupatu Claims Settlement Act 1995*, www.legislation.govt.nz/act/public/1995/0058/latest/DLM369893.html

New Zealand Government. 1998. *Ngai Tahu Claims Settlement Act 1998*, www.legislation.govt.nz/act/public/1998/0097/latest/DLM429090.html

New Zealand Institute of Economic Research. 2003. *Māori Economic Development: Te Ōhanga Whanaketanga Māori.* Wellington: New Zealand Institute of Economic Research. www.scribd.com/document/88803543/Maori-Economic-Development/

Newland, L. 2007. The role of the Assembly of Christian Churches in Fiji (ACCF) in the 2006 elections. In J. Fraenkel and S. Firth (eds) *From Election to Coup in Fiji: The 2006 Campaign and its Aftermath.* Canberra: ANU E-Press.

North Australian Indigenous Land and Sea Management Alliance. 2013. *Indigenous Futures and Sustainable Development in Northern Australia: Towards a Framework for Full Indigenous Participation in Economic Development.* Darwin: North Australia Indigenous Land and Sea Management Alliance.

Norton, R. 2000. Reconciling ethnicity and nation: Contending discourses in Fiji's constitutional reform. *The Contemporary Pacific*, 12, 83–122.

Norton, R. 2004. Seldom a transition with such aplomb: From confrontation to conciliation on Fiji's path to independence. *Journal of Pacific History*, 39, 163–84.

Norton, R. 2007. Understanding Fiji's political paradox. In J. Fraenkel and S. Firth (eds) *From Election to Coup in Fiji: The 2006 Campaign and its Aftermath.* Canberra: ANU e-Press.

Norton, R. 2009. The changing role of the Great Council of Chiefs. In J. Fraenkel, S. Firth and B. Lal (eds) *The 2006 Military Takeover in FIJI: A Coup to End All Coups?* Canberra: ANU E Press.

Norton, R. 2015. The troubled quest for national political leadership in Fiji. *The Round Table*, 104, 113–25.

Nussbaum, M. C. 1987. *Nature, Function, and Capability: Aristotle on Political Distribution*. Helsinki: World Institute for Development Economics Research of the United Nations University Helsinki, Finland.

Oldfield, A. 1990. Citizenship: an unnatural practice? *The Political Quarterly*, 61, 177–87.

Ombudsman, New South Wales. 2016. *Fostering Economic Development for Aboriginal People in New South Wales: A Special Report to Parliament Under s. 31 of the Ombudsman Act 1974*, www.ombo.nsw.gov.au/__data/assets/pdf_file/0019/34138/Fostering-economic-development-for-Aboriginal-people-in-NSW_May-2016.pdf

Orange, C. 1987. *The Treaty of Waitangi*. Wellington: Allen and Unwin, Port Nicholson Press.

O'Regan, T. 2014. The economics of indigenous survival. *ABC Big Ideas*, www.abc.net.au/radionational/programs/bigideas/the-economics-of-indigenous-survival/5832918

O'Sullivan, D. 2005. *Faith Politics and Reconciliation: Catholicism and the Politics of Indigeneity*. Adelaide: The Australian Theological Forum.

O'Sullivan, D. 2007. *Beyond Biculturalism*. Wellington: Huia Publishers.

O'Sullivan, D. 2010. Covenants, treaties and the politics of reconciliation. *Uniting Church Studies*, 16, 29–37.

O'Sullivan, D. 2014. Māori self-determination and a liberal theory of indigeneity. In M. Woons (ed.) *Restoring Indigenous Self-Determination*. e-International Relations, www.e-ir.info/wp-content/uploads/2014/05/Restoring-Indigenous-Self-Determination-E-IR.pdf#page=33

O'Sullivan, J. and Dana, T. 2008. Redefining Maori economic development. *International Journal of Social Economics*, 35, 364–79.

Palmer, G. 1995. Where to from here? In G. McLay (ed.) *Treaty Settlements: The Unfinished Business*, pp. 153–4. Wellington: New Zealand Institute of Advanced Legal Studies and Victoria University of Wellington Law Review.

Parekh, B. 1997. Dilemmas of a multicultural theory of citizenship. *Constellations*, 4, 54–62.

Parliamentary Counsel Office. 1989. *Education Act 1989*. Wellington: Parliamentary Counsel Office. www.legislation.govt.nz/act/public/1989/0080/latest/DLM175959.html

Patton, P. 2005. Historic Injustice and the Possibility of Supersession. *Journal of Intercultural Studies*, 26, 3, 255–66.

Pearson, C. 2006. *Statement to the Permanent Forum on Indigenous Issues Regarding the Declaration on the Rights of Indigenous Peoples: Australia, New Zealand and the United States*. New York: United Nations, http://unny.mission.gov.au/unny/soc_170506.html

Penetito, W. 2011. Where are we now in Māori education: A sense of radical hopefulness. *New Zealand Association for Research in Education*, http://www.nzare.org.nz/portals/306/images/Files/wally-penetito-herbison2011.pdf

Phillips A. 1996. Dealing with Difference: a politics of ideas or a politics of difference? In S. Benhabib (ed). *Democracy and difference: Contesting the boundaries of the political*. Princeton University Press, 139–52.

Phillips, M. 2005. Aboriginal reconciliation as religious politics: Secularisation in Australia. *Australian Journal of Political Science*, 40, 111–24.

Pholi, K., Black, D. and Richards, C. 2009. Is 'Close the Gap' a useful approach to improving the health and wellbeing of indigenous Australians. *Australian Review of Public Affairs*, 9, 1–13.

Plaganyi, E.E., van Putten, I., Hutton, T., Deng, R.A., Dennis, D., Pascoe, S., Skewes, T. and Campbell, R.A. 2013. Integrating indigenous livelihood and lifestyle objectives in managing a natural resource. *Proceedings of the National Academy of Sciences of the United States of America*. 110, 9, 3639–44.

Prasad, J. 2009. The good, the bad and the faithful: The response by Indian religious groups. In J. Fraenkel and S. Firth (eds) *The 2006 Military Takeover in Fiji: A Coup to End All Coups?* Canberra: ANU E-Press.

Prasad, S., Dakuvula, J. and Snell, D. 2001. *Economic Development, Democracy and Ethnic Conflict in the Fiji Islands*. London: Minority Rights Group International.

Prowse, C. C. 1995. *Racist Attitudes Towards Aboriginal Australians in the Light of Contemporary Catholic Concepts of Social Sin and Conversion*. PhD dissertation, Rome: Pontifical Lateran University.

Quiggin, J. 2005. Economic liberalism: Fall, revival and resistance. In P. Saunders and J. Walter (eds) *Ideas and Influence: Social Science and Public Policy in Australia*. Sydney: UNSW Press.

Radio New Zealand. 2016. Judd felt force of anti-Maori racism. 10 May, www.radionz.co.nz/news/national/303537/judd-felt-force-of-anti-maori-racism

Radio New Zealand International. 2006. *Morning Report*, 26 November.

Rata, E. 2003. Late capitalism and ethnic revivalism: A New Middle Age? *Anthropological Theory*, 3, 43–63.

Rata, E. 2005. Rethinking biculturalism. *Anthropological Theory*, 5, 267–84.

Ratuva, S. 2001. *State Induced Affirmative Action, Economic Development and Ethnic Politics: The Case of Malaysia and Comparative Study with Fiji*. Sociology and Social Policy Working Paper Series, Working Paper Number 1/2001. Suva: University of the South Pacific.

Ratuva, S. 2002. Economic nationalism and communal consolidation: Economic affirmative action in Fiji, 1987–2002. *Pacific Economic Bulletin*, 17, 1, 130–37.

Ratuva, S. 2005. Politics of ethno-national identity in a postcolonial communal democracy: The case of Fiji. In A. Allahah (ed.) *Ethnicity, Class and Nationalism: Caribbean and Extra-Caribbean Dimensions*. Oxford: Lexington Books.

Ratuva, S. 2007. The pre-election cold war. In J. Fraenkel and S. Firth (eds) *From Election to Coup in Fiji: The 2006 Campaign and its Aftermath*. Canberra: ANU E Press.

Ratuva, S. 2014. Ethnicity, affirmative action and coups in Fiji: Indigenous development policies between the 2000 and 2006 coups. *Social Identities*, 20, 139–54.

Ratuva, S. 2015a. Protectionism versus reformism: The battle for Taukei ascendancy in Fiji's 2014 general election. *The Round Table*, 104, 137–49.

Ratuva, S. 2015b. The interface between affirmative action and neoliberalism: The case of Fiji. *Cultural Dynamics*, 27, 135–54

Rawls, J. 1971. *A Theory of Justice*. Cambridge, MA: Harvard University Press.

Reeves, P., Vakatora, T. and Lal, B. 1996. Towards a united future: Report of the Fiji Constitution Review Commission. *Parliament of Fiji, Parliamentary Paper* 34. Suva: Government Printer.

Republic of Fiji. 2013a. *Agricultural Investment Guide: Discovering Opportunities, Harvesting Potential*. North Sydney, NSW: Fiji Consulate General, https://pafpnet.spc.int/attachments/article/740/FJ-IGuide.pdf

Republic of Fiji. 2013b. *Constitution of the Republic of Fiji*, www.paclii.org/fj/Fiji-Constitution-English-2013.pdf

Republic of Fiji. 2015. *Supplement to the 2016 Budget Estimates*. Suva: Ministry of Finance, Republic of Fiji, www.finance.gov.fj/s/government-budget.html?download=434:2016-budget-address

Reynolds, H. 1996. *Aboriginal Sovereignty: Reflections on Race, State, and Nation*. St Leonards, NSW: Allen and Unwin.

Robinson, N. 2008. Push for English causes Aboriginal backlash. *The Australian*, http://listserv.linguistlist.org/pipermail/lgpolicy-list/2008-November/008448.html

Rodriguez-Pinero, L. 2005. *Indigenous Peoples*. Oxford: Oxford University Press.

Ross, M. 2009, www.cylc.org.au/cms/index.php?option=com_content&view=article&id=50&Itemid=55

Rowse, T. 2002. *Indigenous futures: choice and development for Aboriginal and Islander Australia*. Sydney: University of New South Wales Press.

Rudd, K. 2008. Apology to Australia's indigenous peoples, *Speech*, By Authority of the House of Representatives, 13 February. Canberra, ACT: House of Representatives, Commonwealth of Australia, http://parlinfo.aph.gov.au/parlInfo/genpdf/chamber/hansardr/2008-02-13/0003/hansard_frag.pdf;fileType=application%2Fpdf

Ruhanen, L. and Whitford, M. 2014. Indigenous Tourism and Events for Community Development in Australia. In E. Fayos-solà, M.D. Alvarez, C. Cooper (eds) *Tourism as an Instrument for Development: A Theoretical and Practical Study (Bridging Tourism Theory and Practice, Volume 5)*. Bingley: Emerald Group Publishing Limited, pp. 183–94.

Ryan, W. 1976. *Blaming the Victim*. New York, Vantage Books.

Sacred Congregation for the Doctrine of the Faith. 1984. *Instruction on Certain Aspects of the 'Theology of Liberation'*, Vatican City, www.ewtn.com/library/CURIA/CDFLIBR1.HTM

Sanders, W. 2004. *ATSICs Achievements and Strengths: Implications for Institutional Reform*. Canberra: Centre for Aboriginal Economic Policy Research, Australian National University.

Sarra, C. 2007. Stronger, smarter. *Teacher: The National Education Magazine*, pp. 32–41.

Sarra, C. 2014. *Strong and Smart: Towards a Pedagogy for Emancipation Education for first Peoples*. London: Routledge.

Savage, C., Tarena, E., Te Hemi, H. and Leonard, J. 2014. *Te Tapuae o Rehua*: Iwi engagement in higher education in *Te Waipounamu*. In F. Cram, H. Phillips, P. Sauni and C. Tuagalu (eds) *Maori and Pasifika Higher Education Horizons*. Bingley: Emerald Books.

Scambary, B. 2013. *My Country, Mine Country: Indigenous People, Mining and Development Contestation in Remote Australia (CAEPR Monograph 33)*. Canberra: ANU E-Press.

Scheyvens, R. and Russell, M. 2010. *Sharing the Riches of Tourism Summary Report: Fiji*. Palmerston North: Massey University.

Scott, C. 1996. Indigenous self-determinaton and decolonization of the international imagination: A plea. *Human Rights Quarterly*, 18, 814–20.

Scott, D. 2003. Culture in political theory. *Political Theory*, 31, 92–115.

Sen, A. 1999. *Development as Freedom*. Oxford: Oxford University Press.

Shaw, K. 2008. *Indigeneity and Political Theory: Sovereignty and the Limits of the Political*. London: Routledge.

Sherriff, J. 2010. *Investigating Factors Influencing the Retention of Maori Students within Secondary Education in Aotearoa/New Zealand*. MEd dissertation, Auckland: Unitec Institute of Technology.

Short, D. 2003. Reconciliation, assimilation, and the indigenous peoples of Australia. *International Political Science Review/ Revue internationale de science politique*, 24, 491–513.

Simpson, A. 2000. Paths toward a Mohawk Nation: Narratives of citizenship and nationhood in Kahnawake. In D. Ivison, P. Patton and W. Sanders (eds) *Political Theory and the Rights of Indigenous Peoples*. Cambridge: Cambridge University Press.

Smith, G., Tinirau, R., Gillies, A. and Warriner, V. 2015. *He Mangopare Amohia: Strategies for Maori Economic Development*. Whakatane: Te Whare Wananga o Awanuiarangi.

Soguk, N. 2007. Indigenous Peoples and Radical Futures in Global Politics. *New Political Science*. 29, 3, 1–22.

Srebrnik, H. 2002. Ethnicity, religion, and the issue of Aboriginality in a small island state. Why does Fiji flounder? *The Round Table*. 91, 364, 187–210.

Statistics New Zealand. 2013. *2013 Census QuickStats about Māori*, Statistics New Zealand, www.stats.govt.nz/Census/2013-census/profile-and-summary-reports/quickstats-about-maori-english.aspx

Statistics New Zealand 2016. *Maori Population Estimates*. www.stats.govt.nz/browse_for_stats/population/estimates_and_projections/maori-population-estimates-info-releases.aspx

Stewart-Harawira, M. 2005. *The New Imperial order: Indigenous Responses to Globalization*. London: Zed Books.

Stockton, E. 1988. Maverick missionaries: An overlooked chapter in the history of Catholic missions. In T. Swain and D. Rose (eds) *Aboriginal Australians and Christian Missions*. Adelaide: Australian Association for the Study of religions.

Stokes, G. 2000. Global Citizenship. In W. Hudson and J. Kane (eds) *Rethinking Australian Citizenship*. Cambridge: Cambridge University Press.

Supreme Court of Canada. 2001. *Mitchell v. Minister of National Revenue*, SCC 33. CanLII, http://scc-csc.lexum.com/scc-csc/scc-csc/en/item/1869/index.do

Taylor, C. 1999. Democratic Exclusion (and its Remedies?). In A.C. Cairns, J.C. Courtney, P., MacKinnon, H.J. Michelmann and D.E. Smith (eds) *Citizenship Diversity and Pluralism: Canadian and Comparative Perspectives*. Montreal and Kingston: McGill-Queen's University Press.

Taylor, C. and Gutmann, A. 1994. *Multiculturalism*, (Expanded paperback edition). Princeton, NJ: Princeton University Press.

Taylor, J. and Scambary, B. 2005. *Indigenous People and the Pilbara Mining Boom: A Baseline for Regional Participation*. Canberra: ANU E Press.

Te Puni Kōkiri 2010. *Beyond 2020: population projections for Maori*. www.tpk.govt.nz/en/a-matou-mohiotanga/search?q=population

Te Puni Kōkiri. 2014. *Māori Economy in the Waikato Region*. Wellington: Waikato Regional Council.

Te Runanga-A-Iwi-O-Ngapuhi 2013. *Whakatupu: for the next generation*. www.ngapuhi.iwi.nz/Data/Sites/3/downloads-folder/annualreports/ar2013_final_web.pdf

Te Runanga O Ngai Tahu. 2008. *Annual Report 2008*. Christchurch: Te Runanga o Ngai Tahu.

The General Secretariat of the Synod of Bishops and Libreria Editrice. 1998. *Instrumentum Laboris, Synod of Bishops for Oceania. Jesus Christ and the Peoples of Oceania: Walking His Way Telling His Truth and Living His Life*. Vatican: The General Secretariat of the Synod of Bishops and Libreria Editrice.

The High Court of Australia. 1992. *Mabo and Others v. Queensland* (No. 2). High Court of Australia, www.austlii.edu.au/cgi-bin/disp.pl/au/cases/cth/high_ct/175clr1.html?query=%7Emabo

The High Court of Australia. 1996. *The Wik Peoples v The State of Queensland and Ors; The Thayorre People v The State of Queensland and Ors*. High Court of Australia, www.austlii.edu.au/au/cases/cth/high_ct/unrep299.html

The National Congress of Australia's First Peoples. 2013. *Submission on the National Aboriginal and Torres Strait Islander Health Plan*, www.austlii.edu.au/au/cases/cth/HCA/1996/40.html

Tully, J. 1995. *Strange Multiplicity: Constitutionalism in an Age of Diversity*. Cambridge: Cambridge University Press.

Tully, J. 1999. Aboriginal peoples: Negotiating reconciliation. In J. Bickerton and A. Gagnon (eds) *Canadian Politics*. Peterborough, ON: Hadleigh.

Turia, T. 2006. *Tariana Addresses ACT National Conference*, www.maoriparty.com/index.php?option=com_content&task=view&id=164&Itemid=28

Turner, B. S. 1993. Contemporary problems in the theory of citizenship. In Turner, B (ed) *Citizenship and Social Theory*, SAGE London, 1–18.

United Nations. 1966. *International Covenant on Civil and Political Rights*. New York. United Nations.

United Nations. 1965. *The International Convention on the Elimination of All Forms of Racial Discrimination*. New York. United Nations.

United Nations. 1966. *International Covenant on Economic, Social and Cultural Rights*. New York. United Nations.

United Nations. 1993. *Convention on Biological Diversity*. New York: United Nations.

United Nations. 1989. *Convention on the Rights of the Child*. New York: United Nations.

United Nations. 1993. *Vienna Declaration on Human Rights*. New York: United Nations.

United Nations. 2005. *Convention on the Elimination of Racial Discrimination*. New York: United Nations.

United Nations. 2007a. *Declaration on the Rights of Indigenous Peoples*, www.un.org/esa/socdev/unpfii/documents/DRIPS_en.pdf

United Nations. 2007b. *Consideration of Reports Submitted by States Parties under Article 9 of the Convention: Concluding Observations of the Committee on the Elimination of Racial Discrimination*. New York: United Nations, Committee on the Elimination of all Forms of Racial Discrimination.

United Nations Committee on the Elimination of All Forms of Racial Discrimination. 2005. *Procedural Decisions of the Committee on the Elimination of Racial Discrimination, New Zealand*, New York: United Nations. http://hrlibrary.umn.edu/cerd/decisions/newzealand2005.html

Uniting Church in Australia. 2012. *Uniting Church Supports Constitutional Change*, www.wa.uca.org.au/blog/uniting-church-supports-constitutional-change

Van Gunsteren, H. 1978. *Notes Towards a Theory of Citizenship*. In F. Dallmayr (ed.) *From Contract to Community*. New York: Marcel Decker.

Van Meijl, T. 2015. The Waikato River: Changing properties of a Living Māori Ancestor. *Oceania*, 85, 219–37.

Waikato-Tainui. 2015a. *Ko te Mana Matauranga*. Hamilton: Waikato Tainui.

Waikato-Tainui. 2015b. *Whakatupuranga Waikato-Tainui*, www.waikatotainui.com/wp-content/uploads/2013/10/WhakatupurangaWT2050.pdf

Waitangi Tribunal. 2014. *Te Paparahi o te Raki Reports*, www.waitangitribunal.govt.nz/inquiries/district-inquiries/te-paparahi-o-te-raki-northland/

Waldron, J. 1992. Superseding historic injustice. *Ethics*, 13, 1, 4–28.

Waldron, J. 2002. Indigeneity? First peoples and last occupancy. *2002 Quentin Baxter Memorial Lecture*, Victoria University of Wellington, 5 December.

Waldron, J. 2004. Settlement, return and the supersession thesis. *Theoretical Inquiries in Law*, 5, 237–68.

Warner, M. 2003. Who's sorry now? *Times Literary Supplement* 1 (August), 10–13.

Watson, I. 2009. Sovereign spaces, caring for country, and the homeless position of Aboriginal peoples. *South Atlantic Quarterly*, 108, 27–51.

Weber, M. 1984. Legitimacy, politics and the State. In W. Connolly (ed.) *Legitimacy and the State*. Oxford: Basil Blackwell.

Webster, S. 2002. Māori retribalization and Treaty rights to the New Zealand fisheries. *The Contemporary Pacific*, 14, 341–76.

Westpac New Zealand. 2014. *Maori Business is New Zealand Business*, www.westpac.co.nz/rednews/business/maori-business-is-new-zealand-business/

White, C. M. 2001. Between academic theory and folk wisdom: Local discourse on differential educational attainment in Fiji. *Comparative Education Review*, 45, 303–33.

Wild Rivers Act 2005 (QLD), www.legislation.qld.gov.au/LEGISLTN/REPEALED/W/WildRivA05_130523.pdf

Williams, D. V. 2005. Unique treaty-based relationships remain elusive. In M. Belgrave, M. Kawharu and D. Williams (eds) *Waitangi Revisited: Perspectives on the Treaty of Waitangi*. Melbourne: Oxford University Press.

World Trade Organization. 2009. *Trade Policy Review, Report by the Secretariat: Fiji*. Brussels: World Trade Organization.

Xanthaki, A. 2008. *Indigenous Rights and United Nations Standards*. Cambridge: Cambridge University Press.

Yabaki, A. 2008. *Indigenous Rights a Must*. Suva: Fiji Times Online, 23 December, www.fijitimes.com/story.aspx?id=109646

Young, I. 1989. Polity and group difference: A critique of the ideal of universal citizenship. *Ethics*, 99, 250–74.

Young, I. 2001. Social Movements and the Politics of Difference. In B. Boxill (ed.) *Race and Racism*. Oxford: Oxford University Press, 383–421.

Index